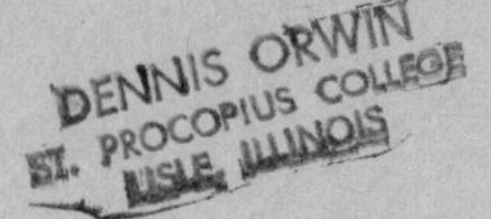

Cervantes - "Don Quixote"

Tues May 16 48-352
Thurs May 18 352-405
Tues 23 406-653
Thurs 25 653-708

THE LIFETIME READING PLAN

BY CLIFTON FADIMAN

Essays and Criticism

Party of One (1955)

Any Number Can Play (1957)

Anthologies, Collections, and Symposia

The Voice of the City and Other Stories by O. Henry (1935)

I Believe (1939)

Reading I've Liked (1941)

The Three Readers (WITH SINCLAIR LEWIS AND CARL VAN DOREN) (1943)

The Short Stories of Henry James (1945)

The American Treasury (ASSISTED BY CHARLES VAN DOREN) (1955)

Fantasia Mathematica (1958)

Inner Sanctum Editions

Leo Tolstoy's War and Peace (1942)

Charles Dickens' Pickwick Papers (1949)

Translations

Friedrich Nietzsche's The Birth of Tragedy (1926)

Friedrich Nietzsche's Ecce Homo (1926)

Desider Kostolanyi's The Bloody Poet (1927)

Franz Werfel's The Man Who Conquered Death (WITH WILLIAM A. DRAKE) (1927)

CLIFTON FADIMAN

The Lifetime Reading Plan

THE WORLD PUBLISHING COMPANY
CLEVELAND AND NEW YORK

Published by The World Publishing Company
2231 West 110th Street, Cleveland 2, Ohio

Published simultaneously in Canada by
Nelson, Foster & Scott Ltd.

Library of Congress Catalog Card Number: 60-5810

The quotations from "Dialogue Between Self and Soul," "Old Ben Bulbun," and "Two Songs from a Play" from *Collected Poems* by W. B. Yeats are reprinted by permission of The Macmillan Company.

The quotation from "In Memory of Sigmund Freud" from *Collected Poetry of W. H. Auden,* copyright 1945 by W. H. Auden, is reprinted by permission of Random House, Inc.

The quotation by Russell Lynes from *American Panorama* is reprinted by permission of the New York University Press.

W

For

Mortimer J. Adler

who first taught me,

and has never ceased

teaching me,

how to listen to

the Great Conversation

Contents

PLAYS

NARRATIVES

PHILOSOPHY, PSYCHOLOGY, POLITICS, ESSAYS

POETRY

HISTORY, BIOGRAPHY, AUTOBIOGRAPHY

SOME CONTEMPORARIES

MISCELLANEOUS

A Preliminary Talk With the Reader

A Preliminary Talk With the Reader

This book was merely completed by me. It was started by William Nichols, the editor-in-chief and publisher of *This Week Magazine*. Some time ago he asked me to prepare a list of books that might be of use to his readers. He laid down no condition other than that the books be of more than transient interest and value. The list, appearing under his title, The Lifetime Reading Plan, was printed in the April 12, 1959 issue. It was a traditional one, consisting largely of those works of Western thought and imagination generally considered of prime importance and excellence. It started with Homer and came down to our own day.

One might suppose that such books would be of no overwhelming interest to the large "mass" audience served by *This Week*. But, despite what some communications tycoons believe, Americans respond more eagerly to the best than to the worst—provided the best is offered them. At any rate The Lifetime Reading Plan drew so many inquiries and letters of all sorts (the credit being due, of course, not to the compiler but to the compilation) that the idea of the present book was proposed to me by my publishers. Here it is, using as its framework the original *This Week* reading list, with a few minor changes and additions.

It could have been written by any one of a great many reasonably well-read Americans. I happened to be drawn into a task that has proved pleasant for me, and whose result will, I hope, prove useful to others.

Its essence lies in Mr. Nichols' title, which he has permitted me to borrow. This is a *Lifetime* Reading Plan. The books herein discussed may take you fifty years to finish. They can of course be read in a much shorter time. The point is that they are intended to be an important part of a whole life, no matter what your present age may be. Many of them happen to be more entertaining than the latest best-seller. Still, it is not on the entertainment level that they are most profitably read. What they offer is of larger dimensions. It is rather like what is offered by loving and marrying, having and rearing children, carving out a career, creating a home. They can be a major experience, a source of continuous internal growth. Hence the word Lifetime. These authors are life companions. Once part of you, they work in and on and with you until you die. They should not be read in a hurry, any more than friends are made in a hurry. This list is not something to be "got through." It is a mine of such richness of assay as to last a lifetime.

The aim is simple. The Plan is designed to help us avoid mental bankruptcy. It is designed to fill our minds, slowly, gradually, under no compulsion, with what the greatest writers of our Western tradition have thought, felt, and imagined. Even after we have shared these thoughts, feelings, and images, we will still have much to learn: all men die uneducated. But at least we will not feel quite so lost, so bewildered. We will have disenthralled ourselves from the merely contemporary. We will understand something, not much but something, of our position in space and time. We will know how we have emerged from three thousand years of history. We will know how we got the ideas by which unconsciously we live. Says Santayana: "Those who cannot remember the past are condemned to repeat it."

Just as important, living in an age which to its cost has abandoned the concept of the Hero, we will have acquired models of high thought and feeling. We will feel buoyed up by the noble stream of Western civilization of which we are a part. This book, then, is a small act of faith, faith in the notion that a great many Americans, despite all the pressures inducing them to do so, have no desire to remain All-American Boys and Girls.

Does this sound schoolmasterish? Let it. The school is a far greater invention than the internal combustion engine. A good schoolmaster is a far more useful citizen than the average bank president, politician, or general, if only because what he transmits is what gives meaning to the life of the banker, the politician, the general. We survive precisely as primitive man survived, that is, by force and cunning. But we live by ideas and faiths of which he had hardly a premonition.

I do not wish to claim too much for The Lifetime Reading Plan. It is not magic. It does not automatically make you or me an "educated man." It offers no solution to life's ultimate mysteries. It will not make you "happy"—such claims are made by tooth pastes, motorcars, and deodorants, not by Plato, Dickens, and Hemingway. It will simply help to make your interior life more meaningful and interesting, as a love affair does, or some task calling forth your deepest energies.

Like many other men, I have been reading these books, off and on, for most of my life. One thing I've found out is that it's easy enough to say that they enlarge you, but rather difficult to prove it in advance. It is less difficult to prove (you'll sense it in short order) that they act like a developing fluid on film. That is, they bring into consciousness what you didn't know you knew. Even more than tools of self-enhancement, they are tools of self-discovery. This notion is not mine. You will find it in Plato who, as with many other matters, thought of it first. Socrates called himself a midwife of ideas. A great book is often such a midwife, delivering to full existence what has been coiled like an embryo in the dark, silent depths of the brain.

For whom is the Plan meant? Not for the highly educated or even (not always the same thing) the very well-read. They would find nothing new in what I have to say. The titles here listed would be perfectly familiar to them. Indeed, they could add many more, and quarrel quite legitimately with some of my choices.

In general the Plan is meant for the American, from eighteen to eighty, who is curious to see what his mind can master in the course of his remaining lifetime, and who has not met more than ten per cent, let us say, of the writers listed. It is also meant for the college graduate who *was* exposed to many of these books during his undergraduate years but who resisted their influence successfully. And it is meant for the college graduate—his name is legion—to whom most of these writers are hardly even names. It is meant also for the high school graduate who might well have profited from a college education but did not have the chance to do so. It is intended for that great and growing army of intelligent men and women who in their middle years are penetrated by a vague, uncomfortable sense that the mere solution of the daily problems of living is not enough, that somewhere worlds of thought and feeling call out for exploration. It is intended for the eager young man or woman of modest means (these books can be bought for little money) for whom the thrills of business competition or homemaking, while valid, are inadequate. It is intended for the retired elderly who have found out that growing roses and looking at television does not leave them mentally exhausted. It is intended for teachers (yes, college teachers too, in some cases) who would like to deepen and extend their knowledge and sensitivity, and so deepen and extend the nonmaterial rewards of their noble vocation. In its small way The Lifetime Reading Plan is a contribution to the solution of the problem of that Leisure Era of the near future that may prove either an opportunity or a horror.

A word about the titles.

This is not in any absolute sense a list of the "best books." There are no "best books." All we can say is that over three thousand years of Western history there has gradually accumulated a body of what has been called "original communications." The schoolroom term is classics, and that is all right with me if we add Carl Van Doren's definition: "A classic is a book that doesn't have to be rewritten." The list of such books changes, though not radically, with each generation. No two scholars would compile identical lists, and no single scholar (I am not one) would find my own list satisfactory in all respects. A Frenchman would include a few more French books. I, an American, find myself stressing books in my own language. Also, while there is fair agreement as to the original communications up to perhaps the year 1800, there is diminishing agreement as we near our own era. Which, Time being the great sifter, is natural enough.

Why one hundred books? There is no magic in the number. But it's an interesting fact that most lists of this sort (this is one of many) tend to vary between about seventy-five and two hundred titles. One must choose some arbitrary number, one must stop sometime; and I feel that for our purposes one hundred books more or less cover the ground. More might well be added. Indeed a supplementary Lifetime Reading Plan might be developed, consisting of those titles that I have omitted or which I may come to see I should have included. But the exact total is of little importance beside the fact that the books here discussed are, with a few exceptions, recognized as having a certain primacy or supremacy or unique excellence.

You will at once note omissions. I have not listed the Old and New Testaments. The Bible, of course, is more important than any book on the list, influencing constantly and deeply the lives of all Westerners, including those who, such as the Communists, claim to be atheists. But I have assumed that anyone who would read this book is already familiar with the Bible. In any case I assume you own one—and the practical purpose of the Plan is to induce you to add to your library.

The great books of the East are not to be found here. Why not?

First, we are Western men. Up to almost yesterday our minds were molded by Western ideas and images, plus those supplied by the Bible. A hundred years from now this may no longer be true. But it is true today; and this book is for now. Besides, to familiarize ourselves with the Western tradition whose children we are is a project big enough for any ordinary lifetime.

Second, I have no competence in any tradition other than my own. It's easy enough to fake competence, but the purpose of this book is not to exhibit the erudition of the writer (limited enough in any case) but to be of service to the reader.

Third, the Eastern classics that I have read (I confess this with some embarrassment) simply light no fire inside me. Limited outlook? Probably so. I have tried Lady Murasaki and the Koran and the *Arabian Nights* and the Bhagavad-Gita and the Upanishads and *All Men Are Brothers* and perhaps a dozen other Eastern classics. Unable to read them with much enjoyment, I cannot write about them with much honesty. Those wishing to find their way into the vast world of Oriental literature are referred to a pair of excellent books, among many: *Literatures of the East* (Grove Press, $1.75), edited by Eric B. Ceadel and *Approaches to the Oriental Classics* (Columbia University Press, $4.75), edited by William Theodore de Bary.

But many Western classics are also omitted. How about Aristophanes, Ariosto, Tasso, to name three that happen to jump to my mind? The difficulty here is one of translation. Even the best versions seem to me to convey too small a proportion of what must be great originals. Read them if you can, by all means. Where they might well be in this book there stands some other title that in my fallible judgment has more to offer. How about Gibbon's masterpiece? It *is* a masterpiece but I don't think I could induce you to go through so much undergrowth in order to come from time to time upon his magnificences. Perhaps I am wrong; add Gibbon to my list if you wish. How about philosophy? I have included as much as I thought the reader could well digest. But I am making you up, I do not know you, perhaps you can take much more. I have had to drop some names: Spinoza, for example, Hegel, Kant. Some seem to me too difficult except for the professional. Some write so badly that they cannot inflame most minds.

Poetry posed a painful problem. The only non-English-writing poets I have suggested for extended reading are Homer and the Greek tragic dramatists, Virgil, Lucretius, Dante, Molière, and Goethe. In these cases the best translations give a good idea of the original, and anyway the men are so overshadowing that they must be included. But I know that Baudelaire is every whit as great a poet as Coleridge. I am quite willing to admit on the authority of men I respect that Pushkin may be greater than either. But there is simply no use in claiming that Baudelaire and Pushkin can be read intensively in English with great pleasure. Robert Frost defines poetry as what is lost in translation, and there is much sense in the statement. I have had to make a common-sense compromise. I have suggested a good anthology of world poetry (see 73) which gives a fair sampling of virtually all the leading non-English-writing poets.

And of course there are other omissions—Plutarch, Bacon, Pepys, many others. I could not include all. I had to call a halt at a given point. I hope that, roughly and generally speaking, my hundred titles give an adequate sense of the mainstream of Western thought and imagination. I am aware that other titles have valid claims. I will not quarrel over them.

Two sections of the book require a word of comment: Some Contemporaries and Miscellaneous.

I discuss only eight leading living writers. Perhaps they are not the right ones. Perhaps I should not have listed any contemporaries at all, for the proper perspective is denied even the best critics. On the other hand, the Western tradition is still alive and kicking. To deny that great writers exist among us would be sheer snobbery. All I can say is that the eight I have chosen represent three important countries. They have worldwide reputations. Their native lands recognize them as great. And their work, in its totality, mirrors a vast area of the modern consciousness. If you prefer others or want to extend your exploration of modern literature, there is no lack of competent guidance.

Miscellaneous, the last section, lists five books with no literary pretentions at all. Three are meant to supply a little needed counterbalance to the Plan's literary emphasis. One (99) is a guide to the kind of reading suggested by the remainder of the Plan. For (100) see the commentary itself.

We come now to the structure of the book, its angle of approach, the way to use it.

I have arranged our hundred entries in a manner that seems reasonably interesting and convenient. We begin with twelve classics, listed chronologically according to type, of Greece and Rome. We continue with three, similarly arranged, from the Middle Ages. If the reader wishes to work on these fifteen first, well and good; a certain useful view of our origins is obtained in that way. But there is no compulsion to do so.

We then talk about five great dramatists of the Renaissance and modern world, arranged in order of date. If you have a special interest in drama, or would simply like to get an over-all view of the peaks in this field, these five may be read as a unit. Again, such rigor is not of the essence.

The largest space is devoted to prose narratives of all kinds and from many countries. Within each country, with one or two exceptions, the writers are grouped chronologically. The same arrangement is followed in the next section (comprising essays, philosophy, psychology, politics) and in the section on English and American poets, except that this is introduced by two anthologies. The pattern is slightly broken in the section on history and biography, but retained in the one listing contemporary writers. It would have been simpler to follow a straight chronological order. But by grouping the books not only by date, but also by country and kind, I hope I have made it possible for the reader to approach the list in various ways, and work out his own personal combinations.

Throughout the commentaries I use a device that may at first seem a bit irritating. Example: talking of Thucydides, I say: "He is the first historian to grasp the inner life of power politics. Hobbes (54), Machiavelli (62), and Marx (59) are, each in a different way, his sons." The idea of the parenthesized numbers, showing that these three men are discussed elsewhere, is not to make you turn at once, or indeed at all, to these references. The purpose is to stop you for a split second. It is to make you realize that the Western tradition is what Robert Hutchins called it, a Great Conversation in which hundreds of powerful or noble or delightful minds are talking with each other, reinforcing each other, refuting each other, recalling each other, or prophesying each other. In that one sense, all these men are contemporaries: "Literature," says Ezra Pound, "is news that stays news." Our nearly one hundred men are not islands. They are all parts of a vast continent. They connect with each other, and finally they connect with us. Those little ( )s are there to point up this fact whenever (and only whenever) it is legitimate to do so. Before rereading or reviewing (and in several cases reading for the first time) these books, I thought I knew many of them, not well, but somewhat. But I was astonished to find something I had not before perceived—that great writers, consciously or unconsciously, are always making gestures toward their peers. Deep calls unto deep: Whitehead talks about Plato, not La Mettrie; Dante glances into the future toward T. S. Eliot, not Vachel Lindsay.

As to the comments themselves: here are simply one hundred brief talks with you, my imaginary reader. They are not true essays, hardly rounded judgments, least of all compendiums of essential facts. What then are they? They are one hundred cards of invitation. Using from five hundred to a thousand words, I have tried to seduce you into reading the book I talk about. That is all; but it is also all I have in mind. My own work is valueless if it does not make you read the book discussed. This is not a critical volume of scope or depth or originality. It is not put forward as such. It is at best a key to open doors. Not the key, but what lies back of the door is what counts. I hope earnestly that these talks are readable and even interesting, and I can at least say that I have tried to pack a good deal into a few words. But their essential job is to be of service to the reader.

And so, in order to seduce you, I have not hesitated to use any method I thought might do the job. Sometimes I have stressed a man's life or personality. Sometimes I have advanced critical judgments. Sometimes I have summarized a man's whole work. Sometimes I have quoted the vivid opinion of a great authority. Sometimes I have warned the reader against common misconceptions. Sometimes I have tried to show a familiar figure, Dickens for example, in a somewhat less familiar light. Sometimes I have stressed the modernity of a man who might too easily be considered stale and dusty. Always I have tried to point out, not always directly, what we mid-twentieth-century Americans may gain from a given book. Why *should* you read Dante? Jane Austen? Lucretius? Voltaire? Because they are great? That is no answer. Their greatness is what we feel *after* we have read them, often years after. I have tried to give a more concrete, less lofty answer to a natural and proper question.

The judgments expressed are largely what is called received opinion. This is not a book of personal crotchets, though I have allowed an occasional prejudice to show through. But where my own judgment is given, that fact is clearly signposted, and the reader is free to ignore me. In any attempt, however, to interest a general, nonexpert audience in one hundred books, most of them acknowledged masterpieces, one is in duty bound to explain why men over many generations have so acknowledged them. Therefore the scholar or critic will find not a word in this book of the slightest interest to him. He has heard it all before. I am not talking to him, though I have learned from him. I am talking to beginners, which is what we all are at some point in our serious reading lives. These brief conversations with the reader are little more than icebreakers. They help to make it possible for you to set out on your own adventures among masterpieces.

You may read this book from first page to last before starting out on your Lifetime Reading Plan; or you may read it in sections, if those sections correspond to the titles you propose to cover as a kind of unit; or you may read the numbered commentary corresponding to the single title you have in mind. I have tried, as I advanced from Homer to our own day, to give some sense of whatever evolution and development we can legitimately detect. Hence the book may be a little more profitable if read as a unit. The essential thing, however, is the use you make of it. If you do no more than read it, you have wasted your time and money. While it is true that it contains a certain amount of information, many famous names, and hundreds of thumbnail judgments, its aim is not educational, but practical. That is, it is intended to spur you to action. Any one of the books it discusses may alter your mind profoundly; but the only alteration it itself can effect is in your will. It aims to direct your steps to the bookstore or library.

In what order should these books be read? Any that you prefer. The order in which I list them has nothing sacrosanct about it. You may wish to start with the moderns and work backward; a fresh perspective is gained that way. You may wish to concentrate for a while on a single group, the poets or the philosophers. You may elect to read the Greeks first, as a whole. You may rove about virtually at random. The Lifetime Reading Plan *is* a plan, not a course. You are not required to pass an examination in it, any more than you are required to pass an examination in your knowledge of your children or parents. If you try a book, say Hobbes's *Leviathan,* and find it too difficult, put it aside for a year or so. Then take it up again. You will find that the other books you have read in the meantime will somehow have made Hobbes a little easier. That is one of the miracles of this kind of reading: each original communication helps us to extract a bit more from all the others.

Remember also that these books are not only to be read. They are to be reread. They are not like a current novel. They are inexhaustible. Plato read at twenty-five is one man, Plato read at forty-five still another. It is not entirely frivolous to say that any great work of art is without question the cheapest thing one can ever buy. You pay for what seems a single object, a book or a picture or a phonograph record. But actually each such object is many objects; the works of Shakespeare do not consist of thirty-seven plays, but more nearly of 370 plays, for *Hamlet* changes into something else as you change into someone else with the passing of the years and the deepening of your sense of life.

Can you read these books without having gone to college? Yes, if you are willing to take pains. But only then. Says Walt Whitman: "Books are to be called for and supplied, on the assumption that the process of reading is not a half sleep, but in the highest sense, an exercise, a gymnast's struggle; that the reader is to do something for himself." There it is: the reader must do something for himself. Reading is not a passive experience, except when you're reading trash or the news. It should be, and is, one of the most vigorous modes of living. A good book, like healthy exercise, can give you that pleasant sense of fatigue that comes of having stretched your mental muscles.

On the other hand, these books, however carefully read, are not to be *studied* as if they were school tasks. Do not try to exhaust their meaning. If you or I can get ten per cent of what Plato has to offer us, we will have done well enough. It happens to be a fact that even a surface familiarity with most of these books will leave your mind better furnished than are the minds of ninety-nine out of a hundred college graduates. But that is a minor argument for The Lifetime Reading Plan; we are not competing with others, we are trying to excel ourselves.

Throughout this book I have tried to be realistic. When a book is hard I've said so. When a book is so odd that it presupposes a preliminary adjustment of your mind, I've said so. And in a few cases when a book is dull, I've said so. Remember that part of the pleasure you get from this kind of reading depends on the attitude with which you approach it. Herodotus can be enjoyed in an informal mood; Thucydides gains if you gird your mental loins in advance. Furthermore, these works cannot all be read at the same tempo. Just as you slow down at curves, so you are forced to slow down at Aristotle or Dewey. You can handle *Candide* in a single evening of delight; but you may find it worth while to spend an equal amount of time over a single short poem such as Yeats's "Sailing to Byzantium." In any case there's no hurry; you have a lifetime.

A word about the two book lists you will find at the end of the volume. The first, called the Bibliography, is meant as a buying aid. It gives the title, author, publisher, and price of each of the titles discussed, from 1 to 100. In most cases several editions are indicated, arranged in order of expense, from the most to the least costly. In the great majority of cases, paper-bound editions are available and are listed. This is important: for the first time in the history of civilization the great classics of that civilization are within every man's reach, a democratic revolution that may prove more far-reaching than the most crucial political or dynastic power changes could ever be. Paper-bound books are easy to buy and easy to shelve. I have made no exact estimate, but I would guess that ninety per cent of our list could be purchased for a minimum total sum of about $150.00, or fifteen dollars a year over a ten-year period, or a little over a dollar a month, which is what we spend on a single magazine of transient value. But of course paperbacks are perishable and you cannot expect the page to be quite as readable or handsome as is apt to be the case with the more carefully produced hard-cover editions.

With respect to translations I have occasionally added a comment indicating which version I have found most satisfactory. But this is a matter of taste and you need not be rigidly guided by my own preferences. Other things being equal, however, choose a modern rather than a Victorian or pre-Victorian version. Ours happens to be a superb age of translation, possibly even greater than the Elizabethan and Jacobean ages.

There are few hobbies more satisfactory than the gradual accumulation of good books. They are timeless; that is, they will be as useful to your descendant to the third or fourth generation as they are to you. No money spent on a good book can ever be wasted; somehow, sometime, somewhere that book will be read, if not by you, then by your children or your friends. And there is a certain satisfaction in completing the purchase of these hundred titles (or others of similar value). It is like seeing your entire past, three thousand years of it, ranged in order on your shelves. But—don't let your past stay there; make it part of your present.

The second list of books at the end of this volume is headed Suggestions for Further Reading. It consists of biographies of the authors mentioned, critical books or essays about them, and related reading aids. It is not only incomplete, it is hardly more than suggestive. But it is enough to start you off in the event that you want to find out more about, let us say, John Donne, after you have become acquainted with his work. Some teachers of the Great Books decry the use of secondary material. I taught these books for many years, so that I am not without experience, and I must state that I do not agree with them. These secondary works should not be used as a substitute for your own opinions. That is why it is better to read them after you have read the original. But they are often most enlightening and frequently works of art. I have tried, as far as possible, to list critical and biographical material by writers who are themselves fine thinkers and stylists, who are themselves parts of the Great Conversation. But without regard to this high criterion, I have listed a great many works that happen to be available in cheap paperbound editions, within the reach of the purses of most of us. Many, however, can only be secured through your library. I should stress again that these Suggestions for Further Reading are not for scholars or specialists, who will find them woefully inadequate. They are for beginners or almost beginners.

The compilation of the Bibliography is in large measure the work of Virginia Iacuzzi of The World Publishing Company. To her, my gratitude.

This has been a long and rambling talk with the reader rather than a formal Introduction. It is that by design. Its tone is informal because the Plan is informal. I would like you to feel The Lifetime Reading Plan as an exciting adventure of the mind, as well as a discipline. If I have communicated to you any of my own enthusiasm (which has persisted and grown over a period of forty years) you are ready to sit down for a lifetime of conversation with some of the liveliest talkers our civilization has produced. On the next page I will start pointing them out to you. That is all I can do. You must make friends all by yourself.

The Beginning

1. HOMER. *The Iliad*

The *Iliad* and the *Odyssey* are two long, ancient Greek narrative poems called epics. They are the first as well as the greatest epics of our civilization. Every time we refer to a siren or Achilles' heel or compare a lovely woman to Helen of Troy we are borrowing from these poems that are perhaps three thousand years old.

I say perhaps. We do not know when Homer lived—maybe between 800 and 700 B.C., maybe earlier. As a matter of fact we do not even know *whether* he lived. We do not know whether the stories were written by one man named Homer; or, as the old joke has it, by another fellow of the same name; or by a syndicate, like *Time*; or even, as Samuel Butler thought in the case of the *Odyssey*, by a woman. These questions are for scholars. The poems are for us.

Originally, it is supposed, they were listened to rather than read. Homer, whoever he or they was or were, recited them. Our radio and TV dramas are a kind of return to this bardic tradition, except that what we see and hear is not worth preserving for twenty-four hours, whereas men have somehow thought it worth while to preserve the *Iliad* and the *Odyssey* over three millennia.

The *Iliad* tells the story of some fifty days of the last of the ten years' siege of Troy (or Ilium) by a number of tribes we loosely call Greeks. This siege resulted in the capture and firing of Troy's "topless towers," which are known to have actually existed. To find out how Troy was taken, see Virgil's *Aeneid* (11).

The *Iliad* is probably the most magnificent story ever told about man's prime idiocy: warfare. The human center is Achilles. The main line of the narrative traces his anger, his sulkiness, his savagery, and the final assertion of his better nature. He is the first hero in Western literature; and ever since, when we talk of heroic qualities, Achilles is somewhere in the back of our minds, even though we may think we have never heard of him.

You can look at the *Iliad* through a diminishing glass. Then it becomes the story of a trivial scuffle, marked by small jealousies and treacheries, fought by long-dead semibarbarians who had hardly advanced beyond the sticks-and-stones era. The wars of the *Iliad*, compared with our splendid planetary annihilations, are petty stuff.

Strangely enough, the lens of this diminishing glass changes when you actually start to read the *Iliad*. It becomes a magnifier. The scale of the war becomes unimportant; the scale of the men and the gods enlarges. The essential quality of the *Iliad* is nobility. Nobility is a virtue connected with magnitude; there are no small nobilities. General Eisenhower's *Crusade in Europe* is a useful book, portraying the greatest single military and naval exploit in all history. It is completely without magnitude, whereas the *Iliad*, portraying a local struggle of little historical importance, moves us so that at its close we feel ten feet high. This is no reproach to General Eisenhower. He is no Homer.

And there has never been another Homer. If a reading of the *Iliad* and the *Odyssey* does nothing else for us, it makes us reflect on the difference between art and science. There has been "progress" in the latter; there is no "progress" in the former. All imaginative artists, but only if they are great enough, seem contemporaries. That is the way to read them.

2. HOMER. *The Odyssey*

The *Odyssey* is a kind of sequel to the *Iliad.* It tells what happened to the Greek heroes after the sack of Troy. More especially it follows the fortunes of one of them: Odysseus, King of Ithaca, also known as Ulysses. It describes what happened to him during his ten years' long voyage home; the search of his son Telemachus for his father (a theme repeated in hundreds of novels since); the arrogant wooing by the suitors of his patient wife Penelope during his absence; Odysseus' return; and his bloody revenge on his enemies. The story is well-known even to those who have never read it. Like the Bible, it is less a book than part of the permanent furniture of our minds.

When we take up the *Odyssey,* after the *Iliad,* we step into a different world. Even its sound is different. That of the *Iliad* is clangorous with the clash of arms; that of the *Odyssey* murmurous or thunderous with the myriad-mooded sea.

But the difference is more basic. The *Iliad* is tragic. It announces a theme repeated in Western literature ever since, and one that obsesses our own private minds: the limitations of even the noblest of men in the face of a world seemingly governed by unchangeable Fate. But the *Odyssey* is not tragic. It stresses not the limitations of man, but his possibilities. Its theme is not courage in the face of death, but intelligence in the face of difficulties. It announces another of the great themes: the power of intelligence, a theme to which we modern men readily respond. Though Odysseus is brave enough, his heroism is of the mind. He is not outsized in passion, like Achilles, but man-sized, like us.

The tone of the *Odyssey* corresponds to this more homely conception of man. Though full of fairy-tale episodes, it impresses us as does a realistic novel; indeed it is the first of all realistic novels, as it is the first of adventure stories, and still perhaps the best.

It is in this spirit that we may read it today, as a narrative of adventures that happened to an unusual man whose mind never stopped working. The mood of the *Odyssey* is more relaxed than that of the *Iliad*. And so should ours be as we read it.

3. HERODOTUS (c. 484–c. 425 B.C.) *The Histories*

Of Herodotus we know mainly that he was born of good family in Halicarnassus, a city in Asia Minor, originally a Greek colony, but under Persian control for half of Herodotus' life. We know also that he traveled widely throughout the entire Mediterranean world, presumably amassing the materials that went into his *Histories*, a word which in the original Greek means inquiries or investigations. His work was famous during his lifetime and has never ceased to be so.

Herodotus states his purpose: to preserve "from decay the remembrance of what men have done" and to prevent "the great and wonderful actions of the Greeks and the Barbarians from losing their due meed of glory." The latter part of his book fulfills his purpose. It gives us as full and objective an account of the titanic struggle between Persia and Greece as was possible for this pioneer historian. With these "actions" we associate such glorious names as Marathon, Thermopylae, and Salamis, battles in a war in possible consequence of which we are today a part of Western rather than Asiatic culture.

But the earlier portions of the book, while all leading up to this grand climax, are really a kind of universal cultural history, mingling fact, anecdote, and myth, of the entire known world during the time immediately preceding and contemporary with Herodotus' own period.

Herodotus, in a manner sometimes confusing, sometimes enchanting, mixes journalism, geography, ethnography, anthropology, fables, travelers' tales, and market-place philosophy and moralizing. Though he writes in prose about real rather than legendary events, he is nearer to Homer and to art than to the modern historian and so-called scientific history. The later Latin critic Quintilian said he was "pleasant, lucid, diffuse." All three adjectives are precise.

Hence the beginning reader should not seek in him a clear and, by present-day standards, correct account of the Greek-Persian Wars. He should be read, at least at first, in great long gulps, almost carelessly. He should be read for the stories, the digressions, the character descriptions, the fantastic oddments of information about the manners and customs of dozens of ancient peoples. And he should be read for the pleasure of meeting Herodotus himself—sometimes gullible, sometimes skeptical, always humane, humorous, curious, and civilized. Don't worry overmuch about who is who and what is where. The absorption of specific facts is less important than the immersion of yourself in the broad, full, buoyant Herodotean river of narrative. The Greek critic Longinus, who said of him, "He takes you along and turns hearing into sight," gives us our cue—just to go along and see things.

4. THUCYDIDES (c. 471 – c. 400 B.C.)
The History of the Peloponnesian War

Called by Macaulay "the greatest historian that ever lived," Thucydides belonged to a highly placed Athenian family and saw Athens at its height under Pericles. He was himself involved as a general in the war he chronicled. In 424 B.C., as a consequence of his failure to relieve the Thracian town of Amphipolis, he was removed from his command and banished, enduring twenty years of exile before being pardoned. In his history he refers to this crucial episode with brief, cold, third-person detachment. During these twenty years he traveled about in Sparta and elsewhere seeking and verifying the facts that form the material of his book. A tradition states that he was assassinated, perhaps in 400 B.C.

Never finished (it breaks off in 411 B.C.) but somehow a satisfying whole, his history records the great Greek Civil War, between the imperial forces of Athens and the coalition headed by Sparta. The emphasis is almost entirely on the second half of the war, of which in his mature years he was a contemporary. This phase began in 431 B.C. and ended in 404 B.C. with the defeat of Athens and the breakup of the most hopeful civilization the world has ever known and to whose purely intellectual eminence we have never since attained. Thucydides knew he had a great because tragic subject. He devoted to it limited but magnificent talents of whose worth he was quite aware. With calm confidence he states that his work will remain "a possession for all times." So far he has not been proved wrong.

Though Thucydides and Herodotus are partially contemporary, they have little else in common. Thucydides does his best to be what we now call a scientific historian. He believes the proper ordering of sufficient facts plus the exercise of a powerful mind can explain historical processes. He rejects entirely all fuzzy explanations, such as Herodotus' childlike notion of an avenging Nemesis, ever alert to punish arrogance like that of the Persians. He scorns omens, oracles, and prophecies; he does not need the gods. He analyzes the motives, rarely idealistic, that impel leaders and so precipitate great events. He supplements his extraordinary psychological insight with considerable understanding, considering his time, of the demographic and economic forces that underlay the Peloponnesian War.

Where Herodotus is gossipy and digressive, he is austere and unified. He is not a cultural historian, but a politico-military one. He is skeptical, charmless—and, let us admit, difficult. He cannot be read except with one's full attention, and is one of those forbidding writers who yield more with each rereading. Finally, he is the first historian to grasp the inner life of power politics. Hobbes (54), Machiavelli (62), and Marx (59) are, each in a different way, his sons.

Yet for all his severity and his aristocratic denial of emotion, he grips the serious reader. Of the forty speeches that he puts into the mouths of his historical personages at least one, Pericles' Funeral Oration (Book II) is a supremely great dramatic monologue. Masterpieces also, though of differing kinds, are his accounts of the Plague at Athens (Book II), the Melian Dialogue (Book V), and the terrible Sicilian Expedition (Books VI and VII) that signalized the end of Athens' dominance.

5. PLATO (c. 427–c. 347 B.C.) *Selected Works*

Plato is less an author than a world of thought. He is probably one of the half-dozen most influential minds in Western civilization. It has even been said that all Western philosophy consists of a series of footnotes to Plato—an exaggeration, but not entirely untrue. The beginning reader cannot hope to explore the entire Platonic world, nor should he attempt it. The suggested readings enable us to make his acquaintance and that of his master Socrates. And that is all.

A wealthy Athenian who lived through his city-state's great and also declining days, Plato experienced one crucial event in his long life: his meeting with Socrates. He had many talents, and was drawn, for example, toward both poetry and politics; but Socrates determined him to a life of thought, undertaken on all conceivable fronts.

The result of this life of thought was a series of "dialogues," long and short, some very beautiful, some dull, and most of them spotlighting his master Socrates. The "Socratic method" was part of the atmosphere of the period. Socrates questioned all things, and particularly the meanings men attached to abstract and important words, such as justice, love, and courage. The questioning was a real thing; the truth was finally approached only through the actual play of minds, that give and take we call dialectic. This mode of thought is exemplified and perfected in the dialogues. They are not mere exercises in mental agility (though occasionally they are that predominantly) but also works of art in which all the resources of a poetical and dramatic imagination are called into play. The reader of Plato is reading an artist, in the same sense that the reader of Shakespeare is.

He should keep in mind three central Platonic notions. The first is that, as Socrates says, "a life without inquiry is not worth living." That lies at the heart of everything Plato wrote. The second notion is that virtue is knowledge; that the sufficiently wise man will also be sufficiently good. The third notion has to do with the kinds of knowledge that are most worth having. Plato believed in "Ideas," invisible, intangible archetypes or prototypes of things and actions and virtues. These latter, as we know them on earth through the distorting veil of the senses, are but faint reflections of the heavenly Ideas. We call this mode of apprehending the universe Idealism; and Plato is its father.

His philosophy, however, is not a consistent whole, and in many respects it changed as he grew older and lost faith in humanity's ability to govern itself wisely. It is suggested therefore that the dialogues be read, not as systematic expositions of dogma, but as the intellectual dramas they are, full of humor, wit, mental play, unforgettable extended similes called "myths," and particularly full of one of history's most fascinating characters, the ugly, charming, mock-modest Socrates.

It might be best to begin with the *Apology*, in which Socrates defends himself against the charges of atheism and corrupting the youth. As we know, his defense was a failure—he was executed, by self-administered poison, in 399 B.C. The dialogue —it's really a long speech—has however been a success for almost twenty-four hundred years.

Follow that with the *Crito*. Here Socrates gives us his reasons for refusing to escape from prison. Then perhaps the *Protagoras*, in many ways the most utterly brilliant of the dialogues, and the perfect exemplification of Plato using all his talents. Some may wish to try the *Meno*, recording Plato's famous doctrine of "recollection." Then comes the *Symposium*, practically a drama in its movement and structure. This deals with love in all its phases, including that accepted Greek passion, homosexuality. It deals also with drunkenness, as well as with more exalted matters.

After this perhaps the *Phaedo*. The sections on immortality may be skimmed or skipped, but the last few pages, describing Socrates' noble death, are required reading. Many good judges have felt them to be the finest short piece of narrative ever written. Finally, absorb as much as you can of Plato's most ambitious and rather difficult work, the *Republic*, which outlines his ideal state and is the ancestor of all the Utopias that have since appeared.

So many of our notions and ways of thought go back to Plato (including some fantastic and even harmful ones) that the man who knows nothing of him knows thereby the less about himself. To discover Plato is not merely to discover a masterly intellect. It is to come face to face, if you are a Western man, with much of the hitherto unsuspected content of your own mind.

6. ARISTOTLE (384–322 B.C.) *Ethics, Politics*

Aristotle tells us that education is accompanied by pain. An education in Aristotle himself certainly involves, if not pain, at least difficulty. Unlike his master, Plato, he is charmless. Furthermore, the fact that we do not possess his original works but only what has come down to us as probably students' notes, does not make for readability. You are warned not to expect from Aristotle the pleasures Plato offers, except that pleasure which comes from following the operations of a supreme brain.

For Aristotle's intellect was one of the most comprehensive, perhaps *the* most comprehensive, on record. He wrote on everything, from marine life to metaphysics. While it is unwise to say that all these writings (many of merely antiquarian value today) can be related under a single system, it is true that Aristotle was a systematizer in the sense that Plato was not. He believed in the collectability and relatability of all knowledge. He spent his life collecting and relating. Our idea of an encyclopedia, a most fruitful notion, goes back to him.

Today we would say he was of upper-middle-class origin. At seventeen or eighteen he left his small native town of Stagira for Athens. Here for twenty years he studied at Plato's Academy. The influence of Plato is marked in his work (often by disagreement or development) but we know nothing about the personal relations between the two greatest philosophers of antiquity.

After Plato's death Aristotle sojourned for five years in Asia Minor and Lesbos, possibly engaged in biological research, for his mental bent was scientific and investigative, rather than artistic and speculative. In 343/2 B.C. he went to Macedon to tutor the future Alexander the Great. There is no evidence, despite all the sentimental romancing, that he greatly influenced Alexander's mind. The one great Alexandrian idea, that of a world imperium, is not Aristotelian.

In 335/4 B.C. Aristotle returned to Athens; organized his own school, the Lyceum; taught, wrote, investigated. In 323 B.C., perhaps because of his suspect connections with the Macedonian party, he found it expedient to exile himself from Athens. A year or so later the mere man Aristotle died in Chalcis, in Euboea. His influence, however, though it has had great downward swoops, has never died, and there is some evidence that he is being more closely studied today than at any time since the Renaissance.

We cannot note here his crucial pioneering in logic—he is credited with inventing the syllogism; or in scientific method; or in metaphysics, which he sometimes called the "First Philosophy"; or in the biological and cosmological sciences; or in esthetics—his *Poetics*, an analysis of classic Greek tragedy, has had an enormous and continuing effect on literary criticism. In general we may say that his whole approach to life is more earthbound than Plato's, less utopian, certainly more geared to the actual nature and abilities of ordinary man.

This is borne out by a reading of the *Ethics* and the *Politics*.

The *Ethics* tries to answer the basic question, What is the Good? It involves an inquiry into happiness and the conditions that attend it; and into virtuous actions, thought of as means between two extremes of conduct. The "Golden Mean" is an Aristotelian catchword.

Ethics is a part of politics, for to Aristotle the individual cannot be thought of fruitfully except as a social and political animal. The *Politics* deals more specifically with men in association. Much of our twenty-four hundred years of speculation as to the best form of government, whether ideal or contingent upon circumstances, traces back to ideas found in the *Politics*. This is not to say that Aristotle gives us universal political "truths"—for example his views on slavery are not much advanced beyond those of certain of our Southern statesmen. But his classification of the forms of government; his sense of the state as a *development*, not an imposed system; and his notion that the state must have a moral aim beyond that of a mere freezing of power: all this makes him alive and pertinent today.

The serious reader (and for Aristotle there is no other kind possible) can handle all of the *Ethics*, if he takes it slowly. You might concentrate on Books I, II, III, VI, and X. Of the *Politics* possibly the first and third of the eight books are the easiest of access.

7. AESCHYLUS (525–456 B.C.) *The Oresteia*

(Ancient Greek tragedy is so different from the plays we are familiar with that the beginning reader will do well first to study some standard book on the subject, or to consult the relevant chapters in a history of Greek literature; or at least to read carefully the notes and introductions usually accompanying the translations. He might also look up the myths associated with the names of the chief personages in the recommended plays.

Classic Greek drama was written in verse, usually in an elevated and formal style. It was presented in the open air at the yearly festival at Athens in honor of the god Dionysus. That means the plays were part of a religious ceremony, attended, as their civic duty, by all or most of the citizens. They were given as trilogies, followed by a shorter play of a comic nature; and the dramatists competed with one another for the laurel of victory. Aeschylus' Oresteia *is the only complete trilogy that has survived.*

It is hard for us to visualize these ancient Greek sunlit productions. They incorporated music, dance, and choral song, and doubtless words were declaimed or chanted in a manner quite dissimilar to our modern realistic conventions. As the plots were usually reworkings of famous legends, they offered no suspense; everybody knew the story in advance. Two features, among others, that seem strange to us were: the Chorus, which acted as a kind of commentary on the action; and the Messenger, who recounted offstage events, particularly if they were of a violent kind. As we approach Greek drama we must try to keep in mind that it is religious in origin and partly so in effect; and that its language and action are not in our sense "realistic.")

Though he did not "invent" Greek tragedy, Aeschylus is generally considered its father, and so the ancestor of all Western tragic drama. He lived through the great days of the growth of the Athenian democracy and himself helped in its ascendancy, for he fought at Marathon and perhaps at Salamis. Born in Eleusis, near Athens, he spent most of his life in and around Athens, dying in Gela, Sicily, from the effects, says legend, of a tortoise dropped by an eagle on his bald head. Of his ninety plays, seven survive.

His last and best work is the trilogy known from its central character as the *Oresteia*. Its theme is one frequently encountered in Greek legend, family blood-guilt and its expiation. The *Agamemnon* is a play about murder, the murder of the returned hero Agamemnon by his faithless wife Clytemnestra. The *Choephoroe (Libation-Bearers)* is a play about revenge, the revenge taken on Clytemnestra by Orestes, Agamemnon's son. The *Eumenides (Furies)* is a play about purification: the tormenting of Orestes by the Furies and his final exoneration by a tribunal of Athenian judges, plus the goddess Athena. The entire trilogy is a study in the complex operations of destiny, heredity, and pride, which produce a tragic knot untied by the advent of a higher conception of law and order.

As the word for Homer is noble so the word for Aeschylus is grand. He cannot be read as modern plays are read. His language is exalted and difficult; it struggles magnificently to express profound ideas about guilt and sin, ideas that have become part of the world of imaginative literature right up to our own day, with Faulkner (89) and O'Neill. Aeschylus is much more akin to the author of the Book of Job than to even the best of our contemporary dramatists. He must be approached in that spirit.

8. SOPHOCLES (c. 496–406 B.C.)

Oedipus Rex, Oedipus at Colonus, Antigone

Sophocles was born in what we would call a suburb of Athens, of upper-class family. He held high office; he was a constant victor in the dramatic competitions; he developed in various ways the relatively primitive playwrighting techniques of Aeschylus; he lived long and, it appears, happily; and he was one of the greatest ornaments of the Periclean Age. Of his more than 120 plays we possess seven. But these suffice to place him among the few truly great dramatists of all time.

Formulas are unreliable. But it is not entirely untrue to say that the beginning reader may best see Aeschylus as a dramatic theologian, obsessed with God and his stern edicts. Sophocles may be seen as a dramatic artist, concerned with human suffering. Euripides may be seen as a playwright-critic, using the legends as a vehicle for ideas current in his skeptical and disillusioned era.

The three recommended plays are all about the same family, that of King Oedipus, but were not written as a trilogy. The order of their composition is *Antigone, Oedipus Rex, Oedipus at Colonus.* (The last, written by a very old man of undiminished powers, was produced in 401 B.C. after Sophocles' death.) If you wish, you may read them in the order of the chronology suggested by their action: *Oedipus Rex, Oedipus at Colonus, Antigone.* Together they are often called the Oedipus Cycle or the Theban Plays.

In his *Poetics,* which you might try if you find Greek tragedy interesting, Aristotle (6) tells us that Sophocles said he portrayed people as they ought to be, Euripides as they are. He might have added that Aeschylus portrayed people as demigods driven by single outsize passions.

Aristotle considers *Oedipus Rex* the ideal play, admiring it especially for its plot and construction. Today we might stress other elements. There is no doubt, however, that it is the most influential Greek tragedy in existence, the one most often revived, the one most universally studied. Its basic myth, that of a man who killed his father and married his mother, suggested to Freud (61) the name for his famous Oedipus complex. After reading the *Oedipus,* you may find yourself asking, among others, two profound questions that continue to be asked down to our own day: First, Is man free or bound? Second, If the intelligence brings tragedy, to what degree is it good? Technically the effect of the play depends in large part on the masterly use of what is called dramatic irony—the device whereby the audience is in possession of crucial facts hidden from the protagonist.

Oedipus at Colonus is a difficult play, even for the learned reader. Unlike *Oedipus Rex,* it is not well-knit; its interest does not lie in its plot. Perhaps it should be approached as a kind of miracle or mystery play, a study of a man more heavily burdened with guilt and knowledge than is normal, and whose life is at last vindicated and given meaning both by the gods and the city of Athens. In the end Oedipus becomes a kind of transcendental hero, like King Arthur; and, also like him, comes to a mysterious end.

The *Antigone* is psychologically the most complex of the three. It has been viewed as a study of the conflicting claims of convention and a higher law of conduct, or, differently phrased, of the state and the individual. It is also one of the many Greek plays about *hubris* or pride—in this case, the pride of Creon—and the ruin that attends such immoderacy of feeling. The reader may have met this notion in Herodotus (3). Before you start the *Antigone* keep in mind that to the ancient Greeks the proper burial of the dead was a matter of overwhelming importance. Also you must accept the Greek idea (or at least Antigone's idea) that a husband or child is replaceable, a brother never.

In the Oedipus Cycle, Sophocles deals with the downfall of greatness. But he is inspired as much by the greatness as by the downfall. We might say that the special Sophoclean emotion is born of the tension resulting from his sad recognition of man's tragic fate on the one hand, and his admiration for man's wondrous powers on the other.

9. EURIPIDES (c. 480–c. 406 B.C.) *Alcestis, Medea, Hippolytus, Trojan Women, Electra, Bacchae*

Though possibly only fifteen years junior to Sophocles, Euripides inherited a different Greek world, torn by intellectual doubt and civil strife. His work seems to reflect the change. In Sophocles' sense of tragedy there is a certain grave serenity; not so with Euripides.

He was born at Salamis, legend says on the very day of the famous naval battle. He appears to have led a retired, perhaps even an embittered life. One story has him living alone in a cave by the sea. Of his eighty or ninety plays, nineteen survive, if the *Rhesus* is genuine. Though they were popular, he won the prize, according to one account, only five times to Sophocles' eighteen.

Of the three great Attic tragedians, Euripides is the most interesting in the sense that his mental world is least alien to our own. A son of the all-questioning Sophists, swayed by the irony of Socrates, he too felt the uncertainty of all moral and religious values. His later career contemporary with the suicidal Peloponnesian War, he too lived in a crisis period marked by fear, pessimism, and political confusion. The development of his genius was irregular and his thought is not consistent, but we can say that his mind was rationalistic, skeptical, and tragic, though not in the exalted Sophoclean pattern. He would today understand without difficulty certain existentialist and even Beat writers.

His plays are generally, though not always, marked by theatricality, even an operatic luridness; by the use of exaggerated coincidence; by the employment at the end of a knot-resolving "god from the machine"; by dialogue which is often debate and oration rather than impassioned speech; by a mixture of tones—Is the *Alcestis* a serious or a comic play?; by unconventional, even radical ideas—the *Trojan Women* empties war of its glory,

Medea can be taken as a feminist tract, other plays portray the gods as either delusive or unlovely; by a remarkable talent for the depiction of women—Phaedra and Medea are miracles of feminine psychology; and finally by a pervading interest, not in the relations between man and some supernal force, but in the weaknesses and passions of our own natures. As a psychologist and vendor of ideas, Euripides is the ancestor of Ibsen (19) and Shaw (20).

And yet Euripides escapes formulas. His plays at times seem to be the broken record of a search for certainties that were never found. He can write realistic, even down-to-earth dialogue —but also choruses and speeches of rare beauty. Plutarch tells us that some Athenians, taken prisoner at Syracuse, were freed because they recited so enchantingly some passages from Euripides. He seems often to be a skeptic, almost a village atheist; yet in his masterpiece, his last play the *Bacchae*, he delves profoundly and with strange sympathy into man's recurrent need for irrationality, even for frenzy. Euripides is not of a piece. Perhaps therein lies part of his fascination for a time which, like ours, specializes in damaged souls.

I have suggested six plays. They are arranged in the probable order of their composition or at least representation. But many others repay study, among them *Heracles*, *Hecuba*, and *Andromache*.

As you read Euripides, see whether you can understand why Aristotle (6) called him "the most tragic of the poets."

10. LUCRETIUS (c. 96–55 B.C.)
Of the Nature of Things

Of Lucretius we know virtually nothing. A tradition states that he was driven mad by a love potion and that he ended his own life. This note of violence is at least not contradicted by the vein of passionate intensity running through his great and strange poem, *De Rerum Natura.*

We do not today cast our explanations of the physical and moral world into hexameters. But in classic times poetry was often the vehicle of instruction and propaganda. Lucretius' poem is such a vehicle.

His temperament was original, his thought less so. As he proudly avers, he borrows his system from the Greek Epicurus (*c.* 342-270 B.C.), who in turn derived parts of his theory from two earlier Greek thinkers, Democritus and Leucippus. The Epicurean philosophy has little in common with our modern use of the phrase. Acknowledging pleasure (or, more accurately, the absence of pain) as the highest good, it rests its ethics on the evidence of the senses. But the pleasures Epicurus recommends are those flowing from plain living and high thinking. Denying the existence of any supernatural influence on men's lives, Epicurus held that the world and all things in it were the consequence of the meeting and joining of refined but quite material atoms.

Lucretius expounds this materialism systematically, explaining everything from optics to ethics in terms of atoms. He empties the world of God; his gods are do-nothing creatures, living in the "interspaces," caring nothing about men. In effect he is an atheist. The origin and behavior of all things are determined by the movement of the atoms composing them. Free will is saved by the idea of the "swerve" of some atoms, a break in the general determinism. The soul dies with the body. Mankind should live without the fear born of superstition. *Of the Nature of Things* is pioneer rationalist propaganda.

The "atomic theory" of Lucretius was less absurd than many other early Greek explanations of the universe, but in all truth it has little resemblance to our modern sophisticated atomic theory, and too much should not be made of the anticipation. On the other hand Lucretius foreshadows much of our own thought in the fields of anthropology, sociology, and evolution. He would have been quite at home in our century.

As we should expect, his poem is knotty and difficult, for physics and cosmology do not translate easily into verse. It is remarkable that he should have succeeded as well as he did. While there are many opaque stretches, they are worth struggling through in order to come upon the frequent passages of intense eloquence and beauty. These flow from Lucretius' ability, unmatched until we meet Dante (14), to hold in his head a complete vision of things and to body it forth in the most concrete, sometimes unforgettable images.

In Virgil's (11) famous line the reference is probably to Lucretius: "Happy is he who knows the causes of things." It is Lucretius' passion for knowing causes, his stubborn refusal to be fobbed off with myth and superstition that, together with his uneven but powerful art, recommend him to our modern temper. No matter how wrong he was in detail, it was a titanic achievement to build a universe out of nothing but matter and space.

11. VIRGIL (70–19 B.C.) *The Aeneid*

The poet called by Tennyson "wielder of the stateliest measure ever moulded by the lips of man" used that measure to celebrate Rome's high destiny, yet was no Roman but a Gaul. He was born near Mantua, situated in what was then called Cisalpine Gaul. His quiet life was marked by study in Rome and by years of contemplation and composition at his Mantuan farm and later on at his residences in Campania. His relatively brief life-span may point to the fragile physique of which we have other evidence. The great Maecenas, minister of the greater Emperor Augustus, was his patron, as he was that of Virgil's friend, the poet Horace.

Labor on his masterwork occupied his entire last decade. He felt the *Aeneid* to be unfinished and, dying, ordered its destruction. This was prevented however by Augustus, whose gesture seems odd to us in an age when heads of state are not only ignorant of literature but not even required to be particularly literate.

Homer may be said to have started European literature, Virgil to have started one of its subdivisions, the literature of nationalism. The *Aeneid* was written with a deliberate purpose: to dramatize, through the manipulation of legend, the glory and destiny of that Rome which had reached its high point in Virgil's own Augustan Era. The *Aeneid* is no more an "artificial" epic than is the *Iliad*. But it is a more self-conscious one. Writing it, Virgil felt he was performing a religious and political duty. Aeneas is called "pious," by which is meant that he was not merely orthodox in religious observance but faithful, like a supremely good citizen, to the overwhelming idea of Roman supremacy. The *Aeneid*'s political center of gravity may be located in the three famous lines of Book VI, in which the spirit of Anchises is showing forth to his son the glorious future of Rome: "Romans, these are your arts: to bear dominion over the nations, to impose peace, to spare the conquered and subdue the proud."

Because this nationalist (but not at all chauvinist) ideal is one of the keys to Virgil's mind, the reader should be aware of it. But for us it is not the important thing. The *Aeneid* today is a story, a gallery of characters, and a work of art.

Its story is part of us. We may not have read Virgil but nonetheless a bell rings if Dido or the death of Laocoön or the Harpies or the Trojan Horse is mentioned. Its personages, particularly the unhappy Dido and the fiery Turnus, have also remained fresh for two thousand years. Its art, hard to summarize, is not always immediately felt. It is based on a delicate, almost infallible sense of what words can do when carefully, often strangely, combined and juxtaposed and subdued to a powerful rhythm. It is this that has made Virgil among the most quoted of all poets. And, back of the story, the characters, the art there shimmers Virgil's own curious sense of life's melancholy, rather than its tragedy, his famous *lacrimae rerum,* which continues to move us though the Rome he sang has long been dust.

One word of counsel: the *Iliad* (1) and the *Odyssey* (2) influenced Virgil decisively. Indeed the *Aeneid's* first six books are a kind of Odyssey, the last six a kind of Iliad, and Homeric references are legion. But Virgil is not as "open" as Homer. He requires more effort of the attention, he does not have Homer's outdoor vigor, and for his master's simplicity and directness he substitutes effects of great subtlety, many, though not all, lost even in the finest translation.

12. MARCUS AURELIUS (121–180) *Meditations*

Marcus Aurelius Antoninus, ruler of the Roman Empire from 161 to his death, is the outstanding, perhaps indeed the only, example in Western history of Plato's (5) ideal Philosopher-King. His reign was far from utopian, being marked by wars against the barbarian Germans, by severe economic troubles, by plague. It will be remembered not because Marcus was a good emperor (though he was) but because during the last ten years of his life, by the light of a campfire, resting by the remote Danube after a wearisome day of marching or battle, he set down in Greek his *Meditations,* addressed only to himself but by good fortune now the property of us all.

The curious charm, the sweetness, the melancholy, the elevation of the *Meditations* are his own. The moral doctrines are those of the popular philosophy of the time, Stoicism, as systematically expounded by the Greek slave (later freed) Epictetus (*c.* 60-*c.* 140). Its ethical content is roughly summed up in Epictetus' two commandments: "Endure" and "Abstain." Stoicism passed through many modifications, but in general it preached a quiet and unmoved acceptance of circumstance. It assumed a beneficent order of Nature. Man's whole duty was to discover how he might live in harmony with this order, and then to do so. Stress was laid on tranquillity of mind (many of our modern "inspirational" nostrums are merely cheapenings of Stoicism); on service to one's fellows; and on a cosmopolitan, all-embracing social sense that is a precursor of the fully developed Christian idea of the brotherhood of man. Stoicism's watchwords are Duty, Imperturbability, Will. Its tendency is puritanical, ascetic, quietistic, sometimes even escapist. Though a philosophy peculiarly suited to a time of troubles, its influence has never ceased during almost the whole of two thousand years. It seems to call out to men irrespective of their time and place—see, for example, Thoreau (67).

We find it at its most appealing in the *Meditations*. This is an easy book to read. We seem to be eavesdropping on the soliloquy of a man almost painfully attached to virtue, with a firm sense of his responsibility, less to his Empire than to the Stoic ideal of the perfect man, untouched by passion, generous by nature rather than by calculation, impervious both to ill and good fortune. Says Marcus, in one of the saddest sentences of a book shadowed throughout by melancholy, "Even in a palace life may be lived well."

Through the years the Golden Book of Marcus Aurelius, as it has been called, has been read by vast numbers of ordinary men and women. They have thought of it not as a classic but as a wellspring of consolation and inspiration. It is one of the few books that seem to have helped men directly and immediately to live better, to bear with greater dignity and fortitude the burden of being merely human. Aristotle one studies. Marcus Aurelius men take to their hearts.

The Middle Ages

13. ST. AUGUSTINE (354–430) *Confessions*

Autobiography would seem to be the easiest of all literary forms, for what could be simpler than to talk of one's own life? Yet, though the Lifetime Reading Plan abounds in great poems and novels, it suggests only three autobiographies: those of Rousseau (85), Henry Adams (87), and St. Augustine. Of all the autobiographies ever written, perhaps the most powerful and influential is the *Confessions.*

In passing from Marcus Aurelius to Augustine we meet a deeper, if less attractive mind. The profundity of Augustine's intellect can be felt only by those willing to spend some time in the vast and obscure forest of his works, particularly his masterpiece *The City of God.* But its intensity, its obsession with God, and its tortured concern with sin and salvation can be felt by anyone who reads at least the first nine books of the *Confessions.*

The Roman citizen, born in North Africa, who became the bishop of Hippo, is probably the most effective defender the Church has had in its long history. Yet, as he tells us, he came to Catholicism only in his thirty-second year, after he had sampled the delights of the flesh (including the thirteen-year possession of a mistress who bore him a son); after he had dabbled in the heresy of Manichaeism; after he had sampled the classical doctrines of Platonism and Skepticism. Readers of the *Confessions* will note the many influences, especially that of his saintly mother Monica, that led him at last to his true vocation. The moment of his conversion in the garden, as described in the twelfth chapter of Book VIII, is one of the pivotal moments in the history of Christianity as well as a crucial instance of the mystical experience.

There is a great deal of theology and Christian apologetics and Biblical exegesis in the *Confessions*, notably in the last four books, dealing with memory, time, the nature of temptation, and the proper expounding of the Scriptures. But the power of the book is exerted even on the nonbeliever. The *Confessions* was originally written to bring men to the truth. For us it is rather a masterpiece of self-revelation, the first unsparing account of how a real man was led, step by step, from the City of Man to the City of God. To the psychologist, to the student of what William James (69) called the "varieties of religious experience," it is endlessly interesting. But, beyond this, it grips us because we cannot shut our ears to the terrible humanness of Augustine's voice. He is trying desperately to tell us the truth, about the events not only of his external life, but of his soul. The *Confessions* is the classic spiritual autobiography. In all our literature there is nothing quite like it.

14. DANTE ALIGHIERI (1265–1321)
The Divine Comedy

Like his time, the life of Dante was disordered, which may in part account for the fact that his masterpiece is the most ordered long poem in existence. During his lifetime his native Florence, and indeed much of Italy, was divided by factional strife. In this struggle Dante, as propagandist and government official, played his part. It was not a successful part, for in 1302 he was banished. To the day of his death, almost twenty years later, he wandered through the courts and great houses of Italy, eating the bitter bread of exile.

To our modern view his emotional life seems no less unbalanced. He tells us that when he was nine he first saw the little girl, Beatrice; and then nine years later saw her again. This is the extent of his relationship with a woman who was to be the prime mover of his imagination and whom, in the last canto of the *Paradiso*, the third part of *The Divine Comedy*, he was to place beside God.

Dante called his poem a Comedy (the adjective Divine was added by later commentators) because it began in Hell, that is, with disaster, and ended in Heaven, that is, with happiness. To the beginning reader it at first seems almost impenetrable. To daunt us there is first its theology, derived from the great thinker Thomas Aquinas (*c.* 1225-1274). There is its complex system of virtues and vices, in part stemming from Aristotle (6). There is the fact that, as Dante tells us, the poem is written on four levels of meaning. There is its constant use of allegory and symbol; with Dante this is not a mere device, but part of the structure of his thought. And, finally, the poem is stuffed with contemporary references, for Dante was one of the few great writers who constantly worked with what today we would call the materials of journalism.

And yet, despite these, and many more, impediments, Dante can still move and indeed overwhelm the nonscholarly reader. Perhaps it is best, as T. S. Eliot (93) advises in his famous essay, to plunge directly into the poem and to pay little or no attention to the possible symbolic meanings. Its grand design can be understood at once. This is a narrative, like Bunyan's *Pilgrim's Progress* (21) of *human* life as it is lived on earth—even though Dante has chosen to make vivid our earthly states by imagining a Hell, a Purgatory, and a Paradise. We too live partly in a state of misery, or Hell. We too are punished for our sins and may atone for them, as do the inhabitants of Purgatory. And we too, Dante fervently believed, may, by the exercise of reason—personified by Dante's guide Virgil (11)—and faith, become candidates for that state of felicity described in the *Paradiso*. Dante's moral intensity, though it is exercised on the life of his own time and within the framework of the then dominant scholastic philosophy, breaks through to the sensitive reader of our own century. Dante is as realistic, as true to human nature, as any modern novelist—and far more unsparingly so.

Furthermore, the poem is open to us *as* a poem. The greatest poetic imaginations are not cloudy, but hard and precise. Concision and precision are the essence of Dante's imagination. He is continually creating not merely vivid pictures, but the *only* vivid picture that will fully convey his meaning. These we can all see and feel, even in translation: Dante is a great painter. Similarly we can all sense the powerful, ordered, symmetrical structure of the poem: Dante is a great architect.

One last word: I would qualify Mr. Eliot's advice to this extent. No harm, and much good, will result from a reading of the introduction to your edition, for Dante's poem and his life and time are inextricably interwoven. Furthermore most editions contain notes explaining the major references. A good way of trying Dante is to read a canto (there are one hundred in all) without paying any attention to the notes. Then reread it, using the notes. Do not expect to understand everything—eminent scholars are still quarreling over Dante's meanings. You will understand enough to make your reading worth the effort.

15. GEOFFREY CHAUCER (c. 1340–1400)
The Canterbury Tales

As Dante's masterwork is called the Divine, so Chaucer's has often been called the Human Comedy. It is a fair distinction. Dante loved God; Chaucer loved human beings, including the imperfect and even sinful ones. Dante fixed his eye on those paths leading to perdition, purification, and felicity; Chaucer fixed his on the crowded highway of actual daily life. Both wrote of journeys. Dante's is a journey through three symbolical universes. But Chaucer takes himself and thirty-odd Englishmen and Englishwomen of the fourteenth century and sets his wayfarers on a real journey on a real English road, starting at a real inn at Southwark, then just outside of London, and ending at the real town of Canterbury. Though Chaucer was greatly influenced by Dante, the two supreme poets of the Middle Ages could not have been more unlike in temperament.

Their careers too, parallel in some respects, turned out differently. Like Dante, Chaucer was a civil servant, serving under three kings. He held various posts, many quite important, as economic envoy, Controller of Customs, Clerk of the King's Works, Justice of the Peace, and others. He seems to have met with one or two brief periods of disfavor but on the whole his life was lived close to the centers of English power; he rose steadily in the world; and all the evidence suggests a successful career, marked by lively contacts with the stir and bustle of his day, and sufficiently relaxed to allow time for the composition of a great number of works in both verse and prose.

He lacks Dante's depth, bitterness, intensity, vast scholarship, and complexity of imagination. Instead he offers more ingratiating if less overwhelming talents: broad humanity, humor, a quick but tolerant eye for the weaknesses of human nature, an unmatched gift for storytelling, a musical gift of a lower order than Dante's but nonetheless superb, and most of all a certain open-air candor that makes us at once eager to claim him as a friend.

As the *Prologue* indicates, *The Canterbury Tales* were originally conceived as perhaps 120 narratives of all kinds, held together by the ingenious device of having a band of pilgrims, bound for Thomas à Becket's shrine, tell stories to while away the tedium of travel. Chaucer completed twenty-one of these, with three left unfinished or interrupted. Several are dull exercises in sermonizing and are well skipped. The *Prologue* of course must be read; it is perhaps the most delightful portrait gallery in the world. Those tales that have been most generally admired are the ones told by the Knight, the Miller, the Prioress, the Nun's Priest, the Pardoner, the Wife of Bath (Chaucer's greatest single character, and comparable to Shakespeare's supreme achievements in comic portraiture), the Clerk, the Merchant, the Squire, and the Canon's Yeoman. I suggest you also read the various prologues, epilogues, and conversations that link the stories. Many readers prefer them to the Tales themselves.

Chaucer is a supreme yarn-spinner, the founder of English realism, and an entrancing human being. He is also full of interesting information. He paints an immortal picture of Catholic medieval England, drawn with all the warts left in, and painted in colors as fresh and lively as though applied only yesterday. He can be read without any apparatus at all, though most editions supply a handful of notes explaining those customs and manners peculiar to his day. His book is an "open" book, like the *Odyssey* (2), and unlike *The Divine Comedy* (14). He makes you feel that a clear-eyed man of the world has taken you by the arm to tell you about the men and women of his time—and, lo, they turn out to be oddly like the men and women of ours. There are no mysteries in Chaucer. Even when he is allegorical, he is plain and downright.

If you are lucky enough to have an exceptional feeling for English words, you may find it quite possible to read a good deal of Chaucer in the original Middle English—at any rate the *Prologue*. But most of us will need a translation, either a sound prose version (I like Lumiansky's) or the remarkable verse rendering by Coghill.

Plays

16. WILLIAM SHAKESPEARE (1564–1616)
Complete Works

Enjoying Shakespeare is a little like conquering Everest: much depends on the approach. Let's clear away a few common misconceptions.

1. There is no Shakespeare "mystery." There was a man named William Shakespeare, we know considerable about his life, and he wrote the plays. His existence is no more conjectural than yours.

2. He was a man, not a demigod. He was not "myriad-minded," even though Coleridge (78) said he was. He does not out-top knowledge, even though Matthew Arnold said he does. He was not infallible—merely a genius, one of many the race has produced. He was also a practicing theater craftsman, a busy actor, and a shrewd, increasingly prosperous businessman. A genius may live a quite conventional life, and Shakespeare (unless you are terribly shocked at his leaving his young wife and children for some years) did so.

3. He is our greatest English poet and dramatist. But he is not always great. He often wrote too quickly, with his eye not on posterity but on a deadline. Some of his comic characters have lost all power to amuse, and it is best to admit it. His puns and wordplay are often tedious. He can be obscure rather than profound.

4. He is not a great original thinker. Few poets are—that is not their business. Those who seek ideas that have changed the world should not go to Shakespeare; they will be disappointed.

5. Finally, we all (including this writer) think we "know"

Shakespeare, when what we probably know is merely what we are supposed to think about him. Hard though it is, we must try to clear our minds of the formulas inherited from the average high-school or college English class. Approaching the plays as "classics" is less fruitful than approaching them with the fresh expectancy with which we attend the opening performance of a new play.

This brief note therefore does not at all suggest what to look for. Even if you are not looking for anything in Shakespeare you will find something.

Read, do not study him. And of course reread him, for the simple approach I have advised will disclose only a part of a complex artist. Many men have spent almost their entire lives on Shakespeare and felt no regret.

To read him complete is well worth, let us say, six months out of the ordinary three score and ten. Yet few of us possess the necessary curiosity. Judgments vary, but of the thirty-seven plays the following dozen may be recommended as minimum reading, to be done not as a block but in the course of your lifetime: *The Merchant of Venice, Romeo and Juliet, Henry IV* (Parts 1 and 2), *Hamlet, Troilus and Cressida, Measure for Measure, King Lear, Macbeth, Antony and Cleopatra, Othello, The Tempest.*

Shakespeare also wrote a sonnet sequence, some of the poems being clearly addressed to a young man, others to an unidentified "Dark Lady." Though the whole forms a kind of loose progression, the sonnets may be read singly, with perfect satisfaction. Some of the more famous: Numbers 18, 29, 30, 33, 55, 60, 63, 64, 65, 66, 71, 73, 94, 98, 106, 107, 116, 129, 130, 144, 146.

The right edition is important. The best one-volume buy for the reader for whom Shakespeare consists of a few dozen quotations plus some vague memories of *Julius Caesar* and *Hamlet* (that includes most of us) is perhaps the complete edition edited by G. B. Harrison (Harcourt, Brace). This contains almost a hundred pages of highly informative introduction, useful illustrations, appendixes, and a reading list. Of Shakespearean commentaries there are literally thousands. In the Suggestions for Further Reading I list a mere seven. Of these Marchette Chute's book is a delightful and trustworthy reconstruction of Shakespeare's life and times. Of the commentaries I like Mark Van Doren's interpretation. It is, of course, his own personal view of the plays.

17. MOLIÈRE (1622–1673) *Selected Plays*

Molière's real name was Jean-Baptiste Poquelin. The son of a prosperous Parisian upholsterer, he received a good Jesuit education, read for the law, and at twenty-one renounced security and upholstery for the chancy and nonrespectable life of the stage. His company failed in Paris. He spent many years, perhaps thirteen, knocking about in provincial inn-yards, mounting farces, learning from the ground up the business both of the theater and of human nature. In 1658 his company re-established itself in Paris under the patronage of the brother of Louis XIV. It was successful and so was Molière, operating as actor, manager, and writer of whatever seemed called for—farces, court entertainments, comedies.

In his personal life he was less fortunate. At forty he married Armande Béjart, who may have been the illegitimate daughter of his former mistress, and, some said, his own daughter, though there is not the slightest evidence for this contention. Half his age, Armande doubled his troubles, which were complicated by overwork, illness, and the many controversies brought on by Molière's to us rather mild satires on affectation, religious hypocrisy, and conventional prejudices. One night, while playing the title role in his own comedy *The Imaginary Invalid,* he hemorrhaged onstage, dying soon after.

There are at least two Molières. Unhappily they are often found in the same play. The first is the play-it-for-laughs commercial hack who knows all the tricks. Molière the gagman and knockabout farce-confector would have no trouble in Hollywood today. Indeed Hollywood, though it does not know it, is still using switches on comedy situations developed or less often invented by Molière.

The second Molière is the strange man who turned his own sad life into comedy: his illness into *The Imaginary Invalid;* his tragic marriage into *The School for Wives;* and I think his own bittersweet view of his society into *The Misanthrope.*

Molière will never be a great favorite of the English-speaking world. His characters are conceived in the French classic tradition (when they are not even simpler reincarnations of the Italian *commedia dell'arte*). That is they are not individuals, as Hamlet and Falstaff are, but walking and mainly talking incorporations of single passions or ideas. From our viewpoint his plays are badly constructed and lacking in action. Finally he has none of the "richness" or unexpectedness of our Shakespeare. Molière is all logic and neatness.

Yet if we are willing to accept the French classic notion of a play as a kind of organized argument, constructed in accord with the rules of rhetoric, Molière is suddenly seen to be a master. But we do not have to know much about the rules he followed (or quite often broke) to enjoy his thrusts at exaggerated conduct, his constant sense of the ridiculousness of human behavior, and the curious sadness that underlies much of his most hilarious comedy. "It's a strange business, making nice honest people laugh," says Dorante in *The Critique of the School for Wives.* Molière must have found it so.

For those who do not know French he offers only moderate enjoyment. Somehow in English he sounds what he was not—simple-minded. My best recommendation is the Morris Bishop version in the Modern Library edition. Of the eight plays there included try: *The School for Wives, Tartuffe, The Misanthrope, The Would-Be Gentleman.* There are four other equally major plays: *The Miser, Don Juan, The Imaginary Invalid,* and *The*

Learned Ladies (Les Femmes savantes). But none of the translations of these latter that I have come across conveys fully either the elegance or the vitality of Molière.

18. JOHANN WOLFGANG VON GOETHE (1749–1832) *Faust (especially Part 1)*

Goethe is often called "the last Universal Man." He possessed the sort of nonspecialized mind that no longer exists, and the lack of which may be leading us to disaster. This colossus lived a long and superbly favored life. He loved plurally. He wrote, brilliantly or tediously, in every possible form. Creative artist, government administrator, scientific researcher, and theorist, he was fantastically versatile. He invented German literature and then dominated it for half a century. Like his contemporary Napoleon he was more a force of nature than a man.

Perhaps he was more a process than either. One key to Goethe is a pair of words: change (he might have said metamorphosis) and development. Although he felt both himself and nature to be wholes, his sense of himself, as well as of nature, was evolutionary. He outgrew women, ideas, experiences, only to incorporate what they had taught him into a new, larger, still growing Goethe. "I am like a snake," he said. "I slough my skin and start afresh." Perhaps we should speak of Goethe as we do of some great country, like the United States. At any moment he is the sum of a complex historical past plus the potentialities of an incalculable future. In his lifelong emphasis on growth, change, striving, activity, and the conquest and understanding of the world, Goethe was himself what we have come to call a Faustian man, typifying a major aspect of our modern Western life-feeling.

His masterpiece grew as Goethe himself did. As a small boy in his native Frankfurt he saw a puppet show based on the old folk-character Faust. From that day to a few months before his death, when he finished Part 2, *Faust* continued to develop in his mind and on his writing table. Part 1 was started in his early twenties and completed almost thirty years later. Neither part is really a play for the stage. Both are changing visions of life, written, as Goethe's own career was conceived, in many different tonalities and styles, from the obscene to the sublime.

Part 1 is the simpler and less profound of the two, and the easier of access. It is familiar to us partly because its legend has attracted so many writers and composers. The Faust-Margaret love story of course inspired Gounod's famous opera.

Part 1 deals with an individual soul, the seeker Faust: his intellectual disillusionments and ambitions; the temptations put in his way by the fascinating, all-denying Mephistopheles; his seduction of Margaret; and the promise of redemption through love. Part 2 deals with the "great world," not of the individual Faust but of Western man. It is really a kind of historical phantasmagoria, with the legendary Helen, whom we met in Homer (1), symbolizing the classic world (see 1 through 12) and Faust himself symbolizing the modern or post-Renaissance world. Heaven, Hell, and Earth are the settings of *Faust* as they are of *The Divine Comedy* (14). But Goethe is not even as clear as Dante, and many of his meanings are still being quarreled over.

In translation Goethe, like Molière, is not entirely satisfactory reading. Yet some acquaintance, however surface, is necessary with this European titan who has influenced hundreds of writers, including the greatest moderns such as Thomas Mann (36).

19. HENRIK IBSEN (1828–1906) *Selected Plays*

You will note that, in addition to the Greek dramatists (7, 8, 9), the Plan suggests only five famous writers of plays, plus T. S. Eliot (93), better known as a nondramatic poet. Of these five Ibsen, though by no means the greatest or most readable, has perhaps had the widest influence on the modern theater. Single-handed he destroyed the lifeless, mechanical "well-made play" which was dominating Europe when he began his life work. He turned the theater into a forum for the discussion of often disruptive ideas. He introduced a new realism. He made plays out of people rather than "situations." And, being partly responsible for Shaw (20), he is the grandfather of modern social drama.

The son of a Norwegian merchant who went bankrupt in Henrik's eighth year, Ibsen passed through a difficult boyhood and youth. In his twenties he began to write poems and romantic historical dramas, but was at first no more successful as an author than he was as stage manager and theater director. In 1864 he left Norway for Rome, on a traveling scholarship. For the next twenty-seven years, except for two brief visits home, he lived abroad, mainly in Germany and Italy. During this fertile period he produced most of the plays that astounded, shocked, or delighted Europe. Mental illness clouded the last few years of his long and probably not very happy life.

There are at least three ways of looking at Ibsen.

To H. L. Mencken and many others he is no iconoclast but "a play-maker of astounding skill," a superlative craftsman without a message, whose originality consisted in taking ideas generally accepted by intelligent people and giving them a novel setting: the stage. Mencken quotes with approval Ibsen's statement: "A dramatist's business is not to answer questions, but merely to ask them."

However, to Ibsen's disciple, George Bernard Shaw, the asking of questions, if they be the right ones, can itself be a revolutionary act; and the Plato (5) who recorded or created Socrates would agree with him. Shaw sees Ibsen's theater as the means by which the nineteenth-century middle class was enabled to free itself from false ideas of goodness, from what Shaw calls "idealism." To him Ibsen is essentially a teacher, we may even say a teacher of Shavianism. Whether or not his interpretation is accurate, it does seem fair to say that Ibsen's plays, particularly those dealing with marriage, the position of women, and the worship of convention, actually had a decisive effect on the ideas of his generation and the succeeding one.

There is still a third Ibsen, and that is Ibsen the poet, whom in translation we can only dimly glimpse. To Norwegians his early *Peer Gynt*, written in verse, is, though it is not at all nationalistic, a kind of epic, an ironic-fantastic résumé of the Norwegian character. It is possible that the so-called "social plays," such as *A Doll's House*, *Ghosts*, and *Hedda Gabler*, will soon be forgotten; and that the more difficult, imaginative, symbolic dramas (*Peer Gynt*, *The Master Builder*, *When We Dead Awaken*) will eventually be ranked among the dramatic masterpieces of the last two centuries.

The plays here recommended are arranged in their order of composition. To my mind the finest are *Peer Gynt* and *The Wild Duck*, but there is no absolute agreement on Ibsen's best work. At any rate try: *Peer Gynt*, *A Doll's House*, *Ghosts*, *An Enemy of the People*, *The Wild Duck*, *Hedda Gabler*, *The Master Builder*, *When We Dead Awaken*.

20. GEORGE BERNARD SHAW (1856–1950) *Selected Plays and Prefaces*

For the better part of a century G. B. S. explained and advertised himself and his intellectual wares with dazzling wit, energy, iteration, and clarity. A man who lives to be ninety-four;

who probably began thinking in his cradle if not in the womb; who left behind him, in addition to a vast library of correspondence, thirty-three massive volumes of plays, prefaces, novels, economic treatises, pamphlets, literary criticism, dramatic criticism, musical criticism, and miscellaneous journalism dealing with every major preoccupation of his time and many trivial ones; and who, like all his favorite supermen, lived forward, as it were, toward an unguessable future—such a man reduces to no formula.

Except perhaps one, and it is his own: "The intellect is also a passion." Whether one agrees with Shaw or not at any point in his long mental wayfaring is less important than the solid fact that he made intellectual passion exciting, or at least modish, for hundreds of thousands, perhaps millions, of human beings. He was a ferment, a catalyst, an enzyme. He left neither system nor school. But one cannot come fresh to any half dozen of his best plays and prefaces without having one's mind shaken, aerated, and often changed.

At the moment the more rarefied critics tend to pass him by, or to stress his lacks: lack of any other than intellectual passion; lack of the tragic sense we find in the Greeks or in Shakespeare; lack of what we call poetry. These dissatisfactions are part of the long process of digesting a titan. My own opinion is that in fifty years his figure will bulk larger than it ever did in the past; that he will be recognized as a supreme prose writer in the plain or unadorned style; and that, merely as a nonstop influential *personality*, he will rank with Voltaire (38), Tolstoy (52), and Dr. Johnson (86).

It will help us, as we read Shaw, to remember a few simple facts.

First, he was Irish—or, as he puts it, "I am a typical Irishman; my family came from Yorkshire." Hence he viewed English life, his immediate world, with a detachment and an irony impossible for an Englishman.

Second, he was a Fabian (antiviolent, gradualistic) Socialist who never recovered from Karl Marx (59). Hence in his work economic knowledge, as he says, "played as important a part as the knowledge of anatomy does in the work of Michael Angelo."

Third, he had a deep faith in the capacity of human beings to rise by effort in the scale of mental evolution. His mouthpiece Don Juan in *Man and Superman* speaks for him: "I tell you that as long as I can conceive something better than myself, I cannot be easy until I am striving to bring it into existence or clearing the way for it."

Fourth, he is probably the greatest *showman* of ideas who ever lived. He is continually using all his resources of wit, paradox, clowning, humor, surprise, invective, and satire, plus a thousand stage tricks, in order to fix firmly in the reader's or playgoer's mind ideas which ordinarily might be found in volumes of sociology, economics, politics, and philosophy that would be inaccessible to the average intelligence. He is always preaching—but from the middle of the center ring of the circus.

Here follow the titles of eleven of Shaw's forty-seven plays. (He wrote ten more than Shakespeare, a man he considered rather inferior to himself as a dramatist—but then he lived almost twice as long.) Always read the prefaces that usually accompany the plays. As prose they are masterly. As argument they are usually more comprehensive and persuasive than the plays—see, for example, the astounding Preface to *Androcles and the Lion* on the prospects of Christianity. Arranged in order of publication or production, this list suggests a little of the evolution of Shaw's mind over his most fertile quarter century, from 1894 to 1923.

Arms and the Man, Candida, The Devil's Disciple, Caesar and Cleopatra, Man and Superman, Major Barbara, Androcles and the Lion, Pygmalion, Heartbreak House, Back to Methuselah, Saint Joan.

Narratives

21. JOHN BUNYAN (1628–1688)
The Pilgrim's Progress

Seventy-five years ago anyone who spoke of a muck-raker or a worldly-wise man or Vanity Fair or the slough of despond or the valley of humiliation would have known he was quoting from *The Pilgrim's Progress.* For over two centuries, starting with the publication of the first part in 1678, it was probably more widely read than any book except the Bible. It cannot, of course, speak to us as powerfully today as it did to the plain, nonconformist people of Bunyan's time, wrestling with their conviction of sin, fearful of Hell's flames, hoping devoutly for salvation. And yet, for all its revivalist theology and its faded Dissenters' devotionalism, it is still worth reading, not alone for its historical importance, but as a work of almost unconscious art.

We marvel that Christianity could have been founded by so few men, most of them obscure and unlettered. The miracle seems a little less baffling if we consider that these men may have been like John Bunyan. Recall his life: the poor tinker and ex-soldier, almost completely unschooled—indeed he tells that at one point he had forgotten how to read and write; converted to the Puritan creed; arrested in 1660 as "a common upholder of several unlawful meetings and conventicles"; spending, except for a few weeks, the next twelve years in Bedford jail; refusing the conditions of release—"If you let me out today, I will preach again tomorrow!"; leaving behind him a wife and four children, one of them blind; spending his imprisonment in writing and in memorizing the Bible and John Foxe's *Book of Martyrs;*

jailed again for six months in 1675, during which time he wrote the first part of *The Pilgrim's Progress;* released once more, only to become one of the most popular preachers of his time.

Written in what is now quaint English, *The Pilgrim's Progress* is a simple allegory for simple people, offering terribly simple answers to the dread question, What shall I do to be saved? It is whole cultures remote from Augustine (13) and Dante (14) whose books it in certain respects resembles. Its faith recognizes only a black-and-white ethic. It appeals to a ferocious piety (though Bunyan himself was kind and tolerant) discoverable today only in our backwoods. And its author, with his dreams and voices and visions and his skinless conscience, was, no doubt of it, a fanatic who would offer Freud (61) a perfect field day.

But it is a remarkable book all the same. It has swayed not only millions of God-fearing plain folk, but sophisticated intellects like Shaw (20). Its prose is that of a born, surely not made, artist—muscular, hard as nails, powerful, even witty. Has a certain kind of business morality ever been more neatly described than by the comfortable Mr. By-ends? "Yet my great-grandfather was but a water-man, looking one way and rowing another; and I got most of my estate by the same occupation." And, if we cannot respond to the theology, it is hard not to respond to the strong rhythm and naked sincerity of that triumphant climax. "When the day that he must go hence was come, many accompanied him to the river side, into which as he went, he said, 'Death, where is thy sting?' and as he went down deeper he said, 'Grave, where is thy victory?' So he passed over, and all the trumpets sounded for him on the other side."

Of all the writers who, listed in this Plan, had preceded him, Bunyan had never read a line. He merely quietly joined them.

22. DANIEL DEFOE (c. 1659–1731)
Robinson Crusoe

Robinson Crusoe is one of the most famous books in the entire world. Its publication however, though successful, was a minor incident in its author's crowded, singular, and not entirely unspotted life. A butcher's son, Defoe traveled widely in his youth; was once captured by Algerian pirates; went bankrupt for £17,000—which he later paid off; supported William of Orange in 1688; served as pamphleteer, propagandist, and undercover agent under four sovereigns; changed his allegiance without ever abandoning what we would today call a liberal political position; got into trouble through his partisan writings and was stood in the pillory, from which rather unliterary vantage point, with true middle-class enterprise, he managed to sell quite a few copies of a broadside entitled "Hymn to the Pillory"; saw the inside of a prison; wrote *Robinson Crusoe,* the first of his novels, when he was almost sixty; in all composed over four hundred books and tracts, very few of which bore his name on the title page; and, according to one account, died hiding out from his creditors. He also married and engendered seven children.

Defoe was perhaps the first truly outstanding professional journalist (or hired hack, if you prefer) in England; the father of the English novel (try his *Moll Flanders,* if you haven't read it); and a master of the trick of making an invention seem so true that to most of us Robinson Crusoe (a figment, though suggested by a real episode) is a living person.

Robinson Crusoe is supposed to be a boys' book. But, like its greater cousin *Huckleberry Finn* (46), it is a boys' book only in that it satisfies perfectly those male dreams that happen to be most vivid in boyhood but continue to lead an underground life in most males until they die. Virtually every male dreams of being completely self-sufficient, as Crusoe is; of building a private kingdom of which he can be undisputed lord; of having that deliciously lonely eminence emphasized in time by the establishment of a benevolent colonial tyranny over a single slave (Friday); of accumulating wealth and power that can never be endangered or vulgarized by competition; of enjoying success through the wholesome primitive use of muscle and practical good sense, as against the effete and troublesome exercise of the intellect; of doing all this in an exotic setting quite remote from his dull daily habitat; and finally of living in a self-made Utopia without any of the puzzling responsibilities of a wife and children. (*Robinson Crusoe* and *Moby Dick* (45) are the two great novels that manage superbly without involving more than one sex. They have never been popular with women.)

Robinson Crusoe has no plot. Its hero, though a sturdy stick, is nonetheless a stick. On reflection its smug mercantile morality seems offensive. All this matters not at all against the fact that it is a perfect daydream, a systematic and detailed wish-fulfillment, indeed the only one of its kind. Its appeal is heightened in that the most romantic experiences are related in the baldest prose. Its utter lack of fanciness makes the daydream respectable. We believe it precisely because it is not "literature."

When we were young we could see only that it was entertaining. Now, rereading it, we can perhaps see why it is also, as books go, immortal.

23. JONATHAN SWIFT (1667–1745) *Gulliver's Travels, A Modest Proposal, Meditations Upon a Broomstick, Resolutions When I Come To Be Old*

Thackeray (29) once said of Swift: "So great a man he seems to me, that thinking of him is like thinking of an empire falling." Swift's mind was not comprehensive, perhaps not even very subtle. But it was extremely powerful, it was the mirror of an extraordinary temperament, and so its frustration, decay, and final extinction do suggest the tragic dimensions of which Thackeray speaks.

Swift, like Shaw (20), was an Anglo-Irishman, born in Dublin and dying there, as Dean of St. Patrick's Cathedral. Like Shaw too he had a genius for exposing the vices and weaknesses of his age. Like Shaw too he was a master of the English language, so that today his prose can be read with pleasure even though much of what he wrote about is of interest only to scholars. But here ends the parallel. Shaw's was one of the most successfully managed careers in history; Swift's one of the least. Shaw died after bestriding his world like a colossus. Swift died much as he foresaw, "like a poisoned rat in a hole."

His century is often called the Age of Reason and he was one of its chief ornaments. He *did* worship reason: *Gulliver* may be seen as a picture of the consequences of man's refusal to be reasonable. The irony is that this apostle of reason should also have been a man of volcanic, baffled passions; that the terrible fits of dizziness and, later, deafness from which he suffered from his twentieth year led him at last to the loss of that reason he so much admired; that some enigmatic lack apparently precluded what we think of as a normal sex life; that his split allegiance (Was he an Irishman or an Englishman?) helped to unbalance him; that his semiexile in Dublin for his last thirty-two years was, even though the Irish loved him as their champion, a permanent cross to his spirit. This man should have been the intellect and conscience of England. But melancholy marked him for her own; ambition denied withered him; and so his life, whose inner secrets we shall probably never know, was what the world called, and he himself called, a failure. Pointing to a blighted tree, he once remarked that he too would die first "at the top," and so he did, a ruined monument to frustration.

He left behind him a vast mass of poetry and prose. Much of it is in the form of political pamphleteering, for he was in large part a journalist and propagandist. Some of it is in the form of his strange letter-diary, addressed to his ward, and known as the *Journal to Stella.* One small part of it is a masterpiece.

When first published in 1726 *Gulliver* was an instant success "from the cabinet council to the nursery." It is one of those curious works to which we may apply Lewis Mumford's sentence: "The words are for children and the meanings are for men." In fact, however, though children have always taken to their hearts at least the first two books of *Gulliver* (Lilliput and Brobdingnag), Swift wrote it with a serious purpose—"to mend the world." *Gulliver* is so rich a book as to bear many interpretations, but I think we may say that Swift wanted to hold up a mirror which would show mankind its true and often repellent face; and by doing so to force men to abandon their illusions, forswear their lies, and more nearly approach that rationality from which his Yahoos are the terrible declension.

In addition *Gulliver* is a political allegory. Its hidden references mean less to us than they did to the Londoners of 1726. The best thing is to pay no attention to the transient satire that threads it. As readers have discovered over almost two and a half centuries, there is plenty left: irony that applies to the human race wherever and whenever found; a biting humor; delightful invention; and an English style of fantastic clarity and power.

Swift's essence you will find in the last book, describing the voyage to the land of the Houyhnhnms. Here the misanthropy flows not from meanness but from an idealism broken under the buffets of fortune. Somehow, despite his ferocity, it is impossible to think of Swift as malicious. His inner contradictions are sorrowfully hinted at in the Latin epitaph he wrote for himself. In St. Patrick's Cathedral he lies at peace at last in a place "where bitter indignation can no longer lacerate his heart."

24. LAURENCE STERNE (1713–1768)
Tristram Shandy

Sterne is an odd bird, a bit gamy, and not to everyone's appetite. You may find yourself one of the many, including the most cultivated minds, who simply cannot read Sterne with pleasure. But the Lifetime Reading Plan cannot well omit his book. It is original in two senses: though indebted to Cervantes (48), Rabelais (37), and Swift (23), there is nothing quite like it; and it is the origin, or at least the foreshadowing, of much great modern fiction.

Sterne was himself something of an original. Born of an unsuccessful English army officer and an Irish mother, he was, after an irregular childhood, educated at Cambridge. He took holy orders, though of neither holiness nor orderliness did he ever possess a scrap. Family connections helped him to obtain a series of livings in Yorkshire. He settled down to the light duties of a typically worldly eighteenth-century parson, punctuated by "small, quiet attentions" to various ladies; a sentimental romance, recorded in his *Letters of Yorick to Eliza;* health-seeking trips to France and Italy, one of which produced his odd little travel book *A Sentimental Journey;* and his death of pleurisy at fifty-five. His external life has no distinction. Everything that matters in it is to be found in *Tristram Shandy,* whose first two volumes burst upon a delighted (and also shocked) world in 1760.

If you can take *Tristram Shandy* at all, the first thing you will notice is that very little happens in it. Not till the fourth of its nine books does its hero even manage to get himself born. It seems one vast digression, pointed up by blank pages, seemingly whimsical punctuation, and a dozen other typographical tricks. Second, you will note that it is a weirdly disguised story about sexuality; in a sense it is one long smoking-room yarn. Sterne's interest in sex is not frank and vigorous, like Fielding's

(25). It is subtle, suggestive, enormously sophisticated, and some have called it sniggering. Certainly it is sly. Third, you will find a quality more highly prized by Sterne's generation than by ours. They called it sensibility or sentiment. To us it sounds like sentimentality, the exhibition of a forced emotion in excess of that normally required by a given situation.

Though *Tristram Shandy* seems a completely whimsical book, it is actually one of the few great novels written in accord with a psychological theory. Sterne was much influenced by the *Essay on Human Understanding* of John Locke (55), with its doctrine of reason and knowledge as derived from sensory experience. *Tristram Shandy* dramatizes this theory, and in the course of the dramatization creates half a dozen living characters: My Uncle Toby, Mr. and Mrs. Shandy, Parson Yorick, Dr. Slop, the Widow Wadman. *Tristram Shandy,* unlike most novels, is not about things that happen. As its full title, *The Life and Opinions of Tristram Shandy,* suggests, it is about thought, about the inner lives of its characters. It is a true psychological novel, perhaps the first. Hence its rejection of straight-line chronology, as well as its odd punctuation, which mirrors the wayward associative crisscrossing paths of our minds and memories. Thus it anticipates Joyce (35), Proust (42), Mann (36), and the modern psychological novel in general, with its flashbacks, abrupt transitions, zigzags, and its serious attempt to reflect the pressures of the unconscious.

Sterne is more than a genius of the odd. He is the most modern, technically creative novelist produced by his century. If *Tristram Shandy* seems strange, it is not merely because Sterne is an eccentric, though he is, and glories in so being. It is because the book is actually nearer to the realities of mental life than a conventional novel is. And this is something that takes getting used to, because we so rarely stop to look at ourselves in the act of thinking, feeling, and remembering. Some awareness of all this may help you to enjoy this strange masterpiece.

25. HENRY FIELDING (1707–1754) *Tom Jones*

Like his fiction, Fielding was open, generous-hearted, full-blooded. Some of his character as a young man is doubtless reflected in Tom Jones himself, as perhaps the adult Fielding may be seen in the wonderful portrait of Squire Allworthy.

Well-connected, well-favored, well-educated, he led the pleasantly unrestrained life of the upper-middle-class youth of his time, getting into the proper improper scrapes with girls. For some years he supported himself by writing successful, worthless plays. The best of the lot, *Tom Thumb*, was at least good enough, it is said, to make Swift (23) laugh for the second time in his life. This career as a playwright Fielding cheerfully abandoned when the Prime Minister, Walpole, engineered a government censorship act directed primarily at him, and which incidentally stultified English drama up to the advent of Shaw. Fielding then turned to the law, journalism, and novel writing, mastering each in turn. Appointed Justice of the Peace in London, he fulfilled his duties conscientiously, even brilliantly, organizing a detective force that later developed into Scotland Yard, and being generally influential in softening the harsh justice of his day. Having abused his body hopelessly, he journeyed to Lisbon in search of health and there died at the early age of forty-seven.

One episode of his vigorous, crowded life is typical. His first wife—she is the model for Sophia Western, the heroine of *Tom Jones*—he loved to distraction. After her death he married her maid, and was condemned for doing so by every snob in England. He married her, however, because she was about to bear his child, and he wished to save her from disgrace. The word for Fielding is manly.

About his best novel little need be said. It lies open for your enjoyment. It has no depths to be plumbed. Its style, though a bit long-winded by our Western Union standards, is transparent. The characters are lifelike and simple—we have forgotten that in real life there actually are simple people. At one time its plot was greatly admired; Coleridge (78) foolishly declared it one of the three perfect plots in all literature, the others being that of Ben Jonson's *Alchemist* and that of Sophocles' *Oedipus Rex* (8). Today the intrigue, turning on Tom's true paternity and maternity, though manipulated with masterly skill, seems rather mechanical.

What we cannot help responding to are the comic genius animating the long, crowded story; the quick-moving panorama of eighteenth-century life in town and country; the colorful procession of picaresque incidents; and especially the zest for and tolerance of human nature which, as Fielding says, was all he had to offer on his bill of fare.

Fielding elevated the novel to the high estate it has since enjoyed. His aim, he tells us, was to write comic epic poems in prose, in which the lives of recognizable men and women of all stations would be presented without fear or favor by means of an organized, controlled narrative. He once described himself as "a great, tattered bard"; and there *is* a little of Homer in him.

Among the other attractions of *Tom Jones* are the essays that precede each section. These should not be skipped. Not only do they exhibit a mind of great charm and health and sanity, but, together with the prefatory remarks to his other three novels, they comprise the first reasoned esthetic of the English novel.

26. JANE AUSTEN (1775–1817)
Pride and Prejudice, Emma

Jane Austen is the first woman writer so far suggested by the Plan. By common consent she is what Virginia Woolf calls her: "the most perfect artist among women." It is only proper to add that the six novels she finished have always been more keenly relished by women than by men; that her genius for small-scale but deadly accurate domestic comedy is feminine rather than masculine; and finally that her central theme—the search for a husband—has been one of the major preoccupations of the fair sex for some time. Supremely feminine is the circumstance that she lived right through all of the Napoleonic wars without mentioning them in her work.

Miss Austen, as it somehow seems proper to call her, was the daughter of a rural rector and one of a large family. Though her own circumstances were always modest, she was well connected with the middling-rich landed gentry of southern England, and it is their traits and worldly interests that she reflects in her novels. Though there is some evidence of a frustrated love affair, she never married. During all the years of her brief life she lived quietly with her family, writing her novels in the midst of the domestic come-and-go, for years on end not even boasting a room of her own. Her social life was pleasant, active, genteelly restricted. While her genius as a whole is a sufficiently bewildering phenomenon, it is particularly hard to figure out how she could have known so much about human life when she saw so little of it.

Among other qualities, Jane Austen had one many modern novelists lack. She knew her own mind. Her novels are not (like those, let us say, of Thomas Wolfe) experiments in self-discovery and self-education. She knew precisely what interested her—"Those little matters," as Emma puts it, "on which the daily happiness of private life depends." She knew that the private lives of her special world turned not on high ideals, intense ambitions, or tragic despairs, but mainly on money, marriage (sometimes but not always complicated by love), and the preservation of a comfortable empty space between class and class. The activities of these limited people she viewed as a comedy, more or less as a highly intelligent, observant, articulate maiden aunt might view the goings-on of a large family. Jane Austen is sensible, rational in the eighteenth-century manner, ironical, humorous. She would think little of philosophers and perhaps not much of poets.

What gives Miss Austen her high rank, despite her limited subject matter, is the exquisite rightness of her art, the graceful neat forms of her stories, the matchless epigrammatic phrasing of her unremitting wit. She has little passion, no mystery, and she preferred to avert her face in a well-bred way from the tragedy that lies on the other side of the comedy she understood so well. She was born to delight readers, not to shake their souls.

There is no agreement as to her best book. *Pride and Prejudice* has perhaps had the most readers, but *Emma,* I think, is a more searching as well as a gayer story; so I have suggested these two. If you have read them try *Mansfield Park* or *Persuasion* or *Sense and Sensibility*. They are all pure Miss Austen, a writer so charming that it seems clumsy to call her a classic.

27. EMILY BRONTË (1818–1848) *Wuthering Heights*

It is unsettling to pass from Jane Austen to Emily Brontë. They do not belong to the same world. They do not even seem to belong to the same sex. All they have in common is that they were both parson's daughters. One is a master of perfectly controlled domestic comedy. The other is a wild demiurge of undomesticated tragedy. One excludes passion, the other is all passion. Jane Austen knew her limited, highly civilized world thoroughly; her novels grew out of needle-sharp observation as well as native power of mind. Emily Brontë knew the Yorkshire moors, her own family, and little else, and we can hardly say what her one novel grew out of.

The three Brontë sisters and their brother Branwell, who was a kind of forerunner of the Beat Generation, lived most of their short lives (Emily died of tuberculosis at thirty) in their father's parsonage at Haworth in the North Riding of Yorkshire. For entertainment they depended largely on their own minds plus the stories they heard about the often violent behavior of the semiprimitive countryfolk of the neighborhood. None of the novels produced by the three sisters exhibits that solid acquaintance with real life that we feel at once in Fielding (25). In their childhood and youth the Brontës invented imaginary kingdoms of extraordinary complication. For years they recorded the history and characters of these fantastic countries, playing with their literary fancies as other children play with toys. Something of this daydream atmosphere is retained in *Wuthering Heights*. But the daydream has become a nightmare.

In many respects *Wuthering Heights* is an absurd book. Its plot, turning on the devilish Heathcliff's revenge on all those who stood in the way of his passion for Catherine Earnshaw, is sheer melodrama. Its story-within-a-story method of narration is confusing. Its characters use a language unconnected with normal speech. And these characters, except for Heathcliff and Catherine, are drawn with no special skill.

And yet somehow people have found the book gripping. Not as a work of art, perhaps, but as a dream is gripping. Its prime quality is intensity. Despite all the old-fashioned machinery of the intrigue, we succumb to this intensity, or at least are made uneasy by it.

When we discussed Bunyan (21) we noted that, though he contributed to the Western tradition, he knew, except for the Bible, little or nothing about it. Emily Brontë is the second figure we have met who stands outside this tradition. She had, it is true, read a few of the romantic poets and romancers of her time, but *Wuthering Heights* owes little to them. It is also true that she may have received some real-life stimulus, when composing her novel, from the crazy love affair through which Branwell was passing at the time. But at bottom the origins of this strange book are untraceable. It was spewed up out of a volcanic, untrained, uncritical, but marvelous imagination. It had no true forebears. It has had no true successors.

28. CHARLES DICKENS (1812–1870)
One or more of the following: Pickwick Papers, David Copperfield, Bleak House, Great Expectations, Hard Times, Our Mutual Friend, Little Dorrit

The comments you have so far been reading average about five hundred words. In writing about Dickens the most economical way to use about fifty or so of those words might be as follows: The Artful Dodger, Fagin, Dick Swiveller, Flora Finching, Sairey Gamp, Mr. Micawber, Sam Weller, Uriah Heep, Mr. Dick, Bella Wilfer, Joe Gargery, Miss Havisham, Pumblechook, Wemmick, Bumble, Pecksniff, Mrs. Nickleby, The Crummleses, Quilp, Podsnap, Toots, Rosa Dartle, Chadband, Miss Flite, Inspector Bucket, the Tite Barnacles, Mme. Defarge, the Veneerings. As soon as a Dickens reader recalls any of these names a mental curtain goes up and he sees and hears living, vivid, talking human beings.

With Tolstoy (52) Dickens is perhaps one of the two novelists who have been accepted by the whole world—and Dickens with the greater joy. Santayana (71), after listing all of Dickens' defects, such as his insensibility to religion, science, politics, and art, concludes that he is "one of the best friends mankind has ever had." That is true. And possibly just because Dickens has been so overwhelmingly popular, it is only in recent years that he has been assessed, not as a beloved household fixture, but as a novelist almost of the stature of Dostoevski (51), with whose passionate, troubled imagination he has much in common.

I assume that in your youth you read at least *David Copper-*

field and were probably forced to read *A Tale of Two Cities,* one of his worst novels. Rereading him, I suggest you consider the following:

1. Dickens, though children love him, is not a writer only for children or the immature. He is enormously easy to read, yet is a serious artist. He is serious, even though one of his main methods of exposing life is that of high (or low) comedy. He is more than a creator of funny eccentrics. For example, see whether you can detect his constant and powerful use of symbolism, almost in the modern manner: the dust heaps in *Our Mutual Friend* furnish a good illustration.

2. Whatever the sentimentality in Dickens may have meant to his time, it is hogwash to us. An understanding of him as a whole will only be blocked if we try to be moved by his mechanical pathos, or indeed pay more than cursory attention to it. Said Oscar Wilde: "One must have a heart of stone to read the death of little Nell without laughing."

3. If Dickens' characters are "caricatures," as some think, why do they stick in the mind and continue to move us so strongly?

4. Dickens was a passionate, unhappy man, who apparently never recovered from his miserable childhood (how many waifs and strays there are in his books!) and who failed signally as husband and father. His passion and unhappiness are subtly reflected in his novels, as is his sense of guilt. Thus as he aged his books grew in depth. Compare the lightheartedness in *Pickwick* (and yet there are those Fleet prison scenes) with the sense of suffering in *Little Dorrit* or the dark, brooding atmosphere of *The Mystery of Edwin Drood,* left unfinished at his death. The notion of Dickens as a kind of jolly literary Kriss Kringle has stopped many readers from seeing all there is in him.

5. If Dickens is merely a "popular" novelist, why is he still read, whereas Scott, who was just as popular in his day, is not?

I am merely hinting that, as with Shakespeare, it is best to abandon most of the notions derived from our childhood and high-school experience with Dickens. There's more in him than met the Victorian eye. It is there for us to find.

29. WILLIAM MAKEPEACE THACKERAY (1811–1863) *Vanity Fair*

Thackeray was a broken-nosed giant of a man, standing six feet four, yet without giving the impression of strength. Unlike Dickens, he was educated as a gentleman. His novels have a sophistication Dickens' lack, though they are greatly inferior in vitality. In 1833 Thackeray lost virtually his entire inheritance of £20,000. For all his natural bent for writing, it is possible that were it not for this misfortune he might never have been forced into the business of grinding out novels and essays to support his family. In 1840 his wife, following the birth of their third child, lost her reason, and never regained it. There's something gruesome about the fact that she survived her husband by thirty-one years. This tragedy contributed to the melancholy suffusing Thackeray's work, and also to his idealization of women, perhaps a mechanism by which he bought off the guilt feelings his wife's insanity would naturally arouse in him.

Thackeray might have been happier among the elegant rakes of the preceding century. But he did not have the temperament to flout his century, as Emily Brontë (27) did. She could do so because she lived outside the great world. Thackeray was very much in it, and so are his novels.

He seems to have given the Victorians just what they wanted, a mixture that both soothed and stimulated. His best book, *Vanity Fair* (the phrase is from Bunyan), is really concerned with the rise, fall, and partial rise again of a high-grade whore. At no point, however, does Thackeray make this explicit; he is a master at saving appearances. Furthermore he is careful to present in his dimwitted Amelia the standard picture of the ideal Victorian female, and to pay his respects at regular intervals to those domestic virtues Queen Victoria had substituted for sterner ones.

But *Vanity Fair* rides two horses at the same time. Even while preserving an atmosphere of respectability and sentimentalism, it is delicately exposing human nature in its weakness, egotism, capacity for self-delusion, and mean genius for compromise. In their secret hearts his readers knew that their England, like that of the Napoleonic period Thackeray was depicting, was a Vanity Fair, with much about it that was ignoble and canting. Thackeray appealed to their critical intelligence and yet at the same time managed to support their conventional prejudices.

The contradiction is covered over in *Vanity Fair* by his art, which is a kind of sleight of hand. How well, how gracefully he tells his story and manipulates what he calls his puppets! How pleasantly conversational is his tone! How easy to take is his irony, that of the tolerant, worldly-wise clubman—and how flattering to our own picture of ourselves as precisely such a charming and superior raconteur! And so, though our conventional prejudices are quite different from those of the Victorians; though our novels are frank about sex while Thackeray is disingenuous—nevertheless we can still enjoy *Vanity Fair*.

We can enjoy the panoramic picture of high life in England and on the Continent around the time of Waterloo. We can enjoy the well-controlled plot. But mainly we can still enjoy the perfect symbol of *Vanity Fair*—Becky Sharp. Becky is of course the ancestress of all the beautiful, immoral female adventuresses (Scarlett O'Hara, for instance) who have since enraptured readers. Only because of Becky Sharp, Thackeray's masterpiece will never completely fade. She resolves one of the simpler contradictions in our human nature. For men will always (if possible) marry good women and secretly admire bad ones. And women, knowing that their job is to keep the race going, will always come out strongly for morality, and always have a furtive feeling that somehow immorality seems darned attractive. Thackeray, who had little depth but much worldly wisdom, understood this division in our natures, and through Becky Sharp exploited it perfectly.

30. GEORGE ELIOT (1819–1880)
The Mill on the Floss

George Eliot is the first writer we have met for whom I feel I should argue. Of late her reputation, among certain influential critics, has risen. But the ordinary reader—recalling the high-school infliction of *Silas Marner*, or possibly merely intimidated by the memory of the author's countenance, so suggestive of a sorrowful, though brainy, horse—still shies away from her. George Eliot is one of the many writers handicapped by the existence of photographers and portrait painters.

In many ways, however, she is a most interesting figure. Born Mary Ann Evans, of a middle-class commercial Warwickshire family (her father was a carpenter who rose to be estate agent), she early evidenced that passion for learning that was to mark her career. In her teens she was deeply and narrowly pious, but wide reading, plus conversations with minds less evangelically committed, soon stripped her of dogmatic faith. Her rejection of a conventional God and of Immortality was however balanced by her devotion to Duty, an abstraction that seems to have taken on for her some of the attributes of the Deity.

After her father's death she removed to London, engaging successfully in highly intellectual journalism and meeting some of the best minds of her time, including Herbert Spencer and John Stuart Mill (57). In 1854 she decided the shape of her life. She formed a permanent, illegitimate but not covert connection with the learned journalist and biographer George Henry Lewes. Lewes' wife had already had two children by another man (ah, these proper Victorians), was mentally unbalanced, and not living with Lewes at the time. The relationship lasted till Lewes' death in 1878 and was both happy and eminently respectable. A year and a half later George Eliot married an American banker, John W. Cross, she being sixty to his thirty-nine. Obviously a strong-minded lady.

The strength of her mind is apparent not only in her courageous, laborious life, but in her novels. To us they may seem rather prosy, supersaturated with reflection and moralizing, and, especially in *Romola*, smelling somewhat of the lamp. Yet they quietly blazed wide trails without which the modern novel would have been impeded in its progress. D. H. Lawrence (34) summed it up: "It was really George Eliot who started it all. It was she who started putting action inside." Perhaps in this respect Sterne (24) preceded her, but the eccentricity of *Tristram Shandy* put it outside the mainstream of English fiction, whereas George Eliot navigated its very center. She did depict the interior life of human beings, and particularly their moral stresses and strains, in a way then quite new to fiction. She also deliberately departed from other conventions such as the Dickensian happy ending and the standardized conception of romance. Finally she poured into her stories something few previous novelists had possessed—the resources of a first-class *intellect*. She included *ideas* in her view of life. She even dared to portray intellectuals—a commonplace proceeding since Joyce (35) but one not to be found in Jane Austen or Fielding or Dickens.

Serious critics consider *Middlemarch* her masterpiece, but if you are to read only one George Eliot novel, I suggest *The Mill on the Floss*. Its partly autobiographical early chapters re-create the special atmosphere of childhood with an insight, tenderness, and charm unsurpassed until we reach *Huckleberry Finn* (46). The minor characters, particularly Aunts Glegg and Pullet, are so solidly conceived that the passage of the society in which they are rooted has not diminished their vitality. The struggle of poor Maggie to express her genius for love in a world that is too much for her is poignant still. And finally *The Mill on the Floss*, like all her fiction, is suffused with a moral seriousness neither prissy nor narrow, but rather the effluence of a large, powerful, pondering, humane mind. In current novels such moral seriousness is rarely found. But a few hours with George Eliot, for all her didacticism, may serve to suggest that it must always be one of the staples of truly grown-up fiction.

31. LEWIS CARROLL (1832–1898) *Alice's Adventures in Wonderland and Through the Looking-Glass*

Some may think Lewis Carroll has strayed into this rather formidable list through some error. But he belongs here, for he proved, doubtless not quite knowing what he was doing, that the world of nonsense may have strange and complex relations with the world of sense. I do not include him because he is a juvenile classic, for in that case we should also have Grimm and Andersen and Collodi and a dozen others. I include him because he continues to hold as much interest for grown-ups as for children.

In actual fact he is more alive today than he was in the sixties and seventies of the last century, when the two *Alice* books were published. He continues to fascinate not only ordinary men and women of all countries and races, but the most sophisticated intellects: critics such as Edmund Wilson, W. H. Auden, Virginia Woolf; logicians and scientists such as Whitehead (58), Bertrand Russell, and Eddington; and philosophers, semanticists, and psychoanalysts by the score.

His real name was Charles Lutwidge Dodgson (pronounced Dodson). The son of a rector, he had seven sisters, a circumstance which may in part account for his seemingly arrested masculinity. His nineteenth year to his death he spent at Christ Church, Oxford, as student, mathematics teacher, and ordained dean. He remained, as far as we know, utterly chaste. His life was proper, pleasant, and donnish, marked by fussy little academic controversies, many hobbies (he was a first-rate pioneer photographer and invented something very much like Scotch tape), and the one dominating passion of his life, which was a pure and tender passion for little girls. In our day, when degeneracy is taken as a matter of course, it is necessary for me to add that there is no irony in the preceding sentence.

He was a dull teacher, a conventional mathematician, but a rather exceptional student of Aristotelian logic—defective syllogisms are among the many slyly hidden features of *Alice*. A queer chap on the whole, kind, testy at times, prissy, shy (he even hid his hands continually under a pair of gray-and-black gloves), with a mind that seems to be quite conventional but which, in his letters and diaries, flashes forth from time to time with some startling insight that it is hard not to call Freudian or Einsteinian.

Doubtless, like many Victorians, he was an internally divided man, and some of these divisions and tensions can be traced by the careful and curious reader. In *Alice* four worlds meet, worlds that he knew either consciously or intuitively. They partly fuse, drift in and out of each other, undergo mutual metamorphoses. They are the worlds of childhood, dream, nonsense, and logic. Their strange interaction gives *Alice* its complexity and, more important, its disturbing reality. The adult reader continues to delight in its fanciful humor, but he feels also that this is more than a child's book, that it touches again and again on half-lit areas of consciousness.

Some years ago I wrote an essay on Lewis Carroll, from which I extract this sentence: "What gives the *Alice* books their varying but permanent appeal is the strange mixture in them of this deep passion for children and the child's world, with an equally deep and less conscious passion for exploring the dream world, even the nightmare world, filled with guilts and fears, which is a major part of the child's life, and therefore a major part of our grown-up life."

32. THOMAS HARDY (1840–1928)
The Mayor of Casterbridge

Thomas Hardy came of Dorset stock and lived the larger part of his life just outside Dorchester. The beautiful, history-packed, and rather desolate countryside around Dorchester (Hardy calls it Wessex) is in a way the main character in his novels. His formal education—he was the son of a builder—lasted only from his eighth to his sixteenth year. He was then apprenticed to a Dorchester, and later to a London, architect. At twenty-seven he started what turned out to be a quarter century of increasingly successful novel writing. The indignation aroused by supposedly shocking situations and passages in *Jude the Obscure* (1895) made the sensitive Hardy turn back to his first love, poetry. At his death he had written over a thousand poems, not including his gigantic cosmic panorama of the Napoleonic wars, *The Dynasts*. Many rate his verse above his novels. Certainly he is one of the two dozen or so English poets you may wish to read most closely in the Auden and Pearson anthology (72).

It may be some time before the cycle of taste returns Hardy to favor, just as it has within a generation brought back Dante (14), Conrad (33), Stendhal (39), Melville (45), and Henry James (47). This Plan, however, is not designed to take more than casual account of fashion. It deals mainly with writers of generally acknowledged long-term influence and interest. Among these Hardy will doubtless occupy a secondary rank. But not a minor one.

He died at eighty-eight. Just as his life linked two centuries, so his work acts as a kind of bridge between Victorian and modern fiction. Bravely (for their time) his novels defied many of the sexual, religious, and philosophical taboos to which even so independent a mind as George Eliot's on occasion succumbed. Hardy, influenced by Darwin and by a generally mechanical-determinist nineteenth-century view of the universe, dared to show man as the sport of Nature. His view is sometimes bleak, sometimes merely sorrowful; and it proceeds not only from theory, but from the bias of his own brooding temperament. His humor and his remarkable sensitivity to the magic of landscape and weather prevent his novels from being merely depressing. But if you find modern fiction on the whole uncheerful, that is partly because Hardy pioneered the battle against the unrealistic optimism of some of his contemporaries.

The Hardy novels most generally admired are *The Return of the Native, Tess of the D'Urbervilles, Jude the Obscure,* and that here suggested. In *The Mayor of Casterbridge* I find in balance the most striking elements of Hardy's art: a complex plot which, despite some concessions to melodrama, such as the secret document, is strongly architectured; that sense of place and of the past that gives his work such deep-rooted solidity; the sympathetic portrayal of rustic character, often compared to Shakespeare's; the ability to work out with relentless elaboration a succession of tragic fates; and finally his special, patented atmosphere of ruminative compassion.

The opening scenes, in which a man auctions off his wife, are extraordinary in their capacity to catch our interest. That interest is sustained, page after deliberate page, as we watch Michael Henchard, "the self-alienated man," devising his own self-destruction and expiating his guilt.

The English critic Desmond MacCarthy, speaking of Hardy, says that "it is the function of tragic literature to dignify sorrow and disaster." By this criterion the creator of *The Mayor of Casterbridge,* for all his faults of style and taste, is a true tragic master.

33. JOSEPH CONRAD (1857–1924) *Nostromo*

The same year, 1895, in which Thomas Hardy gave up novel writing, saw the publication of Joseph Conrad's first book, *Almayer's Folly.* The traditional English novel—a large, loose, free-flowing narrative, depending largely on external action and easily grasped characters—begins to die. A new kind of fiction—original in form, full of technical devices, its tensions flowing from the exploration of mental life—is being born. Sterne, Austen, George Eliot, and Hardy had all helped to clear its path. But it is really Conrad who announces its themes and methods. At this point in our reading we will feel a greater richness if we see Conrad as helping to make possible our understanding of Henry James, D. H. Lawrence, Joyce, Mann, Proust, Faulkner, and others, such as André Gide, not included in the Plan.

Strangeness, somberness, nobility: these mark Conrad's career. He repels affection, he compels admiration. Born a Pole, of a family tragically dedicated to the desperate cause of Polish freedom, he was left an orphan at twelve. At seventeen he turned westward "as a man might get into a dream." Without ever forgetting his aristocratic Polish heritage, he committed himself to a new world. Some years of curious, almost cloak-and-sword adventure followed, during which, for instance, he smuggled arms for the Carlist cause in Spain. Then, adopting the life of a seaman and an Englishman, he spent twenty years in the British Merchant Service, rising to the rank of master. He pursued his vocation on most of the seas of the world, and particularly in the fabled Far East, the setting of many of his stories. At last came the fateful decision which had doubtless been maturing in his mind for years. With a certain reluctance he abandoned the sea and, now a mature man, using a language not his own and interpreting the world as a Continental writer would, this Polish sailor in the end became (this is my own opinion, though shared by many others) one of the half-dozen greatest novelists to use our magnificent tongue.

For years, stoically suffering neglect and, what is worse, misunderstanding, Conrad toiled at his desk. He tested his craft by a set of standards unfamiliar to the Victorians. He sought the perfect *form* for each of his stories. He searched human character in depth, fearless of what he might find there. He sought out wonderfully suggestive symbols (such as the silver mine in *Nostromo*) to mirror large areas of emotion. He consciously forged a style, just as Flaubert (41) did, suitable to his special view of human nature under special conditions of moral stress. He thought of himself as an artist fiercely dedicated to his calling. He had no friendly relation to his "public" as Dickens and Thackeray had. His relation was to the vision within himself.

Nostromo is not an easy novel to read and it is best to take it slowly. It does not tell itself, as *Tom Jones* seems to. It uncoils, retraces its steps, changes its angle of attack. Into it Conrad put his most anxious effort, and if he has a masterpiece this is probably it.

But before we read *Nostromo* it is best to clear our minds of some notions about Conrad still entertained by many.

First, he is not a writer of "sea stories," much less of adventure stories. He is a psychological dramatist who happens to be exploiting material he knew intimately.

Second, though he wrote many tales of the Far East, he is not an "exotic" novelist. Local color is there, of course, laid on with a painter's eye, but again this is subordinate to his interest in the roiled depths of the human heart.

Third, he is not, except superficially, a "romantic." The tests of fidelity, fortitude, and understanding to which he submits his characters are ruthlessly true to the human condition, as seen by a most unsentimental eye. Conrad does not flee or evade, nor, despite his sense that all life itself is a kind of dream, does he take refuge in dreams. He is far more realistic than a Sinclair Lewis.

Critics always quote one sentence from his famous Preface to *The Nigger of the Narcissus.* I will quote it too. But we must understand what Conrad means by the word *see.* He is not talking like an impressionist painter. He means the kind of seeing that has the depth, clarity, and often the agony of a vision, visible only when the mind and the imagination are at full tension. Once we grasp this, the sentence may stand as a shorthand summary of Conrad's ideal relationship to the ideal reader: "My task which I am trying to achieve is, by the power of the written word, to make you hear, to make you feel—it is, above all, to make you *see.* That—and no more, and it is everything."

34. D. H. LAWRENCE (1885–1930)
Sons and Lovers

It is hard to realize that when Lawrence died, of tuberculosis, he was only forty-five. From 1911, when his first novel appeared, to his death in 1930, no year passed without the appearance of at least one book. In 1930 there were six, and his posthumous works (excluding the wonderful *Letters*) total another dozen or so. While producing so fantastically, Lawrence was traveling widely, meeting and influencing large numbers of people, working at various hobbies, and engaging in the unhappy controversies caused by his uncompromising ideas. This frail, thin, bearded man—novelist, poet, playwright, essayist, critic, painter, and prophet—had a central fire of energy burning inside him. He stands out as one of the most alive human beings of his time.

Lawrence was born of a Nottinghamshire coal miner and a woman greatly superior to her husband in education and sensitivity. His early life, dominated by his mother's excessive love and his excessive dependence on it, is portrayed quite frankly in the first part of *Sons and Lovers*. Lawrence excelled at school and became a teacher for a few years. In 1912 he eloped with Frieda von Richthofen Weekley, a member of a patrician German family, and in 1914 married her. The latter part of his life was one of almost continuous wandering. In exotic primitives and unspoiled countries he sought the equivalent in fact of the life feeling that blazes in his fiction.

This life feeling attracts some readers, alienates or shocks others. You will not be able to tolerate Lawrence at all unless you understand that he was neither poseur nor hysteric, but a prophet with a message fervently believed in, a message with which he sought to change the day-to-day behavior of men. The message is implicit even in so early a book as *Sons and Lovers*, which is certainly the one with which to start one's reading of Lawrence. It is to be found more particularly in *The Rainbow*, *Women in Love*, and *Lady Chatterley's Lover*, one of his poorest novels.

We must understand that Lawrence was an absolute revolutionary. His rejections were complete. He made war against the entire industrial culture of his and our time. He felt that it had devitalized us, dried up the spontaneous springs of our emotions, fragmented us, and alienated us from that life of the soil, wind, flowers, weather to which Lawrence was preternaturally sensitive. Worst of all, he thought, it had withered our sexual lives. For Lawrence sex was not merely something to enjoy. It was the key to the only knowledge he prized—direct, immediate, nonintellectual perception of reality. As early as 1912 he was writing, "What the blood feels, and believes, and says, is always true."

He hated science, conventional Christianity, the worship of reason, progress, the interfering State, planned "respectable" living, and the idolization of money and the machine. It is easy to understand therefore why he was forced to live, though bravely and even joyfully, a life of poverty, struggle, defiance. Aldous Huxley (94), who knew him well, describes him as "a being, somehow, of another order." It does at times seem that he drew his genius and his energy from some primal source most of us cannot tap. In this respect as in others he reminds us of the prophet-poet Blake (76).

His books are not "constructed," as we have seen Conrad's were. They flow, eddy, flash, erupt, or sing in accordance with the electric changes in the author's own personality as he composed. Unless you are willing temporarily to accept this personality, his books may seem intolerable.

But Lawrence wants you to do more. His view of the novel was deeply moral. The novel, he passionately believed, "can help you not to be a dead man in life." He wanted nothing less than to change men, to reawaken in them an intensity, a joy in life that he felt they were losing or had lost.

It is hard to say whether a century from now Lawrence will be thought of as a major prophet (as well as a remarkable artist) or merely as an oddity of genius. At the moment his voice, obscured for some years after his death, seems to speak out bold and clear.

35. JAMES JOYCE (1882–1941) *Ulysses*

With *Ulysses* we at last reach a book that seems impenetrable. It is best to admit that this mountain cannot be scaled with a single leap. Still, it is scalable; and from the top you are granted a view of human life of incomparable richness.

Here are five simple statements. They will not help us to enjoy or understand *Ulysses*. I list them merely to remove from our minds any notion that this book is a huge joke, or a huge obscenity, or the work of a demented genius, or the altar of a cult. Here is what a large majority of intelligent critics and readers have come to believe about *Ulysses* during the thirty-eight years since its appearance.

1. It is probably the most completely *organized,* thought-out work of literature since *The Divine Comedy* (14).

2. It is the most *influential* novel (call it that for lack of a better term) published in our century. The influence is indirect —through other writers.

3. It is one of the most *original* works of imagination in the language. It broke not one trail, but hundreds.

4. There is some disagreement here, but the prevailing view is that it is not "decadent" or "immoral" or "pessimistic." Like the work of most of the supreme artists listed in the Plan, it proposes a vision of life as seen by a powerful mind that has risen above the partial, the sentimental, and the self-defensive.

5. Unlike its original, the *Odyssey,* it is not an "open" book. It yields its secrets only to those willing to work, just as Beethoven's greater symphonies reveal new riches the longer they are studied.

These statements made, I have three suggestions for the reader:

1. Read Joyce's *A Portrait of the Artist as a Young Man* first (Viking Press, $1.25). This is written fairly 'straight," as compared with its greater sequel. It will introduce you to Stephen Dedalus, who is Joyce; and to Joyce's Dublin, the scene dominating both novels.

2. In this one case, read a good commentary *first.* The best short one is by Edmund Wilson, the best long one by Stuart Gilbert. (See Suggestions for Further Reading.)

3. Even then *Ulysses* will be tough going. Don't try to understand every reference, broken phrase, shade of meaning, allusion to something still to come or buried in pages you've already read. Get what you can. Then put the book aside and try it a year later.

As you read it, try to keep in mind some of Joyce's purposes:

1. To trace, as completely as possible, the thoughts and doings of a number of Dubliners during the day and evening of June 16, 1904.

2. To trace, virtually completely, the thoughts and doings of two of them: Stephen Dedalus, the now classic type of the modern intellectual, and his spiritual father, the more or less average man, Leopold Bloom.

3. To give his book a form paralleling (not always obviously) the events and characters of the *Odyssey* of Homer (2). Thus Stephen is Telemachus, Bloom Odysseus (Ulysses), Molly an unfaithful Penelope, Bella Cohen Circe.

4. To invent or develop whatever new techniques are needed for his monumental task. These include, among dozens, interior monologue, stream of consciousness, parody, dream and nightmare sequences, puns, word coinages, unconventional punctuation or none at all, and so forth. Ordinary novelists try to satisfy us with a selection from or summary of their characters' thoughts. Joyce gives you the thoughts themselves, in all their streamy, dreamy, formless flow.

Even the attempt to read *Ulysses* can be a great adventure. Good fortune to you.

36. THOMAS MANN (1875–1955) *The Magic Mountain*

Some books (they can be first-rate ones, like Jane Austen's) isolate parts of human experience. Others sum up these parts. Thus the masterpieces of Dante and Homer, though they do other things as well, sum up their cultures. So does *The Magic Mountain.* The reader will get more out of it if he sees it as a synthetic, inclusive work. Mae West once remarked, in a somewhat different connection, "I like a man who takes his time." In his Foreword to *The Magic Mountain* Mann puts it thus: "Only the exhaustive is truly interesting." His great novel is exhaustive, and it is truly interesting.

It is a story about a rather simple-minded young German

who comes to visit a sick friend at a Swiss tuberculosis sanitarium; finds that he is himself infected; stays on for seven years; listens, talks, thinks, suffers, loves; and is at last swept up into the holocaust of the First World War. As you read this story you will feel, slowly and almost imperceptibly, that it is more than the usual narrative of the education of a young man. In dialogue, in symbol, in fantasy and dream, in argument, in soliloquy, in philosophical discourse, Mann is trying to sum up the mental life of Western man.

In my preliminary talk with the reader, I pointed out that all our authors are engaged in a Great Conversation, as it has been well called. A minor proof of this is the number of these authors who have helped to form Thomas Mann and whose ideas are orchestrated in *The Magic Mountain.* I could name dozens. Here are a few acknowledged by Mann himself: Goethe (18), Nietzsche (60), Turgenev (50), Tolstoy (52), Conrad (33), Whitman (80), Ibsen (19), Freud (61). In this sense too *The Magic Mountain* is summatory.

Look at it another way. As you read, try to see the Berghof sanitarium as Europe, the Europe (which means America too) that in 1914 died violently, passing into some other culture whose form is still unclear to us. Think of its characters as being not only themselves but incarnations of powerful modes of thought and feeling: Settembrini is liberal humanism; Naphta is absolutist terror (Lenin, Stalin, Hitler, Mussolini, and all the others still to come); Peeperkorn we have perhaps already met, for his message is not unlike D. H. Lawrence's. And the patients, drawn from so many countries and social levels—what are they but the sickness of the West, which Mann understood clearly in 1924 and which in the latter forty years of our century is bound to reach its feverish crisis?

In this gigantic work Mann touches on a dozen themes and issues that have since come to dominate the thought of our day: psychoanalysis and spiritualism; the links connecting art, disease, and death; the relative nature of time, to which Einstein has accustomed us; the nature of Western man, and particularly of the middle-class man; the relations between the artist and society; the proper education of a human being. Mann's special genius lies in his ability to combine high-level reflection with the more traditional creation of character and atmosphere. *The Magic Mountain* takes place in two worlds. One is a world of ideas. The other is a world of subtle human relationships which we can sense all the more clearly because they are cut off from the confusing contingencies of the "flatland," the clock-bound "healthy" world you and I inhabit.

Now that we have read Conrad, Lawrence, Joyce, and Mann (with Proust and Henry James still awaiting us) we are borne on the full tide of the modern novel. We can begin to see its character: it is marked by enormous self-consciousness, profound delvings into the human spirit, technical innovations of bewildering variety. Its main difference from the simpler fictions of the English authors of the eighteenth and early nineteenth centuries lies in its receptive openness to the whole creative life of man. It intellectualizes without dehumanizing. Its entire drift is perhaps most clearly exemplified in Thomas Mann's masterpiece, one of the most magnificent works of art produced by our unhappy century.

37. FRANÇOIS RABELAIS (c. 1494–1553) *Gargantua and Pantagruel*

I have listed this under Narratives because I don't know where else to put it. It contains plenty of narrative, but it has no plot, is virtually formless, and eludes definition. It takes its place near the beginning of French literature but the French novel does not descend from it. Nothing descends from it. Though it has had imitators, it stands by itself. It is a wild, sane, wonderful, exasperating, sometimes tedious extravaganza. Open to a dozen interpretations, one thing at least can be said of it:

it is the work of a supreme genius of language whose sheer vitality and power of verbal invention are matched only by Shakespeare and Joyce.

About Rabelais' life we know little. He was a monk, a doctor, personal physician to the important Cardinal du Bellay, an editor, and, of course, a writer. At various times his books got him into trouble with the authorities. The more bigoted Catholics of his time attacked him; so did the Calvinists, whose bigotry one cannot qualify in any way. Still, despite his attacks on the churchly obscurantism of his period, there is nothing to prove he was not a good, though hardly strait-laced, Catholic. Anatole France said that Rabelais "believed in God five days out of seven, which is a good deal." Fair enough.

The five books of *Gargantua and Pantagruel* (the fifth may not be entirely genuine) deal with two giants. The first book tells us about Gargantua, his birth, education, farcical war-adventures, and the Abbey of Thélème he helped build, whose only rule was: "Do as you wish." The other four books are concerned with Gargantua's son Pantagruel, his boon companion the rascally, earthy, Falstaffian Panurge, and their wars, travels, quests for wisdom.

The tone varies. It is serious (we have still to catch up with Rabelais' ideas on education), mock-serious, satirical, fantastic, always exuberant. However, even at his wildest, Rabelais evidences two well-blended strains: one proceeding from his humanist conviction that all men desire to know, that all knowledge is a joyous and attainable thing (the book is, among other things, an encyclopedia); the other flowing from his personal conviction that "laughter is the essence of mankind."

Of all the writers we have met or shall meet he is the one most unreservedly in love with life. Even when attacking the abuses of his day, he does so in high, almost lunatic spirits. He would not know a neurosis if he saw one, and most of our gloomy modern novels he would destroy with a guffaw. He is a kind of happy Swift, or perhaps a Whitman with an intellect. His characteristic gesture is the embrace. He can love both

God and drunkenness. His laughter is so free and healthy that only the prudish will be offended by his vast coarseness, his delight in the eternal comedy of the human body.

Pantagruelism he defines as "a certain jollity of mind, pickled in the scorn of fortune." To enjoy him you must be a bit of a Pantagruelist yourself. His is a book you must give, or at least lend, yourself to, not bothering to ponder over every morsel of his gargantuan erudition, and perhaps not trying to read more than a dozen pages at a time.

One final suggestion: read any good *modern* translation—Cohen's or Putnam's or Le Clercq's. Avoid the famous Urquhart-Motteux version—a classic, but not Rabelais.

38. VOLTAIRE (1694–1778)
Candide and Other Works

Voltaire died at eighty-four, the uncrowned king of intellectual Europe, the undisputed leader of the Age of Enlightenment, the most destructive of the many sappers of the foundations of the Old Régime destroyed by the French Revolution. As dramatist, poet, historian, taleteller, wit, correspondent, controversialist, and coruscating personality, he had achieved a formidable reputation. His productivity is unbelievable: he left behind him over fourteen thousand known letters and over two thousand books and pamphlets. Yet he will probably be remembered mainly for an extended little bitter joke that he wrote in three days.

All his tens of thousands of ironies fade before the irony of this one circumstance. And it is an unfair irony. Voltaire—his name was possibly an anagram for François-Marie Arouet—handled his career, including his business affairs, with the capacity of a Shaw. But he made one error. He wrote *Candide*. By doing so he obscured the remainder of his vast production. So much else is brilliant and well worth reading—the *Philo-*

sophical Dictionary, Zadig, Micromégas, The Age of Louis XIV, the *Letters Concerning the English Nation*. Yet *Candide* is what we read, for it is perfection.

Also it is so lucid as to need little commentary. It was partly inspired by one of the events it chronicles, the devastating Lisbon earthquake of 1755. Voltaire uses this—as well as all the other misfortunes of poor Candide, Dr. Pangloss, and their companions—to make fun of what he conceived to be the smug optimism of the famous philosopher Leibnitz, caricatured in the figure of Pangloss. As philosophy *Candide* is oversimplified, indeed shallow, for Voltaire's intelligence was quick and comprehensive rather than deep. But as lightning narrative, flashing with wit, as a pitiless yet funny indictment of the follies and cruelties of mankind, it has not yet been surpassed.

Its form is a favorite one of Voltaire's century, that of the "philosophical romance"—*Gulliver's Travels* belongs to this category, and a good modern example is Thornton Wilder's *Bridge of San Luis Rey*. It anticipates also another of the forms later fiction was to take, that of the "development novel," tracing the education of a young man. We have already seen this form extended and deepened in *The Magic Mountain* (36) and we will meet it again when we discuss *The Red and the Black* (39). Candide's education of course was of a uniquely violent nature, so violent that one can hardly help sympathizing with his rather mournful conclusion that in this far from the best of all possible worlds the most sensible thing we can do is to "cultivate our garden."

The reader, however, must not be misled by this jewel of wicked irony into thinking that Voltaire was no more than a genius of mockery. Like Shaw, he could not help being witty; and like Shaw he was a very serious, courageous, and humane fighter for the liberation of men's minds. The best comment on what was finest in him was made by the Germans during the occupation of Paris in World War II. They cast Voltaire's statue to the earth and melted it down. Voltaire would have predicted it.

39. STENDHAL (1783–1842) *The Red and the Black*

One hundred years ago Stendhal (one of his more than 150 pseudonyms, his real name being Marie-Henri Beyle) would not have been listed among the major novelists of Europe. Fifty years later the situation would have changed: he would have been named among the first half-dozen novelists of France. Today the shift is even greater: many rank him among the foremost novelists of all time and place. Stendhal lived partially in the future, and so he would have foreseen all this. "I have drawn a lottery ticket," he wrote, "whose winning number is: to be read in 1935."

So, though most of Stendhal's stories are laid in Napoleonic and post-Napoleonic Europe, we would expect his feeling for life and his way of expressing it to be modern. And that is roughly what we do find. Some qualifications should be made, however. His plots seem to us to smack of opera. His dialogue is more formal than that our phonographic realists have accustomed us to. And, in the case of his masterpiece *The Red and the Black*, the title refers to forces no longer operative, the Red standing for the uniform of Napoleon's soldiers, the Black for the cassock of the clergy. The hero Julien Sorel wears the black because in his day a poor youth with his special talents could advance himself only through the Church; whereas Julien's heart and imagination belonged to the Napoleonic era which he thought of as more glorious than his own. However, the deeper tensions in Julien are not peculiar to the France of his generation. They are part of our entire modern consciousness.

Stendhal's genius lay partly in prevision. His novels, particularly this one, anticipate many of the motifs and devices we are used to in our modern fiction. That is one reason why he may be called the novelist's novelist. *The Red and the Black*, for example, is the first classic expression of what has been called The Young-Man-from-the-Provinces theme—a theme on which all the books of Thomas Wolfe merely ring changes. Also it heads a long line of novels whose subject is the dissatisfaction of the heroine with an empty society—see Carol Kennicott in Sinclair Lewis' *Main Street* and of course Emma Bovary (41). Though George Eliot (30), as we noted, dared to portray an intellectual, it is in *The Red and the Black* that we first get the type fully and closely studied. And so we can keep on identifying in Stendhal other anticipations of twentieth-century fiction: his systematic rather than intuitive use of psychology, even Freudian psychology; his understanding of what is now called ambivalence; his extraordinary detachment from his characters; and especially his major preoccupation, which is with the outsider, the "being apart" who cannot reconcile himself with his inferior or materialistic or merely boring society.

The reader will perceive all this only *after* he has finished *The Red and the Black*. While reading it he will be caught up in a fascinating love story, which somehow seems far more adult than any we encountered in the Victorian novelists. Furthermore he will experience the sensation only the finest psychological novelists can give—that of actually, for a dozen hours or so, living inside the passionately intense, complex minds of a few invented persons who become realler to us than our own neighbors.

40. HONORÉ DE BALZAC (1799–1850)
Père Goriot, Eugénie Grandet

Unlike Stendhal (of whom he was one of the few to show any early appreciation) Balzac is not widely read today. Everyone admits his achievement but no one is quite sure what it is. Does he rank among the greatest of novelists? The answer is not clear. Certain faults stand out that were not so apparent during his century: faults of taste especially; a weakness for melodrama, almost for detective-story melodrama; an incapacity to portray character as changing and developing; and, most important, rank defects of intelligence. Another trouble is that he never wrote a masterpiece. I recommend two titles, among his best known, but they do not represent him properly. Nor would any other two titles. To be overcome by Balzac (he *can* overwhelm you, though he may not move you) you should read fifty or sixty of his novels; and life is too short.

Balzac was a Stendhalian Young Man from the Provinces. There is a famous scene at the end of *Père Goriot*. The ambitious young Rastignac looks down on the lights of Paris and cries, "Between us henceforth the battle is joined." There was plenty of Rastignac in Balzac. Perhaps that was his central flaw: he did not think and feel like an artist, but like a conqueror. Once, as a young man, he seized a pencil and, under a picture of the Little Corporal, wrote: "What Napoleon could not achieve with his sword I shall accomplish with my pen."

With this ideal of conquest always before him, he lived like a madman and died, utterly exhausted, at fifty-one, perhaps, as has been said, as the result of drinking fifty thousand cups of coffee. He engaged in frenzied financial operations for which he had no talent. He wasted time on one of the most idiotic love affairs in literary history. He piled up huge debts. And always he wrote, wrote, wrote, through the night, incessantly for twenty years and more, from fourteen to eighteen hours a day. Only the scholars know exactly how many books he turned out, perhaps over 350 in all, perhaps a hundred comprising what he called his "Human Comedy." Here is his description of this manic, comprehensive design: "The immeasurable scope of a plan which embraces not only a history and criticism of society, but also an analysis of its evils and an exposition of its principles, justifies me, so I believe, in giving my work the title. . . . The Human Comedy." The implied comparison is, of course, with a man he resembled in virtually no way—Dante (14).

Balzac did not live to complete his vast picture of the French society of his day. *Père Goriot* and *Eugénie Grandet* are merely two bricks of this unfinished edifice. The first is a study in irrational passion, the unrequited love of a father for his two daughters, a kind of middle-class *Lear* (16) minus Cordelia. "A hateful book," said George Eliot. The second is a study in avarice. Both deal with monomanias, as do so many of Balzac's fictions. He had little of Stendhal's sense of the ambivalent and ambiguous in human character.

These two novels, one drawn from the worldly life of Paris, the other a picture of provincial manners, have what is found in all his work—force, emphasis, vitality. They display Balzac's tenacious grip on fact, on raw, vivid detail, a talent that makes him the father of a certain school of modern realism. Finally they both expose Balzac's major obsession, which was money. He lived in a period like our own, of money-making, money-losing, money-loving; a period in which the greatest sin was not treachery but bankruptcy. No other novelist before him had understood the world of money as Balzac did. Thus he may be considered the ancestor of all our contemporary novelists of business and finance.

These are not inconsiderable qualities. To them we must add a demonic power of static characterization. Mme. Marneffe, Grandet, Gobseck, Goriot, César Birotteau—if not complex creations, these are solid ones. And when one looks at the mere formidable bulk of his work, so firm in its grasp of reality, so loaded with hard, vivid detail, so close to so many kinds of life, it is difficult not to take off one's hat to this flawed titan.

41. GUSTAVE FLAUBERT (1821–1880)
Madame Bovary

Before commenting on this novel, I wish to recommend the one translation that does it justice—that by Francis Steegmuller. It will serve to convince the reader that good reasons exist for its author's high reputation.

When *Madame Bovary* was first published in serial form, Flaubert had to defend himself before the Public Prosecutor against charges that it was offensive to morality and religion. He won the case. But the excitement over *Madame Bovary,* though transferred from the moral to the literary plane, has never since quite died down. The novel has continued to agitate many readers and most novelists and critics. I must at once admit that, while I admire it as an unquestioned masterpiece, I nevertheless find it cold and depressing. That, however, is not the general verdict.

Unlike Balzac, Flaubert is the classic type of the pure and dedicated artist. The son of a Rouen surgeon, he pursued, unhappily, brief law studies in Paris; in 1844 suffered a nervous attack; and withdrew to a life of study and writing, varied by intervals of travel and amorous experience. He was not by nature a happy man. His native melancholy was further underlined by the loss of loved ones, by the misunderstanding with which the world greeted much of his work, and by the self-torture administered by his literary perfectionism.

"The Idea," he wrote, "exists only by virtue of its form." Form to Flaubert meant more than a frame or a pattern. It was a complex affair. A few of its many elements were: "the perfect word"; cunningly contrived and varied rhythms; assonance; reverberant or echoing sequences of symbols; and a genuine architectural structure. Over *Madame Bovary* he spent five laborious years. Before his time no novel in French had been so carefully written. That is why I want you to read Mr. Steegmuller's translation: the whole emotional tone and weight of *Madame Bovary* is created by the use of a special language, requiring the most careful carry-over into English.

Flaubert believed that the artist hovered somewhere above the moral universe, that he should not judge, explain, or teach, but merely understand and perfectly record. Insofar as this novel is devoid of sentimentality, as it is of pity, Flaubert succeeded in his aim. Yet it conveys a message, if only a negative one; and that message we have already received in the pages of

Gulliver's Travels (23). Flaubert did not love the human race. *Madame Bovary,* for all its seeming detachment, seems to me a beautifully organized confession of misanthropy.

Whether or not this is true, no one can deny its influence. Most of the later novels that turn on the discrepancy between our ideal lives and the actual gray ones that we live owe much to Flaubert. Madame Bovary is the first Walter Mitty. She has given a name, *Bovarysme,* to her disease, a morbid passion for believing oneself other and better than one is. It is even possible that thousands of young men and women have revolted, in day-dream or in reality, against their environment, not because they were spontaneous rebels, but because *Madame Bovary* infected them—just as young men committed suicide as a consequence of reading Goethe's *Sorrows of Werther.*

There are other sides to Flaubert than those revealed in what is by most critics considered his masterpiece. I recommend particularly a reading of *Three Tales,* of which one, "A Simple Heart," discloses an almost Christian compassion not elsewhere to be found in this great, unhappy writer.

42. MARCEL PROUST (1871–1922) *Remembrance of Things Past*

This is the longest first-rate novel ever written. Its difficulties, like its rewards, are vast. If you respond to it at all (many do not) you may feel quite justified in spending what time you can spare over the next five or ten years in making it a part of your interior world.

Though it shares some features with *Ulysses* (35) and, in a minor way, with *Tristram Shandy* (24), it is basically unlike any novel we have so far discussed. It has a story, of course, and characters, and a clear setting in time and place—and all are most interesting indeed. But Proust is less concerned with these matters than in dramatizing a metaphysical system. Metaphysics tries to answer the question, What is it to be? Proust devoted his life to answering the question in the form of a work of art. Of course he answered only part of the question. He tells us what it means to be Proust. But the answer has enormous scope and range.

He never had to work for a living. His family was moderately wealthy and, from an early age, the brilliant boy had access to the world of fashionable and intellectual Paris, as it was before World War I. His attachment to his mother, a sensitive and finely charactered Jewess, was powerful and neurotic. Though Proust loved women as well as men, there is little doubt that his later subjection to inversion was caused partly by his relationship to Mme. Proust. Her death in 1905, together with his own physical weaknesses (particularly asthma), determined the shape of his life. He withdrew to the seclusion of a dark, vapor-filled, cork-lined room. There, sleeping by day, working by night, with occasional sorties into the outer world (with which he also kept in touch through a huge correspondence) he slowly, painfully elaborated his masterpiece.

The hero of *Ulysses* is a place, Dublin. The hero of *Remembrance* is less the "I" of the narrative than Time itself. To project in art the very "form of Time" was Proust's passion, his answer to the question, What is it to be? He jettisoned completely the methods of the conventional novelist. For him being is not a chronological succession of events. Being is the complete past, "that past which already extended so far down and which I was bearing so painfully within me."

How shall we grasp this past, this reality? Quantum theory tells us that in a sense reality is unseizable because observation itself changes the thing observed. Proust understood this. He therefore gave us the past as well as he could, by a series of approximations, by presenting it to us in a thousand aspects, by showing it for what it really is—not a smooth flow of discrete events, but an unbroken and ever-changing continuum. Parts of our past are continually erupting in us. These parts are felt differently at different times, by different people, under different circumstances. Proust evades none of these difficulties; he triumphs with them.

The past is evocable, we say, by memory. But this memory is not under our control. The taste of a small cake dipped in tea, the outline of some towers against the sky—such small events reawaken in Proust a stream of memories and half-forgotten experiences which color his whole life. We cannot understand ourselves at any given moment, nor are we the static sum of all the moments we have lived—because we are continually reliving them, and so the sum is always changing. Only through a complete evocation of the past can the content of any moment be even approximated. Because this is so, reality, as we say, eludes us, and life seems sad, evanescent, and puzzling. Only art, Proust's religion, by giving life's mutations an orderly form, can give us consolation.

Proust's method, even the structure of his interminable sentences, flows from this conception of time, from this enthronement of subjectivism. In his book time turns and twists upon itself like a snake, the past and present merge, motifs and themes are recalled and redeveloped and answer each other in echo and counterpoint. Every critic has pointed out that the book is less like a narrative than like a symphony.

But had Proust done nothing more than incorporate a metaphysic he would not be as interesting as he is. In addition to his peculiar, neurotic sensibility and his phenomenal memory, he possessed most of the gifts of any first-rate novelist. His book, for example, is a social panorama of unprecedented depth (though not of range); compare his Vanity Fair with Thackeray's (29). He describes the agonies and death of a whole aristocratic and upper-middle-class society. He analyzes, sometimes with intolerable exhaustiveness, the baffling and to him frustrating nature of love, and particularly of homosexual love. He creates at least a half-dozen characters comparable to the most living in the literature of the novel. And he invents a prose, often opaque, but always, in its slow sinuosities and plangent rhythms, proper to his difficult theme. His realism is unlike that of any novelist we have so far met. It is the realism of the symbolist, not the naturalist. When he wishes, he can describe to perfection. But he omits all details that do not re-enforce his conviction that our only reality is the aspect of things remembered. This partial reality is not all we need to know, but it is all we do know; and that limitation is the cause of the tragedy of life.

For some this is the greatest novel in the world. For others it is unreadable. For still others it is, as one good critic wrote, "mammoth but minor." You must pass your own judgment. I will, however, in conclusion quote the considered estimate of the man who is probably the finest living American critic, Edmund Wilson:

"We must recognize in Proust, it seems to me, one of the great minds and imaginations of our day, absolutely comparable in our own time, by reason both of his powers and his influence, to the Nietzsches, the Tolstois, the Wagners and the Ibsens of a previous generation. He has re-created the world of the novel from the point of view of relativity: he has supplied for the first time in literature an equivalent on the full scale for the new theory of modern physics."

43. EDGAR ALLAN POE (1809–1849)
Short Stories and Other Works

Poe may not rank among the greatest writers, but he ranks among the unhappiest. He has become a symbol of unappreciated genius.

His life was made up of misfortunes, some caused by lack of understanding on the part of his time, and many caused by his own disastrous inheritance and weaknesses. The child of wandering actors, he was brought up as the ward of a prosperous merchant with whom he quarreled as soon as it was humanly possible. His education, at the University of Virginia and West Point, was interrupted by his own talent for delinquency. He married his thirteen-year-old cousin, and her early death may have been the deciding factor in his ruin. His first volumes of poems were not noticed. He was a capable journalist but mismanaged what might have turned out a successful career. He engaged in desperate, immature, incomplete love affairs. Drugs, alcohol, overwork, poverty became the staples of his life. He died in utter wretchedness. Of all the writers we have met or shall meet, surely he was the most miserable. Even the bitter Swift (23) for a time enjoyed the company and praise of his equals. Poe never did.

Poe's verse has always been popular and in France it was for a time much more than that. Probably all of it that is worth while can be read in half an hour. The rest sounds thin and affected today, though Poe was better than "the jingle man" Emerson (68) called him.

But his tales, monologues, and some of his critical essays, despite infuriating faults of style, retain their interest. His mind was neither powerful nor balanced—but it *was* original, running creatively counter to the rather insipid thought of most of his American contemporaries. James Russell Lowell's famous estimate may not be too far from the truth: "Three fifths of him genius and two fifths sheer fudge."

What is most notable in Poe is that he either pioneered or originated half a dozen fields. With his three tales—*The Murders in the Rue Morgue, The Purloined Letter,* and *The Gold Bug*—he not only invented the detective story but practically exhausted its possibilities. The critic Howard Haycraft credits him with laying the form's complete foundation and then goes on to name ten elements of the modern detective story, all to be found in Poe. Similarly Poe blazed the trail leading to what is now called science fiction. His theories of "pure poetry" influenced the important French symbolist movement of the latter part of the nineteenth century, and so affected the great modern poet Yeats (79). Poe defined and illustrated the tale of effect and atmosphere. In his strange and morbid stories we find many anticipations of modern psychology, including the motif of the death wish and that of the split personality (see his remarkable *William Wilson*). Poe's prevailing moods of desolation and alienation set the tone for much writing of our own century. Finally, for all his faults, he was our first important literary critic, generally making his judgments on a broad base of first principles.

Many of today's critics see in American writing two major strains that sometimes intermingle. The first is optimistic, practical, democratic. The second is pessimistic, guilt-laden, aristocratic, and deeply involved with the heart's darker concerns. The latter tradition found its first notable figure in Poe, and that is why he is more than a mere writer of gruesome romantic tales.

44. NATHANIEL HAWTHORNE (1804–1864)
The Scarlet Letter, Selected Tales

In any well-considered list of the dozen greatest American novels *The Scarlet Letter* would almost certainly appear. Yet one may wonder at first why this should be so. Its background is seventeenth-century Puritan New England. When Hawthorne wrote about it, the scene was already beginning to appear remote; today it is very far away indeed. Furthermore we are not quite sure that Hawthorne's picture of a sin-obsessed, guilt-ridden society offers even the interest attaching to historical accuracy. Most recent researches tend to show that the Puritans were a far more relaxed people than Hawthorne, their brooding descendant, conceived them to be. Finally, Hester and Dimmesdale's adultery and their expiation appear to have a forceful meaning only within the framework of a dogmatic Christian morality. Many of us, living in a post-Freud, post-Kinsey world apparently dedicated to evil on a really wholesale scale, may read this book for the first time only to exclaim, "What's he making all the fuss about?"

And yet, though we may smile away the Puritan ethic that suffuses it, we somehow cannot smile away the book itself. Its power to move us persists, even though we may admire in it qualities different from those that originally won Hawthorne his reputation. For us this is only incidentally a story of the bitter fruits of adultery. It is even more incidentally a historical picture of a bygone society. What we now seem to be reading is a profound parable of the human heart. It happens to be expressed in symbols that were particularly meaningful to Hawthorne and his time. But they *are* only symbols, and flexible ones at that, applicable to the human condition as it exists everywhere and at all times.

Take that moral which Hawthorne, toward the end of his dark and beautiful romance, puts in a sentence: "Be true! Be true! Be true! Show freely to the world, if not your worst, yet some trait whereby the worst may be inferred!" Though couched in didactic phrases, is not this an indictment of repression, a plea for that purification of our souls that comes only from facing, not deceiving, ourselves? In the same way we feel that Chillingworth's dissolution is inevitable in any man, indeed in any society, that tries to live by life-denying emotions. We feel also, as Hawthorne explicitly says, that love and hate begin to resemble each other when both depend too exclusively, too passionately on the possession of the loved or hated object.

In other words, we no longer read this as a book about how two young people were punished for committing adultery. We read it as the work of a moral psychologist who knows as much about our own hidden guilts and fears as he did about those of his tortured Puritans. I would suggest that if we approach *The Scarlet Letter* in this light it will cease to be the faded classic suggested by its old-fashioned style and its, to us, excessive moralizing. We will begin to see what the critic Mark Van

Doren means when he tells us that Hawthorne's "one deathless virtue is that rare thing in any literature, an utterly serious imagination."

Hawthorne once wrote of his workroom: "This deserves to be called a haunted chamber, for thousands and thousands of visions have appeared to me in it." Much of our lives we pass in the prosaic light of day. But a part of it even the most "normal" of us pass in a haunted chamber. Of this haunted chamber Hawthorne is a classic historian.

I should add that it will repay you to read or reread, in addition to *The Scarlet Letter*, a few of Hawthorne's somber allegorical shorter tales, particularly *Young Goodman Brown, The Minister's Black Veil, The Birthmark,* and *Rappaccini's Daughter.*

45. HERMAN MELVILLE (1819–1891) *Moby Dick*

At twenty-five Melville had already had most of the experiences that were to supply him with the raw materials for his books. As a seaman he had served aboard the trader *St. Lawrence,* the whaler *Acushnet,* the Australian bark *Lucy Ann,* and the frigate *United States.* He had sailed both the Atlantic and the South Seas. He had undergone "an indulgent captivity" of some four weeks with a cannibal tribe in the Marquesas. His adventures had been preceded by an aimless, sketchy education and were to be followed by a little formal travel in Europe and the Holy Land. These external experiences—plus a brooding, powerful, and original genius—were enough to produce not only *Moby Dick* but almost a score of other works in prose and verse. One of these, *Billy Budd, Foretopman,* was published many years after his death, and, if you can, you should read it, along with his masterpiece.

He wrote *Typee,* an account of his stay with the cannibals, when he was twenty-five. It had considerable success. Nothing he wrote thereafter received much popular welcome, and the latter half of his life was spent in obscurity and loneliness. *Moby Dick* (1851) was not precisely unnoticed, it is true, but it was not understood. Not until the twenties of our century, about thirty years after Melville's death, was it resurrected by a few devoted scholars. Then Melville's reputation skyrocketed, and it has never since diminished in the slightest. *Moby Dick* is recognized everywhere as one of the supremely great novels of the world.

"I have written a wicked book and feel as spotless as the lamb," wrote Melville to his good friend Hawthorne (44). It is an interesting sentence. Partly it is light irony. Partly it is a recognition of the fact that *Moby Dick*'s metaphysical and religious defiances would hardly please Melville's strait-laced family. And partly it is a fair description of the book. For, though the intention is of course not wicked, the novel *is* about evil, and it is hardly Christian in tone.

We have already noted at least two works of the imagination that can be read on two or more planes—*Gulliver's Travels* (23) and *Alice in Wonderland* (31). We have still to meet two others of which this may be said—*Huckleberry Finn* (46) and *Don Quixote* (48). *Moby Dick* belongs with them.

With a little judicious skipping boys and girls can enjoy it hugely as a thrilling sea story about a revengeful old man with an ivory leg, pursuing his enemy, the White Whale, to their common death. Grownups of various degrees of sophistication can read it as a tempestuous work of art, filled with the deepest questionings and embodying a tragic sense of life that places it among the masterpieces of Dostoevski (51) and even, some think, Shakespeare (16). And no one at all sensitive to our language can help being moved by its magnificent prose, produced by an organ with all the stops out.

Moby Dick is not a "hard" book. But it is not a transparent one either. We all feel that Ahab and the whale (and the other characters) mean more than themselves, but we may well differ over what those meanings may be. For some Moby Dick himself symbolizes the malignancy of the whole universe, the baffling inexorability of Nature, that Nature from which man, if he be sensitive and energetic of mind, somehow feels himself alienated. That dark nature is always in Ahab's consciousness. Indeed Moby Dick may be thought of, not only as a real whale, but as a monster thrashing about in the vast Pacific of Ahab's brain, to be exorcised only by his own self-destruction. *Moby Dick* is not a gloomy or morbid book, but you can hardly call it an argument for optimism.

Seventeen years ago, writing about *Moby Dick*, I tried to summarize my sense of it. Now, rereading it many years later, I find no reason to change my opinion:

"*Moby Dick* is America's most unparochial great book, less delivered over to a time and place than the work of even our freest minds, Emerson and Whitman. It is conceived on a vast scale, it shakes hands with prairie seas and great distances, it invades with its conquistador prose 'the remotest secret drawers and lockers of the world.' It has towering faults of taste, it is often willful and obscure, but it will remain America's unarguable contribution to world literature, so many-leveled is it, so wide-ranging in that nether world which is the defiant but secretly terror-stricken soul of man, alone, and appalled by his aloneness."

46. MARK TWAIN (1835–1910) *Huckleberry Finn*

Most of us who read *Huckleberry Finn* in our youth still think of it as a "boys' book"—which of course it is, and a very good one too. Against this view place Ernest Hemingway's (90) famous statement: "All modern American literature comes from one book by Mark Twain called *Huckleberry Finn*." Somewhere between these two judgments lies the truth. But that truth lies much closer to the second judgment than to the first.

Mark Twain (real name: Samuel L. Clemens) had a good deal of trouble writing *Huckleberry Finn*. It's doubtful that he knew, when he had finished, that it would turn out to be, along with Thoreau's *Walden* (67), one of the two central and generative books of the American nineteenth century. In a way he wrote it out of his unconscious, through which the Great River that had nourished his early imagination still rolled and flooded. Into it he put his youth—but also, perhaps without quite knowing it, the youth of the Republic. He did more. The division in Huck's mind between his natural social genius (for Huck is a genius as well as a boy; indeed this boy is a great man) and his distaste for "sivilization," mirrored a split in our soul. We too as a people have been torn and are still being torn between a desire, based on our frontier heritage, to "light out for the territory," and our apparently stronger desire to convert that territory into one great productive mill. Furthermore, Huck reflects the tensions still vibrating in the national conscience; and if you don't think so, reread the chapter in which Huck debates whether or not he shall turn in Jim, who is that criminal thing, an escaped slave, but who also happens to be a friend.

In this book there is no sentimentality. The preindustrial "natural" America it depicts is one of violence, murder, feuds, greed, and danger. The River is supremely wonderful but also, as its old-pilot author knew, supremely treacherous and even sinister. Nevertheless no grown-up American who loves his country, its present no less than its past, can read *Huckleberry Finn* without a poignant sense that it is a kind of epic celebration of a lost paradise. We all feel, North and South, that with Appomattox, a certain innocence, a certain fresh and youthful freedom, left us forever, possibly to be replaced by something better. The sophisticated Periclean Greek, reading his Homer, must have felt somewhat the same way. *Huckleberry Finn* is our *Odyssey* (2).

Mark Twain, referring to the greatly inferior *Tom Sawyer*, called it "simply a hymn, put into prose form to give it a worldly air." That is precisely true of *Huckleberry Finn*. It is a hymn to the strange, puzzled but still rather beautiful youth of our nation.

Hemingway implied all this in his statement. But he also meant something less vague. He meant that Mark Twain was the first great American writer to use the vernacular (indeed a dozen vernaculars) creatively. *Huckleberry Finn* deliberately destroyed the conventional English "literary" sentence. It introduced a new rhythm that actually followed the twists and turns of our ordinary speech, without trying for phonographic accuracy. It showed us what can be done with a de-academicized language.

For all his later worldliness and big-city culture, Mark Twain was one of those "powerful, uneducated persons" saluted by Walt Whitman (80). This does not make him any the less a great writer. But it makes him a great writer who heads a tradition radically different from that headed by his contemporary Henry James (47). They reflect two powerful forces in our literature and our thought. The first is native, humorous, and in the best sense popular. The second is Anglo-European-American, deeply analytic, and in the best sense aristocratic.

47. HENRY JAMES (1843–1916) *The Ambassadors*

During his seventy-two years nothing much "happened" to Henry James, brother of the great American philosopher-psychologist William James (69). He never married. Indeed, so far as we know, he had no passionate relations with men or women. He did not, in any truly urgent sense, have to earn his own living. The one decisive external event of his long, industrious life was his decision in 1876 to live permanently in England. There, varying his desk labors with trips to his native country and Europe, plus much dining out, James spent the rest of his days.

It seems a bit passive. Yet on balance James probably lived one of the most active lives of the century. Nothing happened to him except everything—everything he could observe, feel, discriminate, ponder, and finally cast into his elaborately wrought stories. He made everything pay artistic dividends. His books are his real biography.

Conrad (33) called him "the historian of fine consciences," an excellent phrase if we extend the last word so as to include the idea of consciousness. James excels in the careful tracing of subtle relationships among subtle characters. He exhausts all the psychological possibilities of any given situation; and the situations he chooses, at least in his major novels, are dense with meaning. His mastery flows in part from his perfect recognition of his own immense powers. These depend on sensibility, high intelligence, and the ability to find and mold the exactly right form for his ideas and themes. As a pure artist he is the most extraordinary figure in the entire history of the American novel.

James himself thought *The Ambassadors* his finest book. Though written in his late period it does not suffer from the overelaboration of which many readers complain. (One well-known witticism thus describes James's three phases: James I, James II, and the Old Pretender.) All his powers are here held in beautiful balance and suspension. He handles one of his major themes—the impact of Continental moral realism on the rigid and sometimes naive ethical outlook of Americans—on the level of the highest comedy. That last word should not make you think *The Ambassadors* is not a serious work. For all its grace and wit, it is weighty enough, with its grave and reiterated plea for more life, for more perception, for the claims of the intelligence as an instrument for seizing and interpreting experience. "Live all you can," cries Lambert Strether to little Bilham, "life, live!" In Strether, who is superbly equipped to react to the new experience that comes to him, alas, too late, I think James felt he had created a peculiarly American type.

As with most of James's work, *The Ambassadors* must be read slowly. Every line tells. All is measured for its possible effect.

There is no trace in it of what the author called "the baseness of the arbitrary stroke." It may take you ten times as long to read *The Ambassadors* as to read *Tom Jones*—but there is far more than ten times as much in it.

One of the most voluminous of great writers, James cannot be known through any single book. He worked brilliantly in the fields of the novel, the long and short story, the memoir, the biography, the critical essay, the travel sketch, as well as unsuccessfully in the theater. For a representative selection of his short stories see *The Short Stories of Henry James*, edited with an Introduction by Clifton Fadiman (Modern Library, $2.95). *The Portrait of a Lady* (Houghton Mifflin, $0.80) displays James's earlier and simpler manner at its best.

48. MIGUEL DE CERVANTES SAAVEDRA (1547–1616) *Don Quixote*

Don Quixote is perhaps the only book (but see Tolstoy, 52) on our long list that may profitably be read in an abridged (but, please, not a bowdlerized or children's) version. Walter Starkie has done a good job along this line. However, if you use, as I suggest, a complete translation, do some skipping. Whenever (or almost whenever) you come to a goatherd or a shepherdess, some drivel lies ahead. Skip all the interpolated pastoral yarns that pleased Cervantes' audience but bore us stiff. Skip every bit of verse you meet; Cervantes is one of the world's worst poets. Finally, use *only* a modern translation—Cohen's or Starkie's or, best of all, Putnam's. Avoid Motteux's like the plague. Post-finally, do not be put off by an occasional tedious passage or chapter in Part 1. Persist to Part 2. It is by far the greater. Even the finest writers sometimes have to educate themselves through the medium of their own creation, and apparently that is what happened to this poor, maimed ex-soldier Cervantes: from writing about Don Quixote and Sancho Panza he learned how great they really were. Ten years elapsed between the publication of the two parts, and those ten years made a difference in Cervantes' genius.

These warnings are needed because, like *Paradise Lost* and *The Divine Comedy, Don Quixote* is one of those books more reverenced than read, more lauded than enjoyed. It has had its ups and downs. Perhaps it reached its peak of popularity in the eighteenth century—we have seen how much it meant to Sterne (24), for example. It is not so widely read in our time. Still, the brute fact remains that, after the Bible, it is one of the two or three books in the world most widely translated and studied. And for this there must be good reasons.

There are.

Of these reasons Cervantes himself suggests the simplest. He remarks, in the second chapter of Part 2, "No sooner do [people] see any lean hack than they cry out: 'There goes Rosinante.'" In other words, his book is crowded with immediately recognizable human types, and in this case a nonhuman type. The whole world understands at once what we mean when we call someone quixotic or say that he tilts at windmills. There are really only a few literary characters we think of as permanently alive and not a creation of printed letters. Hamlet is one, Don Quixote surely another.

The second reason is no less simple. *Don Quixote,* once you allow for its leisurely tempo, is one of the best adventure stories ever written, perhaps the best after the *Odyssey* (2). That is what makes it a classic for the young. When you reread it years later you perceive that it is also a great adventure story of the mind, for some of its most exciting events occur during the conversations between the Knight and his loquacious Squire, two of the best talkers who ever used their vocal cords creatively.

The third reason sounds simple but is not so. *Don Quixote* is a supremely humorous novel. Some readers laugh aloud, others grin, some smile externally, others internally. And some read it with a curious emotion mingling delight and sorrow. Cervantes' humor is hard to define because it is not a "character trait" in him; it is the man himself, hence a mystery. The best clue to his humor is Walter Starkie's remark. He calls Cervantes a humorist, "which meant that he could see more than one thing at a time."

This brings us to the deepest of all the reasons for *Don Quixote*'s greatness—the fact that, though it is not obscure, its meanings seem to change with each generation, indeed with each reader—and that none of these meanings is trivial.

We all know that Cervantes started out to write a satire on chivalric romances. Or so he seems to say. Don Quixote himself, the lean, grizzled Knight of the Sorrowful Countenance, began his life as a figure of fun. So did his earthy, stocky, proverb-filled squire Sancho Panza. Yet, by the end of the book, both have become something else, as well as more like each other, as Salvador de Madariaga remarks. Together they seem to sum up, roughly, the warring elements in all men: our defiance of society and our acceptance of it; our love of the heroic and our suspicion of it; our passion for creating worlds of the imagination and our rueful compromise with the *status quo*.

And so we come to the Don Quixote "problem," as fascinating as the Hamlet "problem." Is this book a burlesque of chivalry? Or is it the most persuasive of pleas for the chivalric attitude, apart from any specific time or institution? Is it a satire on dreamers? Or is it a defense of dreaming? Is it a symbol of the tragic soul and history of Spain? If so, why does it speak so clearly to men of all colors and races? Is it the author's spiritual autobiography? A study of insanity? Or of a higher sanity? Or is it, couched in terms of picaresque incident, a dramatized treatise on illusion and reality, like the plays of Pirandello? Finally—just to indicate how complex interpretation may become—is Don Quixote, as Mark Van Doren thinks, a kind of actor who chooses his role because by so doing he can absorb life and reflect on it in a way denied to the single, unvarying personality?

I leave you to the golden book that Macaulay thought "the best novel in the world, beyond comparison."

49. NIKOLAI VASILIEVICH GOGOL (1809–1852) *Dead Souls*

This does not seem like a particularly appealing title. (Actually the term refers, as you will discover, to Russian serfs who had died but were still carried, until the next census, on the tax rolls. The book is not as morbid as it sounds.)

Gogol is not a particularly appealing figure either. His family heritage was a poor one, he had an unbalanced youth, he failed at the law, as a government clerk, as an actor, as a teacher. To the end of his short life he remained a virgin, and religious mania clouded his mind in his latter years. As a writer he enjoyed a number of triumphs, but continued to be appalled by the electrifying reaction to his books and plays. He wandered aimlessly over Europe and made a pointless pilgrimage to the Holy Land. During his last days he burned his manuscripts, so that we possess only a fragment of the second part of *Dead Souls,* which when completed was to show good victorious over evil. He died in what seems to have been delirium.

Yet this queer duck, who surely cannot be said to possess a powerful mind, virtually founded Russian prose and gave Russia a masterpiece that became a part of world literature. Speaking of Gogol's most famous short story, Dostoevski said, "We all come out of *The Overcoat.*" One recalls Hemingway's remark about *Huckleberry Finn* (46). Gogol's untraditional genius apparently led him to break up the formalism and rigidity that marked much previous Russian writing, just as Mark Twain performed the same service for our own country. The giants who followed him benefited from this liberation.

I once wrote an Introduction to *Dead Souls* which the brilliant author of *Lolita* termed "ridiculous." I think Mr. Nabokov must have felt queasy over my notion (shared by many) that *Dead Souls* is a great comic novel. He must surely have objected also to my other notion (also not uniquely held) that Gogol in one of his moods—for he did not have a coherent system even of prejudices—was in this book expressing a certain dissatisfaction with the Russian feudal system. But it is also true—this is Mr. Nabokov's emphasis—that *Dead Souls* is a demonic book, as well as a funny one. It does have a nightmare, almost a surrealist tone. Usually likened to Dickens, Gogol is even more akin to Poe. That *Dead Souls* can please me as well as Mr. Nabokov may exasperate Mr. Nabokov, but furnishes at least some slight evidence of the variety of Gogol's appeal.

At any rate, this is a fascinating, almost madly vivid, loosely composed yarn about a great, bland rogue and his travels through what seems, to a mere American, a real, if heavily caricatured, early nineteenth-century Russia. Its laughter is mingled with melancholy—the poet Pushkin, after listening to Gogol's reading of the first chapter, sighed, "Lord, how sad is our Russia."

I cannot command the original but nonetheless dare to recommend one translation, and one only. It is by Bernard Guilbert Guerney. It just sounds right. The others have a stiffness foreign, I am told, to Gogol's spirit.

50. IVAN SERGEYEVICH TURGENEV (1818–1883) *Fathers and Sons*

Of the three great Russian novelists Turgenev seems to wear the least well. Perhaps that is because, as authorities tell us, his style is of such delicacy and evocativeness that no translation does it justice. Or it may be that some of his themes have lost their attractive power: the "superfluous men," the charming but effete Russian gentry of the 1840's and 1850's; the struggle, if the term is not too strong, between the dominating female and the weaker male; the pale beauty of early love, of frustrated love, of remembered love; and, his recurrent motif, the mutations of failure.

Turgenev's mother was a witch out of a dreadful fairy tale. The terror and despair she inspired in her son never left his mind and crept into much of his work. His lifelong passion for the famous, ugly but apparently fascinating singer, Pauline Viardot-Garcia, offered no compensation for his bruised spirit. He followed her about Europe like a dog, enjoyed her ultimate favors only briefly, and obtained what happiness he could by living near her or at times with her and her husband. There is no doubt that she distorted his view of women; he seems either to fear them or to sentimentalize them.

Turgenev shuttled between his estates and Western Europe for many years, and spent the last twenty or so mainly in France and Baden. He was an expatriate, rather like Joyce. Like Joyce he widened his own country's perspective by throwing open to it a view of cosmopolitan culture. Also, like Joyce, this "westernizer" continued to draw his central inspiration from his native land, no matter how alienated his external life became. Turgenev's political position, throughout the century that was preparing for 1917, was that of the unengaged, liberal, enlightened, humane skeptic. Hence his books, while at once winning the admiration of the cultivated, often failed to please either the reactionaries or the radicals.

Some of his shorter works (particularly many of the *Sportsman's Sketches*) are very beautiful indeed. But probably his reputation will continue to rest mainly on *Fathers and Sons*, also translated as *Fathers and Children*. As its title suggests, it was intended to be a study of the conflict between the generations. The theme, in my opinion, has been more powerfully treated by other novelists, including Samuel Butler in *The Way of All Flesh* (Modern Library College Editions, $0.85). To us, however, *Fathers and Sons* appears more interesting as the first classic presentation of that element in the Russian character which has surfaced in our time and now challenges the entire world.

Turgenev lacks Dostoevski's intuitive, indeed terrifying grasp of the revolutionary-terrorist temperament. Yet in Bazarov, the center of his masterpiece, he does give us a clear, almost Olympian picture of the mid-nineteenth-century "nihilist" (the word is Turgenev's invention). In Russia as the years went on the nihilist type was to assume a number of different forms: the terrorist, the anarchist, the atheist-materialist, the science worshiper, and at last the dedicated Communist. Though the book exhibits in relief most of Turgenev's other admirable qualities—particularly his economy and his un-Russian clarity of form—it will stand or fall, I think, with Bazarov. Probably it will stand.

51. FEODOR MIKHAILOVICH DOSTOEVSKI (1821–1881) *Crime and Punishment, The Brothers Karamazov*

Dostoevski's life and work are of a piece. Suffering, violence, emotional crises, and extravagance of conduct mark both. The terrible sincerity of his novels flows in part from the anxieties that clouded the author's whole career. It is well for the reader to know this. To read this great Russian is to descend into an inferno.

Like Flaubert (41) he was the son of a physician. Again like Flaubert he was when young introduced to scenes of suffering, disease, and death, and never forgot them. In his fifteenth year his gentle mother died and not long afterward, in 1839, his father was murdered by his own serfs. Dostoevski was left desolate and defenseless. Perhaps from this period stems the epileptic tendency that was to overshadow his whole life, if also perhaps to give him a certain visionary inspiration. In 1849 his connection with a group of dreamy young radicals caused his arrest. He was sentenced to death, but just before the firing squad was about to do its work, his punishment was commuted. This experience marked him deeply. He then spent four years in a Siberian convict camp, enduring inhumanities partially described in his *Memoirs from the House of the Dead.* Another four years were spent in military service at a remote Asiatic outpost.

His first marriage was to a hysteric, his second to his secretary, who seems to have understood his manias and rages. The utopian radicalism of his youth gave way to a religious conversion. Dostoevski became orthodox, reactionary, Slavophile. Yet none of these labels is fair to him, for his temperament was a contradictory one in which Christ and Satan struggled continually for mastery. At times he seems to talk almost like a "good European"—but a very Russian one. The latter part of his life was not much happier than the first part had been, though his supremacy as a novelist and interpreter of the Russian temperament was generally acknowledged. His epilepsy threatened him continually; debts worried him; for a time he was a compulsive gambler; and there can be little doubt that his sexual nature was unbalanced.

This is the man who wrote some of the most extraordinary novels of all time. They anticipated many of the ideas of Nietzsche (60) and Freud (61); they influenced such non-Russian writers as Mann (36) and Faulkner (90); and they dramatized the terrorist theory and practice that we associate with Lenin, Stalin, and Hitler. Indeed it may be said that Dostoevski had an intuitive sense of what the twentieth century would have to endure; and it is this sense which plays its part in the fascination of his work.

It is hard to pin this strange man down. His central obsession was God. The search for Him, or the attempt to prove His existence, dominates his stories. Tormented by God, Dostoevski seems to approach a vision of love and peace only after long journeying through universes of pain and evil. In his novels the worlds of crime, abnormal psychology, and religious mysticism meet and mingle in a manner difficult to define. He is thought of as an apostle of compassion, but of the true saintly qualities he seems to possess few.

The Brothers Karamazov is generally considered his most profound work. However, if you are going to limit yourself to only one novel, there is something to be said for *Crime and Punishment*. For one thing, *The Brothers Karamazov*, though it does not leave you up in the air, is nevertheless an unfinished book. *Crime and Punishment* is a simpler, more unified one, with a strong detective-story plot of great interest. It can be read as a straight thriller. It can be read as a vision. It can be read on planes in between these two. From its murky, gripping, intolerably vivid pages you emerge with the feeling that you have lived and suffered a lifetime. Its action takes nine days.

52. LEO NIKOLAYEVICH TOLSTOY (1828–1910) *War and Peace*

Though no one knows just what the words mean, *War and Peace*, more frequently than any other work of fiction, has been called "the greatest novel ever written." This need not scare us. However its greatness may be defined, it is not connected with obscurity, with difficulty, or even with profundity. Once a few minor hazards are braved, this vast chronicle of Napoleonic times seems to become an open book, as if it had been written in the sunlight. Just as Dostoevski is the dramatist of the unconscious and what is called the abnormal, so Tolstoy is the epic narrator of the conscious and the normal. His tone is one of almost loving serenity, and his characters, though their names are odd and their time is remote, are our brothers and sisters.

Most beginning readers experience three difficulties:

1. The novel is enormously long. As with *Don Quixote* (though less cogently) some sort of case may be made for an

abridged version. There are several available. I prefer, if you are unwilling to tackle the complete *War and Peace*, Manuel Komroff's abridgment in the Bantam Books edition. In this curtailment you will not get the full range of Tolstoy's mind. But you will get the essential *novelist* in Tolstoy. And you may find him so interesting that you will be encouraged to try the longer version.

2. It's hard to follow both the relationships and the movements of the strangely named, complex cast of characters. This is true. All I can say is that if you persist in your reading, the characters will sooner or later arrange themselves clearly in your mind. Some editions, such as The Inner Sanctum Edition, supply carefully annotated lists of characters, maps, and other aids.

3. It's hard to separate the story from the digressions. This too is true, and many critics have thought it a weakness in an otherwise great novel. Tolstoy was not a formalist, as Turgenev (50) was. He sprawls. He tells you what's on his mind. You must take him as you find him. If you read slowly enough (and you should; the book sets its own proper leisurely tempo) you will probably discover that the digressions are no harder to take than were the essays we found scattered through *Tom Jones* (25).

When I first wrote about *War and Peace* many years ago, I singled out for special praise three qualities: its inclusiveness, its naturalness, its timelessness. Rereading it fifteen years later, I discovered other qualities, particularly Tolstoy's ability to reveal one to oneself. Now, reading it once more, I am impressed with a virtue that may be simple to the point of banality. Tolstoy once said, "The one thing necessary, in life as in art, is to tell the truth." When your canvas is narrow enough, this may not seem so difficult—Hemingway tells the truth about bullfighting. But your task is overwhelming when you take human life for your subject, and human life is actually the real subject of *War and Peace*.

Tolstoy meets his own test. In this gigantic story of the impact of Napoleon's invasion on a whole country, he never fakes, he never evades, he grasps life at the middle, he conveys the essence of a character by seizing upon precisely the true, the revelatory gesture or phrase. That is why, though it deals in part with war and destruction, it seems one of the sanest novels ever written. And its sanity flows from Tolstoy's love for his characters, his love for the "procession of the generations," his love for the spectacle of life itself.

Tolstoy is a very large man. When we read him we too must enlarge ourselves.

53. SIGRID UNDSET (1882–1949)
Kristin Lavransdatter

To conclude our reading in the great noncontemporary masters of Western narrative, I suggest the monumental trilogy which in 1928 won for Sigrid Undset the Nobel Prize. Here are my reasons:

1. It is a superb example of a kind of story that rarely receives serious treatment: the historical novel. *Kristin Lavransdatter* is a long, stately, wonderfully vivid interpretation of life in the first half of the fourteenth century in Norway. It is not about costumes but about people; yet they are people seen against a lovingly studied background. Of this period most of us knew nothing until Sigrid Undset's art and scholarship revealed it to us. Thus an archaeologist's daughter, using the artist's impalpable tools, has retrieved for our civilization a part of its past.

2. Over the years this book has won the affection of the general reader as well as the tribute of the professional critic. It appears to have the scope and weight that make for classic stature.

3. My third reason may not persuade all. The West is supposed to be dominantly a Christian community, the idea of

God being understood as pervasive among us. It is nonetheless a curious fact that of the thirty-three prose narratives we have considered, only two receive their *prime* impulse from the Christian religion. These are *Pilgrim's Progress* (21) and *Kristin Lavransdatter*. In several of the other novels questions of faith or dogma are involved; but only these two seem to be pure and unalloyed testimonials to a faith that is supposed to be basic to the lives of the majority of Westerners. Testimonials alone would not merit a place in The Lifetime Reading Plan. But these testimonials are by artists with power to move us, whatever the form or degree of our religious belief.

4. This story about a medieval woman in a remote part of Europe is by implication an interesting commentary on our own century. Sigrid Undset's imagination turned back to the age of faith and moral authority, not because she wished to escape into a dream world, but because she wished to draw as vividly as possible a picture of a culture sharply contrasting with our own. With impressive dignity *Kristin Lavransdatter* celebrates the sanctity of the marriage tie, the spiritual importance of the family, the retribution that follows the commission of evil, and the case for a life led in accordance with absolute standards of morality. Its characters and story are interesting in themselves; one does not have to be of Sigrid Undset's faith to be attracted by them. (She became a convert to Catholicism in 1924). But as a whole the book's stature is connected with the fact that it is a kind of epic of conservative morality. It seems to me that any group of novels intended to illustrate the entire Western tradition should include at least one modern work of fiction in which this view of mankind is given moving expression.

Philosophy, Psychology, Politics, Essays

54. THOMAS HOBBES (1588–1679) *Leviathan*

The quarrel between Man and the State as to the proper division of power is central to our time. Hobbes is important because he presents the first modern reasoned case for the State as the exclusive holder of power, as long as that State can offer protection to its citizens. Thus all of today's authoritarian regimes, whether Marxist or non-Marxist, may claim Hobbes as one of their earliest and greatest advocates. We read the philosophers not only because they are in themselves interesting, but because their ideas have consequences.

Hobbes received a good classical education at Oxford. He later used his scholarship to prepare a translation of Thucydides (4) in whose work he saw a demonstration of the evils of democracy. For some time he made a living as a tutor in a noble family. In his middle years, apparently as a consequence of reading a proof in Euclid, he turned from the classics to science and philosophy. His political sympathies during the great English Parliamentary struggle were Royalist—for a short period he taught mathematics in Paris to the future Charles II. But his deeper loyalty was to power irrespective of party. Hence, after Cromwell's victory, he made submission to the Protector. During the Restoration, though attacked as an atheist, he managed to survive successfully enough to reach the age of ninety-one.

His fame rests on the *Leviathan.* Published in 1651, it was merely a systematic development of ideas he was already holding some years before the Civil War came to a head.

Hobbes's absolutist theory of the State rests on his antiheroic conception of man's nature. He is a thoroughgoing mechanistic materialist. He does not deny God. But God is irrelevant to his thought. He believes in a proposition by no means self-evident—that all men are primarily interested in self-preservation. In a natural, lawless state this passion results in anarchy, and the life of man, in his most famous phrase, is "solitary, poor, nasty, brutish, and short."

To escape such an existence man institutes a commonwealth or government, the great artificial construct he calls Leviathan. To secure peace, or, as we say today, "security," men should or rather must relinquish their right of private judgment as to what is good or evil, placing that right in the hands of a sovereign or assembly. He prefers a monarchy but his logic would suggest no basic objection to a committee or party, as in the Communist Leviathan. In such a state morality would flow from law rather than law from morality.

Most so-called "realistic" theories of politics find their source partly in Hobbes. Our own democratic doctrine is anti-Hobbesian in its view of human nature. It rests on the notion of a division of powers (Hobbes thought the Civil War came about because power was divided among the king, the lords, and the House of Commons); on a system of checks and balances; and on a vague but so far workable theory of the general will expressed in representative forms. To understand what really separates us from all authoritarian regimes, a reading of the *Leviathan* is most helpful.

Despite his iron doctrine, Hobbes himself seems to have been a pleasant and rather timid fellow.

He writes a crabbed, difficult prose. Save him for your stronger intellectual moods. Read the Introduction and Parts 1 and 2 entire, if possible; Chapters 32, 33, 42, and 46 of the third and fourth parts, in which he argues against the power claims of all established churches; and finally his Review and Conclusion.

55. JOHN LOCKE (1632–1704)

Second Treatise on Government (FULL TITLE: *An Essay Concerning the True Original Extent and Aim of Civil Government*)

Locke's father, a Cromwell man, lost much of his fortune with the Restoration (1660). This may have inclined his Oxford-trained son to balance his wide intellectual interests with various governmental and semigovernmental activities. As he had, among other things, studied medicine he was able to serve as household physician, as well as personal secretary, to the first Earl of Shaftesbury. With the latter's fall from power in 1675, Locke removed to France for four years; returned to England under Shaftesbury again; following the latter's exile and death, sought refuge in Holland; and in 1689 was back in England, favorably received by the new regime of William and Mary. During these years he worked on his *Essay Concerning Human Understanding,* which appeared, together with the two *Treatises on Civil Government,* in 1690. The latter, however, had been written twelve years before and are not, as has been thought, a defense of the Revolution of 1688, except by anticipation.

During the whole of the eighteenth century Locke's influence was marked. Through Voltaire (38) and Rousseau (85) he provided some of the ideas that sparked the French Revolution. Through Jefferson and other Founding Fathers he determined to a considerable extent the ideas that went into the Declaration and the Constitution. His views on religious toleration, education, and politics, though not in every instance original, did much to establish the mental climate of the Industrial Revolution and to promote the advance of democratic government.

His major work, the *Essay Concerning Human Understanding,*

is generally supposed to have founded the British empirical school of philosophy. This rejects the doctrine that ideas are innate but derives them rather from experience. If you have a special interest in the fascinating history of theories of knowledge, you might tackle the famous *Essay*.

For the rest of us it is useful to have at least a rough idea of Locke's *Second Treatise on Government*. Like Hobbes, he addresses himself to the central question: What is the basis of legitimate power? His answer, though on many points open to criticism, clears the way for the development of representative government, just as Hobbes's answer does for authoritarian government. Hobbes's idea of a "contract" centers in the absolute or almost absolute relinquishment of power to an absolute sovereign or assembly. Locke's "social contract" is made between equals (that is, property-holding male equals) who "join in and make one society." Government is not divinely instituted, it is not absolute, and its authority is limited by notions familiar to us: the separation of powers, checks and balances, and the permanent retention by the individual of certain "inalienable rights." For Locke these latter include life, liberty, and property. Against a government which does not guarantee such rights, rebellion is legitimate.

While Locke's specific political doctrines are of great historical importance to us, it is perhaps the general tenor of his thought that, through the Founding Fathers, has continued to influence the American conception of government. Locke is optimistic, as we are. He is relatively undogmatic. He hates bigotry and absolutism. He conceives of society as "open" and experimental. He believes the state should aim to further the happiness of all its citizens. These may seem tame ideas today, but they were inflammatory in his time. And, though few people read Locke, his views continue to exert influence.

56. DAVID HUME (1711–1766)
An Enquiry Concerning Human Understanding

In proportion to its population Scotland has probably produced more first-rate minds than any country in the world except ancient Greece. Of these minds David Hume is surely one.

Intended by nature for abstract reflection, Hume, after short tries, sensibly rejected both the law and a business career. He spent three years in France, wrote his *Treatise of Human Nature* (of whose first part the *Enquiry* is a development), and watched it fall "dead-born from the press." The first volume of his *Essays* (1741) brought him greater success. Following their publication he occupied a number of official posts and one unofficial one, that of tutor to a certified lunatic, who was however a peer. One foreign service job netted him almost a thousand pounds, and he increased this small fortune with the profits from his triumphant and highly partisan *History of England.* In 1769, a rich man, he retired to his new house in Edinburgh and became a sort of Dr. Johnson to that brilliant little capital.

In his interesting *Autobiography* he describes himself as "a man of mild dispositions, of command of temper, and of an open, social, and cheerful humour, capable of attachment, but little susceptible of enmity; and of great moderation in all my passions. Even my love of literary fame, my ruling passion, never soured my temper, notwithstanding my frequent disappointments."

Hume developed Locke's antimetaphysical position and so helped to clear the way for the British utilitarianism of the nineteenth century. His *Enquiry,* clear but not easy reading, deals with the origin and limits of human knowledge. For Hume ideas are composed of the original sensations he calls impressions, and "all probable reasoning is nothing but a species of sensation." He is, as the quotation would indicate, a skeptic. He sees no rational connection between cause and effect, causation in his system being equal to mere sequence.

This central skepticism he applies to the self, which he deems unknowable; to morality, which he separates from religion; and to religion, coming "from the incessant hopes and fears which actuate the human mind."

Hume's balanced and common-sensible temperament would have rejected the great romantics of the century following his. Yet they might well justify their position by appealing to Hume's total skepticism with respect to the existence of rational belief.

This skepticism was not mere academic theory. He philosophized, he admitted, not because he was certain of establishing the truth, but because it gave him pleasure. Few philosophers have been so honest.

57. JOHN STUART MILL (1806–1873) *On Liberty*

Mill is the classic instance of the child prodigy who, despite an abnormal education, manages to live a good and useful life. You will find his story in his sober but extremely interesting *Autobiography*.

The elder Mill was a follower of Jeremy Bentham. Bentham's name is linked with Utilitarianism, an unimaginative if well-intentioned doctrine that stressed utility and reason, two terms it never strictly defined. It taught that the object of social action was to bring about the greatest happiness for the greatest number, and tended to ignore the temperamental and psychic differences among men. Young John was brought up in the shadow of this doctrine, caricatured by Dickens in his Gradgrind.

Educated entirely by his logic factory of a father, Mill was reading Greek at three and starting a history of Roman government at eleven. At thirteen he was about as well-educated as an

English university graduate. This educational force-feeding saved him at least ten of the years our first-rate minds are compelled to waste in our own school system. But it had its drawbacks: "I never was a boy," confesses Mill. The morbid emphasis on reason produced a mental crisis in his twentieth year, from which he was saved partly by the youthful resilience of his own fine mind and partly by his reading. Wordsworth (77) in particular revealed to him the existence of a life of feeling.

His crisis, together with the influence of Mrs. Harriet Taylor, whom he met in 1830 and married twenty-one years later, led Mill to recognize the weaknesses of his father's iron calculus of pleasures and pains. He was to spend much of his life, as writer, Member of Parliament, and social reformer, in liberalizing and humanizing Utilitarianism. Thus, working with the other "philosophical radicals," he helped to create a climate of opinion that led to many of the reform movements of the last hundred years, from woman suffrage to the New Deal.

Mill thought that except for his *Logic* his essay *On Liberty* would outlast his other works. In its own unemotional, English way it is a masterpiece of lucid persuasion and humane feeling. Probably no finer plea has ever been written for the claims of the individual against the state. Mill stresses the need for creating a great diversity of temperaments. He urges the protection of minorities. He advocates the utmost possible freedom of thought and expression. He comes out for the encouragement of nonconformist, even eccentric thinkers. His central principle is, in our state-dominated era, still far from realization, and still worth realizing: "The sole end for which mankind are warranted, individually or collectively, in interfering with the liberty of action of any of their number, is self-protection."

Mill should be read as the representative of the purest liberal English thought of his century. His American brothers are Thoreau (67) and Emerson (68), though he lacks the radical daring of the first and the vivid eloquence of the second.

58. ALFRED NORTH WHITEHEAD (1861–1947)
Science and the Modern World

In the history of Western speculative thought such men as Hobbes, Locke, Hume, and Mill have achieved classic stature. In the case of Whitehead we cannot make this statement; it is too soon. I am suggesting a reading of his *Science and the Modern World*, not because it is an acknowledged masterpiece, for it is not, but because no other single volume of my acquaintance tells us more about what four hundred years of science have done to make us the men we are. Unless we continually correct our impressions of science with the insights of a pure and great mind like Whitehead's, there is always the danger of confusing real science with the delirious Buck Rogers phase through which it is now passing. (This phase is merely an extension of ballistics, or the art of killing people, and is a minor branch of technology.)

Whitehead was the son of an English vicar. Early in life he showed mathematical genius. He became senior mathematical lecturer at Trinity College, Cambridge. With Bertrand Russell he wrote the monumental three-volume *Principia Mathematica* (1910-1913), a translation of mathematical concepts into logical terms and a landmark in the important field of symbolic logic. An interval of teaching at London University was followed by his moving in 1924, when he was sixty-three, to Harvard, where he assumed a professorship in philosophy. Just as Mill had no boyhood, Whitehead had no old age. His most fertile period now began and continued to his death. His training was primarily that of a mathematician. But his mind took no account of compartments. He wrote on education, religion, metaphysics, and particularly on science in its broader aspects.

He is not easy to read, for he operates on a plane of high abstraction and uses a terminology which, though clear, is uniquely his own. Nevertheless *Science and the Modern World* can be penetrated by any serious reader. It will prove enormously rewarding. Whitehead's combination of talents (he is not only a good mathematician and a powerful speculative thinker, but a beautifully trained humanist) makes him the ideal analyst of the impact of science on our age. Without some understanding of this impact we cannot understand who we are and how we got here.

The general slope of Whitehead's mind marks him off sharply from the British empirical school with which we now have some slight acquaintance. His conception of nature is opposed to the "common sense" variety. He points out again and again that our senses offer us a delusive picture of reality. He welcomes the Einsteinian physics that replaces empty space with fields of force and discrete bits of matter with energy. He is antimaterialist. More important, he is antidogmatic and an enemy of all closed systems of thought. The words "process," "organism," and "adventure" crop up continually in his writing and serve to suggest the color of his thought, which emphasizes change and continuous evolution rather than systems and certitudes. "Philosophy begins in wonder," he writes. "And, at the end, when philosophic thought has done its work, the wonder remains." The pleasure of reading Whitehead is quite different from that of reading Locke or Mill, for he opens perspectives that enlarge the imagination and are closely akin to those of poetry. It is in this spirit that I suggest you approach him.

59. KARL MARX (1818–1883) AND FRIEDRICH ENGELS (1820–1895)
The Communist Manifesto

Earlier in this book the simple statement was made that ideas have consequences. In no case can this be more clearly shown than in that of Karl Marx. He would perhaps have denied it. He would have said that the victory of the proletariat being inevitable, his life and work were devoted merely to clarifying the issues and perhaps slightly accelerating the outcome of the struggle. Nevertheless the history of the entire world since 1917 seems to have confirmed the judgment expressed in the first sentence of Isaiah Berlin's book: "No thinker in the nineteenth century has had so direct, deliberate and powerful an influence upon mankind as Karl Marx." It is for that reason alone that a reading of *The Manifesto of the Communist Party* (for which his co-worker Engels is partly responsible) is here suggested. Marx was a highly unpleasant person and most of us reject his doctrines, but to have no acquaintance with him or them is to remain forever partially blind.

Up to 1849 Karl Marx, a German-Jewish middle-class intellectual, spent most of his mature years in subversive journalism in Cologne, Paris, Brussels, and Cologne again. Forced to leave Prussian territory, he emigrated to England. The last thirty-four years of his life were spent there, mainly in the British Museum, which may therefore claim to be the physical incubator of the Communist Revolution. Marx's life was uneventful; it has become far more eventful posthumously.

His major work is of course *Capital*. There is no sense in recommending that you read it, unless you are a very earnest student indeed. Its difficulties are formidable; and, in addition to its impenetrable German style, much of it has been rendered utter nonsense by the passage of time and the movement of Marx's revered history. But you should read a good, calm summary of its doctrine. The Suggestions for Further Reading lists a number of helpful books.

The *Communist Manifesto*, however, is quite readable. Indeed one might wish it had been less so. It is not a work of literature, nor even an example of ordered thought. It is propaganda, but epochal propaganda. Its original function was to supply a platform in 1847 for the Communist League, as it was then called. Its continuing function has been to supply propaganda for the entire Communist movement, particularly as it developed after 1917. In clear, if deliberately rhetorical terms, it presents the main theses of classical Communism: that any epoch as a whole is explainable only in terms of its mode of production and exchange; that the history of civilization is a history of class strugggle; that now the stage has been reached in which the proletariat must emancipate itself from the bourgeoisie by means of a total overturn of society, and not merely a political revolution.

The *Manifesto* begins with one of the most famous sentences ever written: "A spectre is haunting Europe—the spectre of Communism." It concludes with three sentences no less famous: "The proletarians have nothing to lose but their chains. They have a world to win. Workingmen of all countries, unite."

The history of both the free and the Communist world has already demonstrated that Marx's concluding sentences are untrue. But the *influence* of the *Manifesto* still remains one of the iron realities of our time.

60. FRIEDRICH WILHELM NIETZSCHE (1844–1900) *Thus Spoke Zarathustra, Selected Other Works*

The rhapsodic singer of the strong, triumphant Superman led a life of failure, loneliness, obscurity, and physical pain. Son of a Lutheran pastor in Saxony, he was brought up by pious female relatives. A brilliant student, he specialized in classical philosophy. At twenty-five he was professor of Greek at Basle University, but resigned in 1879 because of poor health. One of the major influences in his life at this time was Wagner, whom he at first adored. (Bertrand Russell remarks: "Nietzsche's superman is very like Siegfried, except that he knows Greek.") Gradually, however, as Wagner succumbed to philistinism, anti-Semitism,

German racism, and the religiosity of *Parsifal,* Nietzsche drew away from the great composer, and at last broke with him. From 1879 to 1888 he wandered about Germany, Switzerland, and Italy, living a lonely, depressed life in seedy boardinghouses. Yet during these nine years, working under the most agonizing conditions, he produced most of his famous books. In December of 1888 he was found in a Turin street, weeping and embracing a horse. His mind had given way. For the remaining eleven years of his life he was insane, possibly—there is no proof—as a result of general syphilitic paresis.

Nietzsche is still a controversial figure. At times he writes like a genius. At times he writes like a fool, as if he had never been in touch with the ordinary realities of average human living. (His views on women, for example, are those of a man who simply didn't know any.) And so, though he has been dead for sixty years and has been the subject of countless commentaries and interpretations, there is still no generally agreed upon judgment of this extraordinary man. Those naturally inclined to moderation, decent intellectual manners, rationality, or plain common sense, find him ridiculous or even hateful. Others see in him a prophetic figure, a constructive destroyer of false moral values, an intuitive psychologist who anticipates Freud (61). And positions in between these extremes have been set up all along the line.

One practical suggestion: use the edition called *The Portable Nietzsche,* published by the Viking Press. The translations are intelligent, the notes and other apparatus helpful. I suggest that you read the whole of *Zarathustra,* uneven as that strange work is; the selections from *Beyond Good and Evil, Toward a Genealogy of Morals,* and *Ecce Homo*; and perhaps *The Antichrist.*

One general misconception is worth mentioning. The Nazis and Fascists in general did exploit, often by falsifying, Nietzsche's celebration of the virtues of war, ruthlessness, blood-thinking, and an elite class—or presumed celebration, for his admirers translate these words rather differently. But Nietzsche would have despised Hitler and all the little Hitlers. He was not anti-

Semitic and he condemned German nationalism. "Every great crime against culture for the last four hundred years lies on their conscience" is his summing up of the Germans; and were he alive today he would probably amend the "four hundred years" to "almost five hundred years." Nietzsche in one of his aspects was a "good European," a defender of the culture the Germans hated. It cannot be denied that his political influence has been deplorable. But this is not the same as saying that he was a protofascist.

Yet, good European that he may have thought himself, Nietzsche in a certain sense stands outside the Western tradition to which this book is devoted. He is a total revolutionary, more total, if the phrase be admitted, than Lawrence (34) or Marx (59). At times he seems to reserve his admiration for only a few: the pre-Socratics, Socrates himself, and a few "artist-tyrants," such as Frederick II of Sicily. He indicts Christianity as a "slave-morality." He rejects the traditional virtues of compassion, tolerance, mutual accommodation in favor of the "will to power," a phrase variously interpreted. He detests the liberal democratic humanitarianism of Mill (57) whom he called, with typical courtesy, "that blockhead." He exalts the heroic, the "Dionysian," and, it would seem, the irrational and intuitive elements in the human mind. He has no interest in the ordinary conception of progress, substituting for it a somewhat misty doctrine of eternal cyclical recurrence, and stressing the positive power of heroic suffering, exultant pessimism, and tragic experience. On the whole, not a comfortable chap.

No one can deny his extraordinary, though uncontrolled, gift for language; his command of invective and irony; the variety of his poetical images; and the torrential paradoxical inventiveness of his tortured mind. If taken in large, uncritical doses he can be not only antipathetic but dangerous; the God he denied seems to have formed him to attract the lunatic fringe. On the other hand it is true that, like Ibsen (19) and Shaw (20), he helped to point out to his century and ours many of our shams, cowardices, and hypocrisies.

61. SIGMUND FREUD (1856–1939)
Selected Works

Freud died September 23, 1939. In his memory W. H. Auden wrote a superb poem from which I quote:

> To us he is no more a person
> Now but a whole climate of opinion.

That is the heart of it. To the discomfiture or horror of many, Freud is one of the major components of our mental world. There is hardly an area of thought, and there are few of conduct, untouched by him, his disciples, his ex-disciples, or his opponents. You will have to determine for yourself whether this a good thing, a bad, or a mixture of both.

When we talked about Shakespeare it was suggested that most of us think we "know" him when what we really know is some handed-down opinion of him. That is true of Freud. Many of us still vaguely believe that his doctrines encourage sexual license, or that "he sees sex in everything," or that he did little beyond shifting the confessional from the grating to the couch. A reading of his major works will clear up these and dozens of other vulgar misconceptions.

Freud began his training in medicine, specializing in clinical neurology. In 1884 he became interested in some work done by Breuer, with whom he later worked. Breuer had with some success treated a female hysteric by encouraging her to "talk out" her past under hypnosis. The case is classic; it marked the birth of psychoanalysis, whose actual origin Freud, himself no humble type, always credited to Breuer. By replacing hypnosis with "free association" Freud found the key that unlocked his system. By 1896 he had named it psychoanalysis. The rest of his life was devoted to the widest possible development of the new conception of mental processes. Against misunderstanding, abuse, and moralistic prejudice he worked unceasingly, deepening his insights as he extended his experience. In 1938 his books were burned by the Germans. As he was already suffering torture from cancer of the mouth, the Germans waived their usual methods of dealing with the weak, the good, the great, and the non-Aryan. In return for a large ransom they permitted Freud to remove to England where he passed the last months of his fantastically productive life.

Psychoanalysis claims to be two things. It is a science (at least to its adherents) and it is a method. It is a theory of mental life and a specific technique for the cure of neuroses. Both theory and technique base themselves on a few fundamental discoveries. They seem trite to us now, but they were not so fifty years ago. Among them are: the unconscious; the mechanism of repression; the formative power of infantile sexuality (Freud did not invent the Oedipus complex, he observed it); the dream life as the disguised expression of fears and desires; and, more generally, the frightening power of the irrational in determining human behavior.

Sometimes with insufficient caution, Freud and his followers applied their novel insights to fields seemingly remote from mental disease: religion, morality, war, history, death, humor, mythology, anthropology, philosophy, art, and literature. Particularly in the latter area Freud has had an overwhelming influence, not always for good.

With respect to your choice of reading, two difficulties present themselves. The first is the vast volume of Freud's work. The second springs from the fact that his thought changed and developed so that an early (yet still valuable) book may be in part superseded by a later one. I list herewith seven titles. Experts will quarrel over all of them, and doubtless champion others. The first four books, arranged chronologically, contain much of the general theory. The last three, similarly arranged, are more specialized or exemplify Freud's thinking on a philosophical level.

The Origin and Development of Psychoanalysis
The Interpretation of Dreams
A General Introduction to Psychoanalysis
New Introductory Lectures on Psychoanalysis
Beyond the Pleasure Principle
The Ego and the Id
Civilization and Its Discontents

Rickman's *A General Selection From the Works of Sigmund Freud* offers a sound but necessarily brief "Epitome" of the development of Freud's thought. It consists largely of well-chosen excerpts and does not claim to be a substitute for a reading of the major works.

62. NICCOLÒ MACHIAVELLI (1469–1527)
The Prince

Machiavelli is commonly linked with Hobbes (54) as one of the two great early modern "realistic" theorists of political power. They would have understood each other, yet they diverge in some ways. Hobbes is by far the greater theorist. Indeed Machiavelli is hardly a theorist at all; he is an observer, an analyst, and an instructor. Hobbes lays down a doctrine of "legitimacy"; Machiavelli is interested only in expediency. Finally Hobbes is an absolutist. But Machiavelli (in his *Discourses on Livy*, a profounder but less influential book than *The Prince*) prefers republicanism, and anticipates several of the devices of modern parliamentary democracy. Yet the two may profitably be read in association. Together they help to explain the careers of such antimoralists as Richelieu, Napoleon, Lenin, Mussolini, Hitler, Stalin. Also they help to explain the continuous though prettily disguised power struggle that goes on in all democracies, including our own.

Machiavelli was a practical politician. Under the Florentine

Republic he held office for fourteen years, serving efficiently as diplomat and army organizer. In *The Prince* he incorporated the concrete insights he had gained during his observation of the Italian city-states and the emergent nations of Western Europe, particularly France. When in 1512 the Medicis regained power in Florence, Machiavelli lost his. Unjustly imprisoned and even tortured, he was exiled, and retired to his farm. There (compare Thucydides, 4) he employed his time in writing. He achieved some reputation as historian, playwright, and all-round humanist man of letters. But it is as the author of *The Prince,* by which he hoped to regain political favor, that he is best known.

His reputation, an odd one, has given us the adjective machiavellian. During the Elizabethan era "Old Nick" was a term referring as much to his first name as to the Devil. Iago in *Othello,* and a dozen other Italianate Elizabethan villains are the consequence of a popular misconception of Machiavelli. He became known as a godless and cynical defender of force and fraud in statecraft.

All Machiavelli did was to cry out that the emperor had no clothes on. He told the truth about power as he saw it in actual operation, and if the truth is not pretty, he is hardly to be blamed for that. He himself seems to have been a reasonably virtuous man, no hater of mankind, neither devilish nor neurotic.

Also it should be remembered that *The Prince* is a description of political means, not political ends. What Machiavelli seems really to have wanted (see his Chapter 26) was a united Italy, free of Spanish and French domination. Cavour and the nineteenth-century unifiers of Italy owe much to him; from a certain aspect he may even be considered a liberal. Yet there is no denying that his ideal Prince (he admired the ineffable Cesare Borgia) must separate himself from all considerations of morality, unless those considerations are themselves expedient. As for his view of the relationship between religion and the state: "All armed prophets have conquered and unarmed ones failed."

The Prince is a manual. It tells the ambitious leader how he must gain, maintain, and centralize power. Once this power is established there is nothing, in Machiavelli's view, to prevent the state from developing just and free institutions. What is involved here, of course, is the whole question of means and ends, and Machiavelli does not resolve the problem.

Because the politics of European nationalism have been in part guided by this icy, terrifyingly intelligent book of instruction, it is well worth reading.

63. MICHEL EYQUEM DE MONTAIGNE (1533–1592) *Selected Essays*

Many names on our list are far greater than Montaigne's. But the view of life he represents is so deeply rooted in our human condition that, when more powerful minds retain interest only for scholars, he may still be read. He appeals to that part of us more fascinated by the questions than by the answers.

Montaigne, one of the pioneers of modern French prose, was of good merchant-family stock. Apparently there was sufficient money in the family to permit him, on his thirty-eighth birthday, to semiretire to his round tower on the family property. In a period when educational experimentation was generally popular, his own education was unusual. Until he was six he spoke only Latin. He tells us that he was awakened each morning by "the sound of a musical instrument," an anticipation of our radio clocks. He studied law, occupied a magistrate's seat in the Bordeaux Parliament, served in various capacities under three French kings, and during his later years wasted some of his genius on a job, the mayoralty of Bordeaux, fit only for mediocrity. His real life is preserved in his *Essays*. Of these there are 107, if we include the book-length *Apology for Raymond Sebond*. As far as we can determine, they were written, or rewritten, from his thirty-ninth year, after he had withdrawn to a life of tranquil study and contemplation, to the year of his death.

As he says in his preliminary word to the reader, they were composed not for fame, favor, or fortune, but merely to portray himself, in all candor and indiscretion. For this purpose he invented a new form of literature, as important in its way as that of the internal combustion engine, and far more pleasant. The French word *essai* means literally a trial or attempt. Each essay is a trial of the content of his mind, an attempt to find out what is there, so that, though he may know nothing else, he may at least know himself.

Montaigne's essays are not like those we find in our better magazines today. They are formless, they rarely stick to the announced subject, they are chock-full of classical quotations; for Montaigne, in addition to being a man of practical affairs, was a learned humanist. The modern reader will at first find these obstacles irritating.

However, if the experience of almost four centuries is any evidence, you will eventually be won over by Montaigne's charm, wisdom, humor, style, and mental slant. He began as a Stoic (see Marcus Aurelius, 12) but soon developed a generally skeptical, though never cynical or negative, view of mankind. He was interested in everything, convinced of nothing. His motto was "What do I know?", his emblem a pair of balances. He remained a good Catholic, because he was born one, and died in the odor of sanctity. But the tendency of his extremely influential writings has been to encourage the growth of free thought. In his characteristic gesture of suspended judgment dogmatists will find little pleasure.

Montaigne's charm inheres in his style, that of the frankest, freest conversation, "simple and unaffected, the same in writing as on the tongue." He is particularly candid on matters of sex, and those of us who are used to the naive obsessions of some modern novelists may find it interesting to see what a grown-up man has to say on the subject. Montaigne is not only the first informal essayist but incomparably the best. His art is always concealed. The man he gives you is never an improved version submitted for public approval, but always and forever himself.

He writes as if he were continually enjoying himself, his weaknesses and oddities and stupidities no less than his virtues.

You may wander about almost at will in Montaigne. He should be read as he wrote, unsystematically. However, time has winnowed out certain of the essays as superior or more important. For the nearest thing to a reasoned defense of his skeptical position, see the rather long-drawn-out *Apology for Raymond Sebond.* In addition you might tick off the following, whose very titles will give you a good foretaste of Montaigne:

From Book 1: That intention is judge of our actions; Of idleness; Of liars; That the taste of good and evil depends in large part on the opinion we have of them; That to philosophize is to learn to die; Of the power of the imagination; Of custom, and not easily changing an accepted law; Of the education of children; Of friendship; Of moderation; Of cannibals; Of solitude; Of the inequality that is between us; Of ancient customs; Of Democritus and Heraclitus; Of vain subtleties; Of age.

From Book 2: Of the inconsistency of our actions; Of drunkenness; Of practice; Of the affection of fathers for their children; Of books; Of presumption; Of a monstrous child; Of the resemblance of children to fathers.

From Book 3: Of the useful and the honorable; Of three kinds of association; On some verses of Virgil; Of the art of discussion; Of vanity; Of experience.

Try to get a modern translation, either Trechmann's or, best of all, Donald Frame's. Avoid Cotton's version; it is an antique.

64. RENÉ DESCARTES (1596–1650)
Discourse on Method

Descartes is often termed "the father of modern philosophy." Even if this were not so, he would still be well worth reading for the elegant precision of his prose and the mathematical clarity of his reasoning. These two qualities, more than his specific doctrines, have deeply influenced the French character. French schoolboys study Descartes and so learn how to train their minds, just as ours study comics with the same result.

Descartes' family was of the minor nobility and he never had to support himself. This was as it should be; we shall never know how much genius has been lost to the world by reason of the need to make a living. We willingly provide free board and lodging for lunatics, but recoil before the idea of doing so for first-class brains.

Descartes received a good Jesuit education. As his health was poor, his masters, who were intelligent men, allowed him to stay late in bed, instead of compelling him to play the seventeenth-century equivalent of basketball. This slugabed habit he retained all his life. It was responsible for much calm, ordered thought.

Even as a young man Descartes had begun to distrust the foundations of everything he had been taught, except mathematics. This skepticism (which did not conflict, it appears, with conventional piety) was reinforced during his Paris and Poitiers years (1614-1618) when he read Montaigne (63). He finally abandoned study and set off on a career of mild military adventure and travel. He was resolved, he says, "no longer to seek any other science than the knowledge of myself, or of the great book of the world."

His great creative years, from 1629 to 1649, were spent mainly in Holland, at that time a general asylum for intelligence. His fame grew to such proportions that Queen Christina of Sweden invited (that is, commanded) him to visit her and teach her philosophy. In Sweden Descartes was forced to rise at 5:00 A.M. in cold weather in order to converse with the queen. Naturally a few months of such barbarism were enough to kill him. Had not this Swedish female caused his death just as directly as if she had shot him, the world might have had another twenty years of Descartes' mind.

However, he managed to do pretty well. Though the two

talents were inextricably connected, Descartes was an even greater mathematician than philosopher. One morning, while he was lying in bed, the idea of co-ordinate geometry, which married algebra to geometry, came to him. On this point see Whitehead (97). He also worked in physics, though with less distinction.

Descartes' doctrines, dualistic and materialist in tendency, are both interesting and influential. But it is as the creator of a new, or at any rate fresh, method of thought that his position was secured. He threw aside much, though not all, of scholastic reasoning and, as it were, started from scratch. He began by doubting everything. The progression of doubt, however, ended at the point where he found that he could not doubt the existence of his own thought. "I think, therefore I am" is the famous formula with which he begins. (In a somewhat different form, it is found in Augustine too, but Descartes made it do work and Augustine didn't.) He then proceeds to build a system of thought, using four main principles you will find described in his *Discourse on Method*. "Cartesian doubt," however, describes not only a method but an attitude of mind, and this attitude was to influence profoundly post-Cartesian speculation, whether scientific or philosophical.

We read Descartes, then, because as the first supremely great mind to receive his stimulus from the new physics and astronomy of Copernicus, Galileo, and others, he incorporates the outlook of the tremendous renaissance of science which, partly contemporary with him, was to reach a high point with Newton.

65. BLAISE PASCAL (1623–1662)
Thoughts (Pensées)

Pascal is a seeming oddity, for he possessed in the highest degree a number of traits that are not usually linked in a single personality. First and foremost, he is a scientific and mathematical genius. Second, he is a master of prose style; indeed he is often thought of as the norm of classic French prose. Third, he is an acute though unsystematic psychologist. Fourth, he is a god-thirsty, tormented soul, a kind of failed saint. To a freethinker, such as Eric T. Bell, author of the fascinating *Men of Mathematics*, Pascal ruined his life by his preoccupation with religious controversy: "On the mathematical side Pascal is the greatest might-have-been in history." It is hard to make a sensible judgment. Pascal was Pascal. The man who in love and terror cried out for God, and the man who thought of the omnibus and invented the syringe are somehow indivisible.

At twelve, before he had been taught any mathematics, Pascal was proving Euclid for himself. At sixteen he had written a trail-blazing work on conic sections, of which we possess only fragmentary indications. At eighteen he had invented the first calculating machine. At twenty-four he had demonstrated the barometer. He did classic work in hydrostatics, and most of us remember Pascal's Law from high school, provided we were lucky enough to attend a high school that offered physics. In mathematics he is famous, among other matters, for having discovered and shown the properties of a notable curve called the cycloid. This has been termed the Helen of geometry, for its beauty and also for its power to excite controversy.

His major contribution, not merely to science but to thought in general, is probably his work in the theory of probability, the glory of which he shares with another mathematician, Fermat. It is interesting to recall that the ascetic Pascal was stimulated to his great mathematical discoveries by a gamblers' dispute involving the throw of dice. The ramifications of probability theory, writes Bell, "are everywhere, from the quantum theory to epistemology."

As mathematician and physicist, Pascal will rank higher than he will as moralist and religious controversialist. Yet in these latter fields his influence has been considerable. Just as Montaigne (63), who both fascinated and repelled Pascal, stands for one mood of mankind, so Pascal stands for another. Montaigne lived at ease with skepticism; Pascal's heart and mind cried out for certainties. Montaigne contemplated the sad condition of man with interest, humor, and tolerance. Pascal, who had brilliant wit but no humor, regarded it with terror and despair, from which he was saved only by throwing himself on the breast of revealed religion.

His finest, but to us not most interesting prose, is contained in his *Provincial Letters*, which you will find in most editions that print the *Pensées*. These are masterpieces of polemic, directed against certain tendencies of the Jesuit order of Pascal's day, tendencies he and his associates of the Jansenist movement considered too tolerant of man's moral frailties. (Jansenism was a kind of puritanical sect within Catholicism, stressing predestination and asceticism, but also inspiring new and brilliant techniques in the education of children.) This controversy, which made Pascal a best-seller, is today of interest mainly to theologians and historians of religion.

The *Thoughts, or Pensées*, are in a somewhat different category. They consist of a series of scrappy, often unfinished notes, originally intended to serve as parts of a grand design, a reasoned defense of the Christian religion against the assaults or the lethargy of freethinkers. Into them Pascal put his painful sense of the inadequacy, even the absurdity of man, as measured against the immensity of the universe, the endless flow of eternity, and the omniscience and omnipotence of God. A great deal of modern antihumanist pessimism flows from Pascal. Those who reject man as the center of the universe, whether they are religionists or nihilists, find the *Pensées* to their taste. That is what I meant by saying that he represents one profound mood of mankind, that which finds man glorious in his powers yet in the end pitiful and incomprehensible to himself.

The nonscientific Pascal is preserved by his style and by his emotional intensity. As a psychologist of the soul his genius is measured by the fact that he can still move many who are quite unable to sympathize with his sometimes noble, sometimes merely frantic devotionalism. There are two Pascalian sentences, or cries from the heart, that are frequently quoted. The first is: "The eternal silence of these infinite spaces terrifies me." The second is: "Man is but a reed, the weakest thing in nature; but he is a thinking reed." Between them these two statements suggest moods common to all Western men, whether they be Christian, agnostic, atheist, or of some other creed.

66. ALEXIS DE TOCQUEVILLE (1805–1859)

Democracy in America

Had this Lifetime Reading Plan been compiled fifty, even twenty-five years ago, Tocqueville probably would not have been represented. From the appearance of the first part of his masterpiece in 1835 he has never ceased to be read and studied. But it has taken considerably more than a century to disclose him in his true proportions, as one of the few supreme sociological and political observers and theorists of the Western tradition.

Tocqueville's family was of the lesser French nobility. Thus he preserved all his life a deep attachment to the virtues of conservatism and aristocracy. The inexorable logic of his mind compelled him to discern in democracy the "wave of the future," while his roots in tradition helped him to measure the origins and dimensions of that wave with a certain useful and lucid detachment.

On May 11, 1831, the young Tocqueville, accompanied by a brilliant colleague named Beaumont, reached our shores. Their avowed purpose was to observe and report on the American penal system. The pair traveled seven thousand miles in our country and Canada. They sailed home on February 20, 1832. In the course of these nine months Tocqueville saw us during one of our most interesting and critical periods, that of the earlier phase of the Jacksonian Revolution. The outcome was the publication, in 1835 and 1840, of the two parts of his monumental work. This, together with his briefer but no less seminal *The Old Régime and the French Revolution* (Doubleday, $0.95), embody the enduring Tocqueville. I might add that he wasted a certain amount of time from 1839 to 1848 serving as a member of the French Chamber of Deputies, and later held brief office as Minister for Foreign Affairs.

Tocqueville may be described, very roughly, as a liberal aristocrat, a kind of Lafayette with brains. *Democracy in America* had a double purpose: to describe and analyze the democratic (which seems to have meant to him largely egalitarian) system in America; and to turn that observation and analysis into a guide for political thought and action for the future Europe, and particularly for his native land. Many good judges believe his book is still (and by far) the deepest, wisest, and most farseeing ever written about this country.

He made, of course, many errors of observation. Nor have all of his prophecies come true. Yet no thoughtful American can read his book today (and, by the way, it is a masterpiece of elegance and organization) without marveling at his sympathy, his understanding, his balance, and his prescience. Though in his day our modern capitalist structure was still only in embryo, he understood its future, its strengths, its weaknesses, and its capacities far better than did the later Marx (59). More than 120 years ago he warned us against "the possible tyranny of the majority." He outlined the mass age in which we live. But he also saw how our system could mitigate and control the perils of political and social conformity, and he recognized in it one of the broad paths his century and ours would largely follow.

His basic intuition is revealed in the statement: "A new science of politics is needed for a new world." Such a new science, he felt, was developing, not always harmoniously, not without travail, in the United States. And he knew quite well what he was doing: "I have not undertaken to see differently from others, but to look further, and while they are busied for the morrow only, I have turned my thoughts to the whole future."

What probably interests us most, as we read Tocqueville, is the startling applicability of his insight to our present condition. He foresaw, while America was still largely an agricultural country, the attraction that business and industry would have for us all. He foresaw our materialism, but also our idealism. He foresaw the inequities industry would bring in its train. And, most important, he foresaw our future power and, let us hope, our future greatness. Of all his prophecies the most hair-raising is probably his quiet comparison of Czarist Russia and Jacksonian America: "There are at the present time two great nations in the world, which started from different points, but seem to tend toward the same end. I allude to the Russians and the Americans . . . All other nations seem to have nearly reached their natural limits, and they have only to maintain their power; but these are still in the act of growth. . . . The principal instrument of (America) is freedom; of (Russia), servitude. Their starting-point is different and their courses are not the same; yet each of them seems marked out by the will of Heaven to sway the destinies of half the globe."

The words were written in the thirties of the last century.

67. HENRY DAVID THOREAU (1817–1862)

Walden, Civil Disobedience

Thoreau seems to have spent almost his entire life talking to himself; and since his death he has been talking to millions. Perhaps, indeed, hundreds of millions, for the program of Gandhi and the policies of the British Labour Party were both profoundly influenced by Thoreau's ideas. Now, almost a century after his death, it is safe to say that *Walden* (with which we may group *Civil Disobedience*) is one of the most influential books not only of its century, but of ours; that today, defying everything our industrial society lives by, it speaks to us more urgently than ever; and that it and *Huckleberry Finn* (46) are probably the two *central* American statements in our literature. If I add that Thoreau's prose is as enjoyable, as crackling, as witty, as full of sap as any yet produced on this continent, I shall have listed the essential reasons for reading *Walden* and as many other of the major essays as you care to try.

Thoreau had no time to waste in making money. Early in life he decided to do not what society suggested for him, but what he himself wanted. At various times he earned his bare keep by schoolmastering, surveying, pencil-making, gardening, and manual labor. He also appointed himself to certain jobs such as inspector of snowstorms and rainstorms. He wrote tirelessly (this man was no idler—he worked harder than any fifty leading Board chairmen), mainly at a vast journal, some of it still in manuscript. From his books and journalism he made little. His first book was printed in an edition of one thousand copies, of which fewer than three hundred were sold. He remarked, "I have now a library of nearly nine hundred volumes, over seven hundred of which I wrote myself." He spent his life in occasional converse with Emerson and other Concord literati and transcendentalists; more often talking to hunters, trappers, farmers, and other plain folk who lived close to the natural world he loved; most often with himself, tramping the woods and fields around his home, noting with two of the sharpest eyes that ever existed the behavior of the earth, water, and air, of which men's lives seemed to him extensions; and, at all moments, thinking.

He really lived the life Emerson so beautifully preached, of self-reliance, nonconformity, simplicity, plain living, and high thinking. Of external events there were few: a pallid, unsuccessful romance (there is no question that though Thoreau was a great man, he was a defective male); the two crucial years at Walden Pond, where he built a house for twenty-eight dollars and fended almost completely for himself; the overnight jailing for a refusal to pay his poll tax to what he considered an immoral government; his brave public defense of John Brown.

Thoreau needs little commentary; he is an expert at explaining himself. But let there be no misunderstanding: this man is dangerous. He is not a revolutionary but something far more intense —a radical, almost in the sense that Jesus was. He does not, like Marx (59), want to overturn society. He would say that Marx's life-denying state is no better than any other life-denying state. He simply opposed *himself* to the whole trend of his time, as well as to that of ours, whose shape he foresaw. By withdrawal he set his face against invention, the machine, motion, industry, progress, material things, associations, togetherness, cities, strong government. He said it all in one word: Simplify. But if that word were taken by all of us as literally as Thoreau himself took it, our entire civilization would change overnight.

Knowing that "the mass of men lead lives of quiet desperation" (how often the phrase is quoted nowadays), he determined to live entirely by his own lights, in fact to *live* rather than to adjust, accumulate, join, reform, or compete. His rejection of our values is far more complete and, many will think, far saner than that of the one man we have met he is most akin to—Lawrence (34). His private notion of living may not appeal to some of us, who may lack his genius for enjoying and interpreting nature; but the force of his general doctrine of the meaning of human life does not rest on the private notion.

It is a fair guess that this queer Yankee semihermit, this genuinely rugged individualist who distrusted the state and treated July 4 like any other day, may turn out to be, oddly enough, not only the most American of all our writers, but the most enduring.

68. RALPH WALDO EMERSON (1803–1882)
Selected Works

Thoreau's power over us has increased as his friend Emerson's has declined. Thoreau, reaping the reward of greater daring and a firmer grasp on rude fact, casts the longer shadow. Yet Emerson, for all his gassiness and repetitiousness, was, in the first place, one of the central American thinkers of his century; secondly, a formulator of certain attitudes that seem permanently American; and finally a writer, at his best, of quite wonderful force, wit, homely vividness, and freshness—surely one of the finest epigrammatists in English. For these reasons we read him. But beware of overlarge doses. At times he offers fine words in lieu of fine thoughts, and he never understood how to organize or compress large masses of material.

Emerson was the leader of the Concord Transcendentalist school, which taught a curious hodgepodge of fashionable idealisms. After graduation from Harvard, he became a teacher, then a preacher. When he found that he "was not interested" in the rite of Communion, he left the ministry. He never ceased, however, to be both teacher and preacher, developing into a kind of benevolent pastor without portfolio, dispensing spiritual goods without benefit of theology and indeed without the support of any concrete idea of God. As itinerant lecturer and unsystematic sage he purified the moral atmosphere of his restless, expansive era more effectively than did all the ordained ministers combined. And this power, however diminished, he still wields.

Emerson is the first important spokesman for those elements in the national character we vaguely term optimistic, idealistic, democratic, expansive, individualistic. He preached the self-reliance on which we pride ourselves. In *The American Scholar* he issued what the elder Holmes called "our intellectual Declaration of Independence," a note we have since continually and sometimes raucously sounded. Emerson stresses the newness, the freshness of the American viewpoint; he invites his countrymen to "enjoy an original relation to the universe"; he emphasizes what up to twenty-five years ago was one of our proudest boasts, "the infinitude of the private man," the integrity of the individual mind.

Emerson believed the universe was good. Most Americans think so too, though not always for Emerson's reasons. At any rate his emphasis on the power of the will, on inspiration, on an open-ended future, has always appealed to us. Sometimes we have vulgarized his affirmative doctrine. It is but a step from Ralph Waldo Emerson to Norman Vincent Peale.

I suggest you read the short book called *Nature*, published in 1836, which contains most of Emerson's informal philosophy; *The American Scholar*; the essays on "History" and "Self-Reliance"; the essays on Plato and Montaigne from *Representative Men;* the essay on Thoreau; and, best of all, *English Traits*, written for its time but which seems to me by far the most durable of all Emerson's work.

69. WILLIAM JAMES (1842–1910)

The Principles of Psychology (Chapters 1, 4, 7, 9, 11, 21, 26, 28); Pragmatism and Four Essays from The Meaning of Truth (in one volume); The Varieties of Religious Experience

The psychologist-philosopher William James was the slightly elder brother of the novelist Henry (47), whom we have already met. A warm affection linked two very different beings. Henry's nature was fastidious; it concerned itself with the relations existing among other rarefied temperaments; and, though reflective, it was not speculative or able to handle high-order abstractions. William was, like Emerson, a natural democrat, hearty, humorous, with a deep interest in problems of science, religion, and morality. Henry was the pure artist, affecting men by his books alone. William was a vital teacher whose personality still exerts great influence. Henry opted for upper-class and intellectual English society. William delighted in the vigorous, growing America of his time and entered into its public life in a way that would have been difficult for his more detached brother. Whitehead called William "an adorable genius." The noun would apply to Henry; the adjective (though he did have a fussy charm) never.

A word about the suggested reading. Very little of James is nonrewarding, but these three books will give you a fair idea of both his personality and his ideas. *The Principles of Psychology,* though now partly superseded, remains James's most permanent work. Difficult in parts, it succeeds wonderfully in dramatizing the life of the mind. James himself later spoke of its content as "this nasty little subject," but the world has not accepted his judgment. *Pragmatism* should be read not only because the word is so closely connected with James, but also because the idea behind the word is so closely connected with our character as a people. If you have read Mill (57) you may find it interesting to figure out why the book is dedicated to him. James's most purely *interesting* book is *The Varieties of Religious Experience*. One of the cornerstones of the literature of religious psychology, it illustrates concretely what he meant by the pragmatic test.

The pragmatic test sounds simple and to many it is at once convincing. However, it is open to philosophical objections into which it is not our present business to go. Briefly, James argues that an idea's meaning and truth depend on its practical consequences. A problem is real if its solution makes a difference in actual experience, if it performs an operation on our behavior. Thus James stresses not origins but results. In the *Varieties* he asserts that the religious states he is describing are, like all states of mind, neurally conditioned. But he goes on to say that "their significance must be tested not by their origin but by the value of their fruits." Thus religion, whether or not determinably "true," is valuable to the individual and therefore to the race. Its truth is not absolute but functional. Ideas are good only as instruments, and it is by their instrumentalism that we must judge them. To sum up, "an idea is 'true' so long as to believe it is profitable to our lives." James's moral ideals were of the highest and purest; "profitable" does not refer to the market place; nor is it fair to vulgarize James's pragmatism by saying that what he meant was "Anything is O.K. if it works."

There is more in James, far more, than the pragmatic idea, though it is central both to him and to our vague national philosophy, if we may be said to have one. One should understand it. But that is not the main reason for reading him. The main reason is the man himself. He is one of the most attractive figures in the history of thought—vital, alert to the whole world of experience, mentally liberating, emotionally refreshing. In addition he is master of a style of great freshness and clarity. One may disagree with the pragmatic test (believers in fixed religious and moral values are bound to do so) and still emerge from reading James feeling more alive and hopeful than before. He is the philosopher of possibility. By his own pragmatic test, he is apt to succeed with the reader. Reading him can make a difference.

70. JOHN DEWEY (1859–1952)
Human Nature and Conduct

Years ago, when I attended John Dewey's class at Columbia, I thought that he looked like an intelligent, benevolent janitor. Dewey was an unimpressive, rather dull lecturer; and to tell the truth he is, superficially, an unimpressive, rather dull writer. Compared to that of William James (69), whose pragmatism he developed and deepened, his personality is drab. Yet this quiet drawling Vermonter has been far more effective than his predecessor. Indeed, except for the Founding Fathers, it is possible that he is the most influential thinker America has produced. His mind has been felt not only in philosophy, but in law, economics, politics, esthetics, and especially in education.

If the word for Whitehead (58) is "process," that for Dewey is "society." His general outlook he called instrumentalism. By this he meant that the full meaning of an idea is apparent only when it is *applied*, and applied socially. Compare him with James. James stressed the individual, particularly the individual's interior emotional and religious world. As a young man he suffered an inner crisis akin to Mill's (57). Also, his generation was greatly troubled by the agnostic movement precipitated by Darwin and evolution theory. The more balanced Dewey came on the scene a little later, when the religious turmoil of the nineteenth century had partly died down, and when it was society, then in bewildering transformation, rather than the private man, that clamored to be understood.

Of all our abstract thinkers Dewey seems the most American.

That is because, despite his colorless style, he is not essentially abstract. He faced squarely a changed world. He recognized that the planet was soon to be industrialized. He asked the question, How shall we deal with a changed planet (and therefore, he thought, a changing man) actively and intelligently? He began by initiating reforms in education, first here, then in the Near and Far East. If authoritarian instruction and learning by rote and the separation of the school from society are not popular with us, that is John Dewey's work. The excesses of progressive education, however, should not be laid at his door. It would be fairer to say that his liberating influence has made possible the present constructive controversy as to how American children should be taught.

But in his constant endeavor "to change the world through action," Dewey advanced into a dozen other fields. Philosophy for him was not an academic exercise. He thought it "has no call to create a world of 'reality' *de novo,* nor to delve into secrets of Being hidden from common sense and science." He wished to apply to the social disciplines, as well as to such practical activities as politics and law, the methods and insights that had been so successfully used in the sciences, particularly in biology. He made philosophy go to work. All his books were meant to act as bridges between the academy and the growing, changing democratic society he saw around him, and in whose life he actively participated. He made experience the test of theory, and experiment a calculated part of experience. Thinking to him meant inquiry; and belief, as with James, was to be judged by its effects.

There are many whose temperaments cannot sympathize with Dewey's conception of man as essentially a social, sharing, nontragic animal, and who are not at all sure that the environment is there to be changed or "improved." On the whole, however, he has won more supporters than antagonists. He is now part of the American mental world.

I have suggested that you read *Human Nature and Conduct.* His profounder thought is doubtless to be found in other books but this one seemed to me on the whole to be the one most open to the general reader. Also it is typical of Dewey's activist pragmatic thought. As a treatise on morals you may find it rather different from some we have already encountered, such as the *Meditations* of Marcus Aurelius (12). All conduct, for Dewey, is *interaction* between human nature and a changing environment, in our case an environment dominated by science, industry, and democracy. He mediates between the traditional doctrine of fixed moral values and that easy subjectivism which affirms that the good is merely what one happens to like. In this book morals and human nature are again and again, in a hundred different aspects, brought together with consequences each reader will have to judge for himself.

71. GEORGE SANTAYANA (1863–1952)
Skepticism and Animal Faith, Selected Other Works

Santayana was born in Spain, of Spanish parentage. From 1872 to 1912 he lived in Boston, passing twenty-three of those years mainly at Harvard. While his American period was not precisely forty years of wandering in the wilderness, there is no doubt that he was happier during the next forty, spent as an itinerant student in Europe. At eighty-nine Santayana died, quite in character, in a Roman convent, mourned by the gentle nuns whose faith he had never abjured, whose dogmas he had never accepted except as poetry.

He offers a striking contrast to his contemporary Dewey (70) and his teacher and later colleague William James (69). Though he understood us, particularly our weaknesses, well enough, America left few traces in him. He regarded this country with a kindly, slightly patronizing interest. He was unable to sympathize with our dominant Protestantism, optimism, restlessness, and passion for "progress." The practical philosophies of James and Dewey held no charm for him. Perhaps he thought them, as he did the poetry of Whitman (80), barbarous. His real home was not even the Europe he preferred to the United States. It lay more nearly in the classical Greece he loved—the author of *The Last Puritan* has been called the last Greek. Perhaps even more truly this solitary aristocrat was at home only among those timeless objects of intuition he calls "essences." The modern world he thought of as a host to whom he happened to be paying a brief visit.

Santayana lived so long and wrote so superbly in half a dozen fields that no one book adequately reflects his complex, ironical temperament. As a philosopher he discussed metaphysics, morals, epistemology, politics, and particularly esthetics. But he also wrote first-class literary essays, philosophical dialogues, social criticism, and one extraordinary novel, as well as some youthful poetry still represented in the anthologies. No matter what you decide to read, however, it is well to bear in mind that of all the philosophers we have met he is the only one who is centrally an artist. It is not merely that he writes beautiful prose. It is that he is at all times open to concrete impressions of beauty, humor, and tragedy that are generally received only abstractly by such thinkers as Locke or Mill or Dewey. From this fact arises a fascinating paradox. He seems at one and the same time to be living in a timeless world of contemplation and in our own world of vivid color, loveliness, and sorrowful contingency. He is both remote and, despite his elegant snobbery, intensely human.

Basically Santayana remained a naturalist in the Greek sense. "All life," he says, echoing Aristotle (6), "is animal in its origin and spiritual in its possible fruits." He is skeptical of the exalted claims of reason, calling it, in his philosophy, "only a harmony among irrational impulses." Religion, science, art he thinks of as the crowns of human endeavor; yet at bottom they are not carriers of absolute truths, but only creative myths—religion is "sublimated poetry." In politics, as in other areas, he is profoundly conservative, and Deweyan liberals find him hard to stomach.

No reader of Santayana will ever be spurred on by him to change or improve the world.

Skepticism and Animal Faith, not the easiest of his works, is probably the single volume most adequately presenting his central thought. His one novel, *The Last Puritan,* published when he was seventy-two, is not only interesting as a portrait of the New England conscience, but suggests, in highly readable form, many of Santayana's favorite doctrines. His most sheerly beautiful writing, I think, will be found in *Dialogues in Limbo* and a lecture-essay called "The Unknowable." As essayist and aphorist Santayana ranks among the greatest. This aspect of his genius may be glimpsed in many of his books, particularly *Interpretations of Poetry and Religion.* If you continue to find Santayana interesting, you will want to read his three little books of autobiography, the fruit of his old age. Collectively they are called *Persons and Places.* The separate titles are: *The Background of My Life, The Middle Span,* and *My Host the World.*

Poetry

72. *Poets of the English Language,* EDITED BY W. H. Auden (1907–) AND *Norman Holmes Pearson* (1909–)

We have already met, though under other headings, many of the world's supreme poets: Homer, the Greek dramatists, Virgil, Lucretius, Dante, Chaucer, Shakespeare, Goethe. Numbers 74-80 suggest seven additional English and American poets (others might well have been chosen) for extensive and intensive reading. Frost (88) and Eliot (93) are the two living poets who are often (there is no common agreement) considered the finest in their respective countries. The anthology noted above, together with (73), comprises a mop-up operation.

The Auden-Pearson collection is in five handy volumes, titled as follows:

I: Langland to Spenser
II: Marlowe to Marvell
III: Milton to Goldsmith
IV: Blake to Poe
V: Tennyson to Yeats

It ends with the opening of World War I; for post-Yeats poetry see the Suggestions for Further Reading.

Each volume contains a brilliant Introduction, rich in unconventional and often controversial ideas. Each also contains a useful "Calendar of British and American Poetry," listing in two tables the leading events of both the poetical and the politico-socio-cultural worlds of the particular period. There are several other reader's aids. The main virtue of this anthology—beyond the fact that its editors are men of taste and learning—is that they have given themselves room in which to move around. Many long poems are printed in full; there are no snippets; and a great many minor poets are well represented. In general the whole tradition of British and American verse is intelligibly and intelligently covered.

Only the heroic reader who is ruled by a systematic mind will want to start at the beginning and read this vast collection straight through, though much profit lies in doing so. You may pick and choose at random; or concentrate on a single period for a year or so; or read the verse corresponding in time with the prose work you are reading; or simply obey your mood, for poetry is a more mysterious as well as more rigorous form of communication than prose. A poem will talk to you at one time and avert its face at another.

Two suggestions:

First, remember that a poem, if it is a good one, is good in itself. If you are reading a great deal of Voltaire, it may help you to remember that he was much impressed with Newton. But if you are reading Hopkins' "The Wreck of the Deutschland" it will help only the tiniest bit to know the sources of his special theory of versification. Poems are only incidentally parts of history. They are essentially self-enclosed, complete messages from individual minds. In some cases, however (see Yeats, 79), single poems reveal much more when read in connection with a larger body of the poet's work.

Second, if you can't or won't read this anthology entire, concentrate on the larger figures. Major poets are so-called for sound reasons. In addition to our Numbers 74-80, therefore, try to give more time to at least the following: Spenser, Marlowe, Jonson, Herbert, Crashaw, Vaughan, Marvell, Herrick, Dryden, Pope, Burns, Byron, Shelley, Keats, Tennyson, Browning, Arnold, Dickinson, Hopkins, Hardy, Robinson. Several of these, such as Dryden, Pope, Byron, and Hardy, may well be read more extensively. You have plenty of time—this is a Lifetime Reading Plan.

One final word, addressed only to those of my readers who learned to dislike poetry in school and have never read a line since. Poetry is not an esoteric art, cultivated by dreamy young men in open collars and wispy beards. Its finest masters have always been men of outstanding energy and great, though by no means common, sense. Poetry is the most economical way of saying certain things that cannot be said in any other way. At its most intense it expresses better than do other forms of literature whatever is left of a man when he is not involved in instinct-following, surviving, competing, or problem-solving. Its major quality is not, as some suppose, beauty. It is power. It is the most powerful form of communication. It does the most work per syllable, operating on a vast field—that of our emotions. It gains its efficiency from the use of certain levers—rhythm, music, rhyme, metaphor, and many others—for which other forms of communication are less well adapted. Some poetry, especially modern poetry, is difficult. But just as our American ears have accustomed themselves to difficult music (some progressive jazz is as complex as Hopkins or Dylan Thomas) so our understanding, if we are willing to make the effort, can accustom itself to the most condensed and superficially strange verse. At one time poetry was as democratic an art as the novel is nowadays. It can be so again, if we are willing to make it so.

73. *An Anthology of World Poetry,* EDITED BY Mark Van Doren (1894–)

Let us admit at once that the full power of poetry generally resists translation. Hence, unless we command the original, our choice is clear. We may ignore completely the existence of great Continental verse. Or we may settle for the secondhand, unsatisfactory acquaintance given by translations.

Assuming you prefer the latter course, I suggest Mr. Van Doren's 1,467-page anthology. From the Plan's viewpoint it is not as vast as it sounds. It prints four hundred pages of English and American verse, much of it already represented in (72). It also contains 250 pages of translations from Oriental tongues, which lie outside our province. That leaves about eight hundred pages of poetry drawn from most of the major European languages: Greek, Latin, Italian, Spanish, Provençal, French, German, Old Norse, Danish, Norwegian, Swedish, Russian, Gaelic. There is nothing from the Welsh, nothing from the Portuguese, and only a token representation from the Gaelic. These minor lacks can be remedied by the use of the specialized anthologies listed under Suggestions for Further Reading.

Mr. Van Doren's anthology is not strictly representative. Where he finds no good English versions, as in the case of the classical Pindar, he omits the poet. Major names, such as Heine, are usually allotted generous space; but this is not always true. The criterion is always readability, or a reasonable facsimile thereof.

The latest edition is dated 1936. This means that, unavoidably, no advantage has been taken of the remarkable translations made mainly by American scholars during the last quarter century, particularly in the classical tongues. Again, you may supplement Mr. Van Doren with other anthologies listed in the Suggestions.

Perhaps you will wish to concentrate on the major names in the European poetical tradition. Here, omitting those we have already met, are a few: Sappho, Aristophanes, Catullus, Horace, Ovid, Cavalcanti, Petrarch, Saint John of the Cross, Villon, Ronsard, La Fontaine, Hugo, Baudelaire, Mallarmé, Rimbaud, von der Vogelweide, Schiller, Heine, Stefan George, Rilke, Pushkin, Lermontov, Leopardi. To this list should be added the great fourteenth-century Welshman Dafydd ap Gwilym. You will find him in Creekmore's *Lyrics of the Middle Ages* (see Suggestions).

Not all of these sound in translation like the fine poets they are, or we are told they are. Don't shoot the translator: he's doing his best.

74. JOHN DONNE (1573–1631) *Selected Works*

Had The Lifetime Reading Plan been compiled in 1900, Donne and Blake (76) would have been less prominent. The shift in emphasis is more than a matter of fashion, though both men do happen to be fashionable in literary circles. It is a matter of taste; and taste, when it mirrors a real change in man's view of himself, can be a profound thing.

Neglected for some generations after his death, Donne seems important to us today because he speaks to our condition, as Milton (75) does not. In another fifty years or so this may no longer be true. At the moment, however, Donne seems to us a great writer, not merely because he has so powerfully influenced modern poetry, but because his voice is that of a modern man. It is no accident that in 1940 Hemingway (90) should have drawn the title of his novel *For Whom the Bell Tolls* from one of Donne's *Devotions*, published in 1624.

Born of a Roman Catholic family, Donne was on his mother's side related to the martyr Sir Thomas More. Some years at Oxford and Cambridge were followed by the study of law, by a period of worldly and amorous adventure in London, by foreign service, and by a marriage—injudicious from the practical viewpoint—with the highborn niece of his employer, Sir Thomas Egerton. Donne's career prospects darkened and for a decade the young couple endured discouragement and poverty. At forty-two Donne, after much serious reflection, forsook the family faith and took orders in the Anglican church. He rose until he became Dean of St. Paul's in London, and the most famous preacher of his time. The daring young spark of the earlier love poems was now a God-tormented man, assailed by visions of death and the indignities of illness. He rejected "the mistress of my youth, Poetry" in favor of "the wife of mine age, Divinity." His mortality obsession grew with the years. Today you may visit the crypt in St. Paul's and see Donne's statue, sculpted during his lifetime, wrapped in a winding sheet. As his last hour neared he contemplated from his bedside a painting of himself in a shroud, his eyes closed as if death had already touched him.

Donne's *Devotions* and sermons are quite unlike conventional religious literature. They are works of art, combining an almost frightening spiritual intensity with cunning elaboration of rhythm and metaphor. The *Devotions* are addressed to himself. The sermons were delivered before large audiences, often before the king. No Sunday pieties, they were designed deliberately to work upon the emotions. They can still do so, with their art if not with their doctrine.

Donne's poetry is at once highly sensuous (often highly sensual), uncompromisingly intellectual, and startlingly personal. By the use of metaphor, sometimes complex, sometimes brutally direct, Donne merges sense and intellect in a manner to which our own taste seems curiously receptive. At his worst his figures of speech are the ingenious conceits that annoyed the downright Dr. Johnson (86). At his best they seem identical with the thought itself.

His love poetry by-passes not only all the Elizabethan conventions, but all the standard sentiments that had been the staple of erotic verse up to his day. "For God's sake hold your tongue, and let me love." A man who begins a poem that way is imitating no one. He is not writing exercises. He is a real man speaking, and his voice is in the room. Donne can be shocking, outrageous, tender, learned, colloquial, fantastic, passionate, reverent, despairing; and sometimes he is several of these in a single love poem. It is his awareness of the complexity of emotion that recommends him to our un-simple time. And what is true of his love poetry is true of his devotional verse, which often seems to have an erotic tinge: it is the work of the whole man, including the physical man. Two often-quoted lines condense a great deal of John Donne:

> Love's mysteries in souls do grow,
> But yet the body is his book.

We may, very roughly, liken Donne's poetry to El Greco's painting. As El Greco distorts line, so Donne distorts language, not out of any lust for experiment, but to achieve calculated effects of emphasis, intensity, and directness obtainable in no other way. Just as El Greco's colors at first seem harsh and unnatural, so Donne's rhythms are broken, un-smooth, the agitated reflection of emotions themselves broken and un-smooth. The spiritual pain and tension that we feel in El Greco we feel also in Donne. His faith was not serene; it was shadowed with anxieties, perplexities, contradictions that seem to anticipate the climate of our own sorely beset time.

Donne produced much writing of interest mainly to the scholar. For the beginning reader, who may be familiar with only a few anthology pieces, I might suggest: the *Songs and Sonnets,* the *Elegies,* the *First and Second Anniversaries,* the *Holy Sonnets,* the *Devotions Upon Emergent Occasions,* and perhaps a few of the *Sermons.* At first this "angel speaking out of a cloud" may seem far-fetched and needlessly difficult. But, behind his odd metaphors (often drawn from the trades and sciences) and his seeming extravagances of style lie sound reasons. Careful reading will soon make these reasons apparent, and his personal idiom will become less and less alien as it becomes more and more fascinating.

75. JOHN MILTON (1608–1674)

Paradise Lost, Lycidas, On the Morning of Christ's Nativity, Sonnets, Areopagitica

Milton's life opened on a fair prospect and closed in darkness. At Christ's College, Cambridge, the delicate-featured boy was called, half in scorn, half in admiration, "The Lady of Christ's." He found his vocation early: poetry and classical scholarship. A period of reading and study at his father's country house (1632-1638) was followed by a year or two of Continental travel. During this time he was a humanist not greatly different from other humanists of the Renaissance. Then came twenty years of stormy political and religious controversy. Some magnificent prose resulted, but little happiness; and some may think these years a waste of his genius. Championing the Parliamentary cause, hating "the bishops," he served as Latin Secretary to Cromwell for over a decade, overlaying his original humanism with puritan doctrine. From his forty-third year to his death he was blind; none of his three marriages turned out well; and with the Restoration all his political hopes and dreams were dashed. Nothing was left him but poetry, and his personal Christianity, a kind of dissidence of dissent.

This was the man who wrote *Paradise Lost*, receiving twenty pounds for the effort of justifying the ways of God to men; who told us that poetry should be "simple, sensuous, and passionate," but did not always follow his own prescription; whose *Areopagitica* is the classic defense of free speech and who fiercely supported Cromwell's rigid Puritan theocracy; whose views on divorce were three hundred years ahead of his time and whose views on women were those of a dimwitted barbarian; who was a supreme master of the language and yet may be said to have written English as if it were Latin or Greek.

The average reader, approaching this unhappy Samson, meets two obstacles. The first is Milton. The second is Miltonese.

It is hard to like John Milton. Suffering the penalty of charmlessness, of humorlessness, he has been less read than admired, less admired than merely accepted. The "God-gifted organ voice of England," as Tennyson thought it, is a pretty intimidating voice as well. Milton was a man of the utmost courage; but it is not the kind of courage that kindles the imagination because it is not married to much humanity, and has about it the smell of stubbornness. His pride was too magnificent for any alloy of mere conceit; yet we are made uncomfortable by his "elaborate assumption of the singing-robe," by his flat statement that he will pursue "things unattempted yet in prose or rhyme." He is a hard man to live with. Shakespeare, even Dante, had not only the uncommon but also the common touch. Milton lacked it. Making due allowance for Samuel Johnson's Toryism, it is hard not to agree with his view of Milton: "an acrimonious and surly republican."

And the style is suited to the man. It has, as Milton proudly states, "no middle flight." It can be grand; it can be windy; it can be sublime; it can be pompous. It is never charming, restful, or easy, except in the minor poems and even then infrequently. It is difficult, un-English in syntax and vocabulary, uncompromising in its elevation.

Perhaps I have persuaded you to skip Milton. That was not my intention. For all the mustiness of his theology and morality, for all his mannerism (though it was no mannerism to him), for all the negative magnetism of his personality, he remains a very great artist in both verse and prose. With rocklike—he would say adamantine—grandeur he continues to impose himself even in our age which laughs at grandeur, at the noble style, and at erudition.

It is worth while to make a special, even a painful, effort of adjustment in order to read Milton. If he is a museum piece, he is a rare, a precious one. If you cannot stomach his "message" in *Paradise Lost*, at least read it for the gorgeous sound, the elaborate imagery, the portrait of Satan, that fallen god with whom Milton himself had so much in common. No one will ever again write like this. No one will ever again conceive such perfect, rolling periods as are to be found in his most eloquent prose.

When we step inside our first great Gothic cathedral, our feelings are mixed. It seems alien, it seems too complicated, it does not seem quite human. But gradually we accustom ourselves to what the builders had in mind. Little by little the structure and sweep and decoration and color become familiar. Soon two clear emotions begin to arise in us, different in nature, yet capable of blending: the emotion of awe, the emotion of esthetic pleasure. Milton is a little like that. He cannot give you these emotions all the time, nor should one be too obstinate in seeking them continually. But they are there for you, if you read him in small doses, skipping when he is too wearisome, or too exalted for our commoner clay.

76. WILLIAM BLAKE (1757-1827)
Selected Works

Once, William Blake tells us, he walked to the end of the heath and touched the sky with his finger. At four he screamed upon perceiving God's head at the window. He saw angels in boughs and the prophet Ezekiel under a tree. His wife once remarked, quite placidly, "I have very little of Mr. Blake's company. He is always in Paradise." Perhaps an exaggeration, wives being what they are, but there is no doubt that Blake felt himself on familiar terms with spirits. He is the supreme type, at least in modern times, of the visionary poet.

Toward this strange, baffling man of streaky genius one has a choice of attitudes. You may put him down as a faker, though the sweetness and honesty of his whole life belie it. Some of his contemporaries, quite celebrated then, quite forgotten now, called him a harmless lunatic. A psychologist will talk of Blake's "eidetic vision," which is simply a specialized ability to project into the external world images we usually hold in our minds. Many children have this power, Joan of Arc may have had it, and rationalists cite it when trying to explain the visions of saints and even Jesus. Finally you can ponder Blake's sly and, from the viewpoint of the professional artist and poet, quite practical advice to his friends: "Work up imagination to the state of vision."

It doesn't matter. By the pragmatic test (see William James, 69, and Dewey, 70) Blake is a success. His paintings, drawings, and engravings, though not of the highest order, are beautiful and moving. His finest verse, of which there is not a great deal, is original and unforgettable. His ideas, long mocked or neglected, appeal with increasing force to those who have lost faith in materialism's ability to bring happiness to the race.

Blake was that odd thing, a completely spontaneous human being. "A man without a mask," a friend called him. Living and dying in poverty, he was probably one of the most energetically joyful men of his time. He had some secret of ecstasy denied to most of us, and at times it stimulated quite non-gray-flannel behavior: he and his wife were once discovered in their little arbor, stark naked, reading *Paradise Lost* aloud.

In his rejection of most of the institutions of his time (as well as in his crankiness) he resembles other figures we have met, such as Thoreau (67), Nietzsche (60), and Lawrence (34). His romanticism is a far deeper thing than that of the Romantic poets who followed him—Wordsworth (77), Keats, Shelley. "Man is all imagination," he tells us. "God is man and exists in us and we in him." And again: "We are led to believe a lie when we see *with*, not *through*, the eye."

His scorn of what is called common sense led him to champion freedoms of all kinds, in the religious, political, and sexual spheres. Calmly, in a memorable sentence, he anticipates Freud: "Sooner murder an infant in its cradle than nurse unacted desires." For him "Exuberance is Beauty." Nonconformists of all stripes love to quote "Damn braces. Bless relaxes." He hated all those virtues arising out of measure and calculation: "The tigers of wrath are wiser than the horses of instruction."

Blake has the defect of his qualities. His interior world was so vivid that he often lost touch with the exterior world. He may wrap piercing truth in a cloud of frenzy. But the cloud is there; he can be a bad communicator. His private mythology is contained in the so-called *Prophetic Books*. Scholars keep on trying to unravel these. To most of us they will seem like delirium interrupted by gorgeous eloquence.

Blake's nature mingled high natural intelligence and piercing intuition. In his aphorisms and his best verse the two elements are held in balance. His poetry is not artless—Blake was an excellent craftsman with his pen as well as with his pencil and graver. But in the best sense it is childlike—that is, pure, flowing, simple in diction, wildly imaginative. T. S. Eliot's severe and just judgment is really a tribute: "Dante is a classic, and Blake only a poet of genius."

For all his extravagance and seeming mooniness, Blake must be seen as essentially a moralist, of the prophetic rather than the reflective order. His defense of imagination and instinct is religious in tone. Whether he writes about children or spirits his concern is "to cleanse the doors of perception." His thought can be merely odd or ill-balanced. Blake shows that uncertain sense of proportion often possessed by self-educated geniuses. But just as frequently it goes straight to the heart of what is wrong with an industrial society, disfigured by its "dark, Satanic mills." Yet there is no do-goodism in Blake. He is a hard-core rebel, like Shaw, and, like Shaw, a dangerous man.

Of his verse I suggest you read *Poetical Sketches, Songs of Innocence, Songs of Experience, The Everlasting Gospel,* and the *Preface to Milton.* To get some notion of the principles by which Blake lived his quietly rebellious life, see *The Marriage of Heaven and Hell, All Religions Are One,* and *There Is No Natural Religion.* His ideas on art may be understood through his divertingly ill-tempered Annotations to Sir Joshua Reynolds's *Discourses.*

77. WILLIAM WORDSWORTH (1770–1850)

The Prelude; Selected Shorter Poems; Preface to the Lyrical Ballads, 1800

In a famous parody of one of Wordsworth's sonnets the English humorist J. K. Stephen writes:

> Two Voices are there: one is of the deep; . . .
> And one is of an old halfwitted sheep
> Which bleats articulate monotony . . .
> And, Wordsworth, both are thine . . .

My Wordsworth contains 937 closely printed pages. Of these, possibly two hundred are in the accents of the Voice of the deep. The remainder are bleatings. Wordsworth, who never understood how to cut things short, persisted to his eightieth year. Of these years only the first half were, from posterity's viewpoint, worth living. The last forty were of great interest to Wordsworth; of considerable interest to the three female acolytes who took care of him; and of some interest to literary scholars attracted by the problem of the decay of genius.

The main influence on Wordsworth was Wordsworth. I know of no major literary figure who was so continuously and so favorably impressed by himself. This highly successful love affair dried up in him the springs of self-criticism; and, as he never had any humor to start with, four-fifths of his work turned out to be a crashing bore.

Of the non-Wordsworthian influences the most important was the English countryside, which he may almost be said to have discovered. It touched something in him deep, pure, and unselfish, releasing some of his finest verse. The second influence was the superior intelligence of Coleridge (78). Their friendship produced the epochal collaboration of the *Lyrical Ballads* (1798) and the no less epochal Preface to the edition of 1800.

The third influence was Wordsworth's sister Dorothy, a remarkable neurotic whose eyes and ears were far better than her brother's and whose alertness to the face of nature provided him with many lines and insights for which he is usually given full credit. At this late date it would be prissy to deny that the relation between Dorothy and William was unconsciously incestuous, at least on Dorothy's part. This has no bearing whatsoever on the value of his work.

Minor influences were the French Revolution and Annette Vallon, a Frenchwoman who seems to have stimulated Wordsworth to something mildly approaching passion. At first the eager young poet was a partisan of the Revolution. Its excesses, plus his own deep quietistic bias, plus what seems to be plain cowardice (compare Milton, 75) combined to change Wordsworth into a dull reactionary. The connection with Annette Vallon, resulting in an illegitimate daughter, he did his best to hide from posterity. His whole conduct in the affair (compare Fielding, 25) is unmanly, even callous. This again has nothing to do with the value of his work.

The odd thing is that, though Wordsworth's poetry and manifestoes really did help to liberate men's emotions (see Mill, 57), his own emotions were limited in number and even in depth. He wrote beautifully about nature, children, the poor, common people. Our attitudes toward all these differ today from the attitudes of the neo-classic eighteenth century against which Wordsworth courageously rebelled; and this change we owe in part to a poet most of us have never read. Yet he himself never observed nature with the particularity of a Thoreau (67). He does not seem to have understood children—the sonnet "On the Beach at Calais" is supremely lovely, but there is no real child involved (even though he is writing about his own daughter), but merely a moving sentiment about an abstract, Wordsworthian idea of childhood. For all his influential theories about using "the real language of men," he does not seem to have the slightest idea of how humble folk really talked. And, except perhaps for the Annette Vallon affair, in which he conducted himself like a poltroon, he was incapable of a strong, passionate love for a woman.

And now that I have said all this, an open confession of my intense dislike of Wordsworth, I must make two other statements far more to the point. The first is that he wrote some great verse, though I think virtually all of it is contained in his long poetical autobiography *The Prelude,* plus *Tintern Abbey,* the *Ode on the Intimations of Immortality, Michael, Resolution and Independence,* the *Ode to Duty,* and a scattering of superb sonnets and shorter lyrics.

The second statement is that he opened the eyes of poets and ordinary human beings to the possibilities of a fresh approach to nature, to the life of feeling, and to the English language. With Coleridge, he diverted the course of English and American poetry. He helped to release it from conventionality, stock epithets, city-pent emotions. His famous definition of poetry as "the spontaneous overflow of powerful feelings" arising from "emotion recollected in tranquillity" is limited and partial. But as a corrective to the petrifactions of the eighteenth century it was badly needed. For all its excesses the romantic protest has proved valuable to the Western tradition.

It is probable that Wordsworth will in perspective be seen to be greater as a historical event than as a poet. But he is great enough in both categories to warrant some acquaintance with this humorless, mentally and emotionally straitened egomaniac who in a few short years wrote verse that helped to "cleanse the doors of perception."

78. SAMUEL TAYLOR COLERIDGE (1772–1834)
The Ancient Mariner, Christabel, Kubla Khan, Biographia Literaria, Writings on Shakespeare

In a moment of self-forgetfulness Wordsworth called Coleridge "the most *wonderful* man he had ever known." Shelley hailed this "hooded eagle among blinking owls." His good friend the essayist Charles Lamb spoke of him as "an Archangel a little damaged" and of his "hunger for eternity." The scholar George Saintsbury ranks Coleridge, as literary critic, with Aristotle (6) and Longinus. Mill (57) remarked, "The class of thinkers has scarcely yet arisen by whom he is to be judged," and many thoughtful students feel the statement, made over a century ago, still stands. Such judgments could be multiplied by the score.

They were made about the greatest might-have-been in English literature. For the fact is that Coleridge's reputation and influence are both far more imposing than his work. His mind, a Tuscarora for depth, a Pacific for vastness, was never quite able to pull itself together. Though the *Biographia Literaria* comes nearest to it, he wrote no single, complete prose masterpiece. Like Wordsworth's, much of his verse, though more intensely felt, is balderdash. Of the three poems by which as a poet he will live, only *The Ancient Mariner* is a finished whole. Often ranked as the finest Shakespearean critic that ever wrote, he never imposed order on his mass of essays, lectures, notes, and conversational remarks.

At no time in his incoherent life did Coleridge show any notable common sense. There are many men, often of the highest order of mind, who should be exempted from the pressures of "normal" living. Coleridge was one of them. He had no capacity for marriage, little for fatherhood, not much for earning his board and lodging. He tried soldiering, preaching, periodical journalism, lecturing, even foreign service under the Governor of Malta. During his latter years he wasted part of what might have been productive energy in incessant and apparently uniquely brilliant monologues. ("The stimulus of conversation suspends the terror that haunts my mind.") Tortured by neuralgia and other ills, plus intense melancholy, he sought relief in laudanum, and became an addict. For the last eighteen years of his life, withdrawn from his wife, he lived under the medical care of a kindly friend, James Gillman.

In a sense the "person from Porlock" who interrupted him as he was writing down the dream-dictated lines of *Kubla Khan* was a real-life reflection of his own inner disorder. He was continually interrupting himself. His mind was too active and associative for him to complete any project. His whole life is like a mass of notes, undigested, erratic, sometimes baffling, more often profound, rich in wonders.

The fruitful association with Wordsworth produced the *Lyrical Ballads*, to which Coleridge contributed his lone undisputed masterpiece, the *Ballad of the Ancient Mariner*. Here, as also in the unfinished *Kubla Khan* and *Christabel*, he successfully achieved "that willing suspension of disbelief for the moment which constitutes poetic faith" and so contributed to the mainstream of Romanticism. That magic, eerie note he never again quite sounded.

What fascinates in Coleridge is that, along with his genius for the fairy tale (these poems, though not for children, belong to the literature of the fairy tale), he possessed a speculative mind of the rarest power. He wrote on metaphysics, politics, theology. Never reducing his insights to a system, he nonetheless remains a psychologist of most original gifts. And as a literary critic of the Romantic school he has no peer in the language.

When you think of Coleridge you may quite naturally think also of Poe (43). Neither was able to dominate practical life. Both took drugs. Both wrote verse ruled by unworldly beauty and strangeness. Both had minds that worked as well in the area of ratiocination as in that of dream. But there the parallel more or less ends. Poe's erudition was spotty, Coleridge's incredibly vast ("I have read everything"). Poe's mind was acute; Coleridge's brooding, penetrating, and hungry for vast unities. Poe was an interesting minor failure. Coleridge was a fascinating major failure. But he was so fascinating and so major that even as a failure he bulks larger than his admired friend Wordsworth, who finished work he never should have started and ended as poet laureate, while Coleridge died in poverty.

79. WILLIAM BUTLER YEATS (1865–1939) *Collected Poems, Collected Plays, The Autobiography*

Exclusive of certain other major figures, such as Shakespeare, the Plan suggests for extended reading seven noncontemporary English or American poets. Among these posterity will assign Yeats his proper rank. That he will not be at the bottom of the list we may be sure.

Yeats offers difficulties. He is a complex man and, of all the poets we have met, he is the one who offers the least enjoyment when read in anthological snatches. Also, he is more than a poet. Among his tremendous output are poems, plays, memoirs, essays, literary studies, folk and fairy tales, mystical philosophies, letters, speeches, translations from Sophocles. Like Goethe's (18) his long life comprised a series of evolutions. There is a vast space between the aged poet of the *Last Poems and Plays* (1940) and the young Celtic dreamer of *The Wanderings of Oisin* (1889). To bridge this space the reader must absorb a great deal of Yeats and also know something about the Ireland whose soul he tried to find and form.

That is why I suggest his *Autobiography*, a one-volume omnibus. It contains reminiscences of his life through 1902, together with extracts from a diary kept in 1909, some notes about the death, in 1909, of the great Irish dramatist Synge, and an account of his reception in Sweden which he visited in 1923 to receive the Nobel Prize.

Yeats grew and changed and deepened; his life is not simple, any more than his thought. We may name a few influences: his early childhood in the beautiful Sligo country; his readings in the Romantic English poets; the mythology and folklore of Ireland, together with the Irish Literary Revival that he led; theosophy, spiritualism, occultism, astrology, and Indian philosophy; the beautiful Irish revolutionary Maud Gonne, whom he loved in vain for twenty years; the psychic powers of his mediumistic wife; and toward the end such cyclical theories of history as are to be found in Vico, Spengler, Toynbee.

The major movement of his creative life is away from the delicate, suggestive, vague but often beautiful lyricism of the early verse toward the hard, spare, condensed, intellectual, tightly passionate, often obscure poetry of his later years. The change was already apparent in a poem called "September 1913," with its plain statement: "Romantic Ireland's dead and gone." Yeats's evolution is exactly opposed to Wordsworth's: aging, he became greater as man and as artist. The growth was fed by deep conflict, not only personal but political and social, for he despised much of our world ("this filthy modern tide") and used it as nourishment for his noble rage.

The bias of his mind is aristocratic (even feudal), mystical, symbolical. Though the symbols are not as wildly private as in Blake (76), who greatly influenced Yeats, they cannot be understood without a considerable knowledge of his work and life. Unless this is frankly admitted, the reader is apt to be at first puzzled, then irritated, finally antagonistic.

Yeats often seems esoteric, remote, impersonal, wrapped up in his symbolical world of strange images drawn from antiquity or the East or his own occult thought system or Irish legend. But the more one lives with him, the more clearly one feels his unflinching closeness to reality. He may be taken in by visions; but he is not taken in by illusions. In his mature work there is a bracing tragic bitterness:

> Whatever flames upon the night
> Man's own resinous heart has fed.

His wisdom is not for children, optimists, or the comfortable:

> I must lie down where all the ladders start,
> In the foul rag-and-bone shop of the heart.

In the final lines of one of his last poems, "Under Ben Bulben," he compresses his seeming arrogance, his patrician elevation of spirit, his horror of self-pity. He is leaving instructions for his own gravestone:

> No marble, no conventional phrase;
> On limestone quarried near the spot
> By his command these words are cut:
> *Cast a cold eye*
> *On life, on death.*
> *Horseman, pass by!*

80. WALT WHITMAN (1819–1892)

Selected Poems; Democratic Vistas; Preface, 1855, to First Issue of "Leaves of Grass"; A Backward Glance O'er Travel'd Roads

I hear America singing. I celebrate myself. I loaf and invite my soul. I wear my hat as I please indoors or out. I find no sweeter fat than sticks to my own bones. I am the man, I suffered, I was there. Do I contradict myself? Very well then I contradict myself. Passage to India. I sound my barbaric yawp over the roofs of the world. A woman waits for me. When I give I give myself. The long brown path before me leading wherever I choose. The never-ending audacity of elected persons. Pioneers! O Pioneers! Out of the cradle endlessly rocking. When lilacs last in the dooryard bloomed. O Captain! My Captain! Who touches this, touches a man. I think I could turn and live with animals. A great city is that which has the greatest men and women. The mania of owning things. These United States. To have great poets, there must be great audiences, too. Leaves of Grass. Powerful uneducated persons.

I have omitted the quotation marks around these lines and phrases because the marks hardly exist in our minds and memories. It is Whitman's language rather than his message that exerts power. He worked with all his soul to become a national bard, the voice of "the divine average," the Muse of Democracy. But we have no national bards; the average man does not feel divine, nor wants to; democracy prefers to get along without a muse. Whitman loved his country and often wrote thrillingly about it; but it is probable that he never really understood it. He has penetrated not because he is accepted by the "powerful uneducated persons" he idealizes, but because he is a poet in the original sense, a maker, a coiner of wonderful new language.

His ideas, if you can call them that, he borrowed from many sources, including Emerson (68), who was among the first to hail his genius. Even his rhythms echo, among other books, the Bible. Nonetheless he is a true revolutionary in poetry. His free-swinging, cadenced, wavelike verse, his fresh (even if often absurd) manipulations of language, his boldness of vocabulary—all helped to liberate American poetry, and have had a profound effect abroad. And there is no doubt also that his erotic candor, however "abnormal" its source, was useful in the revolt against the genteel tradition.

The first three issues of *Leaves of Grass* (1855, 1856, 1860) contain ninety per cent of his best work. After that he tended to repeat himself or to create poses rather than poetry. There is no longer any sense in denying that Whitman was a bit of a charlatan; if you want to be fancy you can say that he wore masks. There's also no sense in denying that he was a homosexual. His verse, and particularly his odd notion of democracy, cannot be understood except in the light of his bias toward males.

Whitman had an original temperament, a certain peasant shrewdness, but only a moderate amount of brains. He can excite us with his rhapsodic, prophetic note. He can move us with his musical threnodies of death. He can cause to pass before our eyes a series of wonderful tiny images of men and things in action. These are not small gifts. They are enough to make him by far the greatest of American poets, until we come to our own time.

On the other hand, he tries too hard to make a virtue of his deficiencies. He was poorly educated, his experience of life (despite the legends he busily circulated) seems to have been limited, and he depended too much on the resources of his own rich temperament and too little on the common stock of three thousand years of the Western tradition. This makes him parochial when he thinks he is being daringly American. It lends a certain hollowness to his boast that he is "non-literary and non-decorous."

Ignoring scales of values, he embraces and celebrates all creation—often with infectious passion, often ridiculously. Everything in Whitman seems to be equal to everything else; everything becomes equally divine. Sometimes the reader, fatigued by so many unvarying hosannas, is inclined to agree with the poet Sidney Lanier. Whitman argues, said Lanier, that "because the Mississippi is long, therefore every American is God."

All these criticisms have been made often, and more severely. Yet Whitman somehow remains. England and the Continent, anxious to believe that his barbaric yawp is the true voice of America (it satisfies their conventional romantic notion of us), appreciate him more widely than we do. But reasonably cultivated Americans, though not Whitman's beloved workers, also acknowledge his curious and thrilling spell. It is not because his is a truly native voice—a poet like Frost is a hundred times more authentically American. It is rather because his chant is universal, almost Homeric, touching in us primitive feelings about death and nature and the gods who refuse to die in even the most civilized among us. Trail breaking in form, Whitman seems to be preclassic, pre-Christian in feeling, though he thought of himself as the trumpeter of a new time.

In addition to the three important prose works suggested, the reader might tick off, for minimum reading, the following poems: his masterpiece, *Song of Myself; I Sing the Body Electric; Song of the Open Road; Crossing Brooklyn Ferry; Song of the Answerer; Song of the Broad-Axe; Out of the Cradle Endlessly Rocking; As I Ebbed with the Ocean of Life; When I Heard the Learn'd Astronomer; By the Bivouac's Fitful Flame; As Toilsome I Wandered Virginia's Woods; The Wound-Dresser; When Lilacs Last in the Dooryard Bloom'd; There Was a Child Went Forth; Proud Music of the Storm; Passage to India; Prayer of Columbus; A Noiseless Patient Spider; Years of the Modern.*

History, Biography, Autobiography

81. WILL DURANT (1885-)

The Story of Civilization

In the Suggestions for Further Reading you will find listed a number of one-volume histories of the world. Many more exist, few without some merit. There is no acknowledged single classic covering this vast field; perhaps there can be none ever. Nor is there any recommendation I could make, including this one, over which some reputable scholar will not shake his head.

After much hesitation and pondering I have concluded that for the special purposes of this Plan I can do no better than suggest Durant's monumental panorama. It is long. It is expensive. It is incomplete. But its scale allows the learned author to supply truly generous perspectives. Its style is always highly readable and at its best brilliant, for Durant is a master of the neat phrase and the vivid detail. Above all it is marked by an absence of dogmatic theory, by a warm humanity, by a constant sense that the career of the human animal turns on far more than the outcome of battles and the rise and fall of kings. It moves. It is a narrative.

Volume I, *Our Oriental Heritage,* deals with the civilization of ancient Egypt and with the complete history of India, China, and Japan. It lies outside our scope, though the section on Egypt, one of our ancestors, may be read with profit.

The titles of the remaining five volumes—they may be bought separately—point to the content:

II: The Life of Greece
III: Caesar and Christ
IV: The Age of Faith
V: The Renaissance
VI: The Reformation

In his Foreword to the last-named, Dr. Durant, as of May 12, 1957, writes: "If the Reaper will stay his hand, there will be a concluding Volume VII, *The Age of Reason,* which should appear some five years hence, and should carry the story of civilization to Napoleon." As I know Dr. Durant to be made of enduring stuff the reader may with some confidence place an advance order for Volume VII, to be delivered in 1962.

That will bring us to Napoleon. Hundreds, perhaps thousands, of excellent books exist on the nineteenth and twentieth centuries. From my viewpoint it is the better part of valor to let you discover some of them for yourself. For our particular purposes I feel that the six volumes of Durant dealing with, or to deal with, Western civilization will suffice the average Lifetime reader.

Each volume is conceived as a unit and may be read as such. However, that's quite a large dose of history. You may prefer, as you proceed with the Plan, to select for special attention those sections that supply background for the classic you happen to be busy with. Thus your understanding of Homer (1, 2) will be increased if you preface him with the sixty-five pages of Volume II dealing with Greece up to 1000 B.C. *The Story of Civilization* should be constantly on hand, to be used as a tool. This is not to minimize its other virtues, which are multiple.

82. GEORGE MACAULAY TREVELYAN (1876–) *History of England*

It is for obvious reasons that the Plan suggests the reading of a good history of England. Without reference to the Mother Country our own cannot be understood. From her we drew our language, our early culture, much of our political philosophy, and many of our basic unconscious gestures of the mind and heart. To our great good fortune we have absorbed many racial strains. But Anglo-Saxon attitudes still largely prevail. The United States is not ruled by any single ethnic group. Yet —a somewhat different thing—it is *run* to a great extent by those of Scottish and English blood, though that picture may be slowly changing. I may also point out that of the hundred entries comprising the Plan, thirty-five bear the names of Englishmen, Scotsmen, Irishmen, or, as in the cases of Conrad and T. S. Eliot, by men to all intents and purposes English.

Of histories of England hundreds exist. I suggest Trevelyan. It is available in three handy cheap volumes. It is by a recognized master, the grand-nephew of the great Macaulay. The style is clear, concrete, often lively, and the idiom that of one who loves and knows literature as well as documents. The viewpoint is roughly English Liberal.

Trevelyan is not a "scientific" historian. He believes that the reading of a historical work "should breed enthusiasm." In his fine essay, "Clio: A Muse," he writes: "I cannot abandon the older ideal of History, that the same book should make its appeal both to the general reader and to the historical student." He is essentially a narrative social historian. While dynastic and narrowly political events are not neglected, the sharpest focus is reserved for the life of the people as a whole. Finally, though first published in 1926, the latest reissue of the *History of England* is dated 1953. Thus the story is forwarded almost to our own day.

The volumes are titled:

I: From the Earliest Times to the Reformation
II: The Tudors and the Stuart Era
III: From Utrecht to Modern Times: The Industrial Revolution and the Transition to Democracy.

As with (81) I suggest you use the Trevelyan not only as a classic in itself but as a tool to help you acquire background as you proceed with your reading of English fiction, philosophy, poetry, and biography.

83. ALLAN NEVINS (1890–) AND HENRY STEELE COMMAGER (1902–)
A Short History of the United States

I know of no relatively brief popular history of the United States as outstanding in its field as Trevelyan (82) is in his. Nevins and Commager are first-rate scholars and clear writers. The same may be said of other American historians. Several are listed in the Suggestions for Further Reading.

For the purposes of our Plan all I had in mind was the proposal of some sound, convenient, readable brief account. This one will do well enough, though it has no literary pretensions. The authors "have not conceived American history to be primarily political or economic, or as a series of problems, but as the story of the evolution of a free society." That story they carry up to 1944, which is far enough; beyond that point perspective is as yet lacking.

This book is built on a small scale (you can easily discover others that supply greater detail). Hence it is unavoidable that the authors should skimp the part of our history that was made by the creative imagination. There is no mention, for example, of Thoreau, Melville, Poe, Hawthorne, either of the Jameses, Dewey, or Santayana.

84. *Basic Documents in American History,* EDITED BY Richard B. Morris (1904–); *On the Constitution: Selections from the Federalist Papers,* EDITED BY Ralph H. Gabriel (1890–)

This entry needs little commentary. Much as they have been modified, our basic political ideas are still to be found, classically expressed, in a very few documents: the Declaration, the Constitution, the Virginia Statute for Religious Freedom, the Gettysburg Address, and a few others. Many handy collections of our important state papers exist; Mr. Morris' is quite serviceable. He prints forty-seven documents, from the Mayflower Compact to President Eisenhower's Disarmament Proposals of July 21, 1955. Most are of interest only to students of history. As examples of the use of the language they get progressively worse after Lincoln, a fact from which the reader may draw any conclusion he prefers.

The *Federalist Papers,* by Hamilton, Madison, and Jay, represents American political thought and expression at a peak of elegance and power it has never since attained. Conceived originally as journalistic letters intended to mobilize New York State public opinion in support of the proposed Federal Constitution of 1787, they are not merely historical documents but in many cases masterpieces of reasoning. In 1788 Jefferson wrote to Madison praising them as "the best commentary on the principles of government which was ever written." It is illuminating to study them in connection with your reading of Aristotle's *Politics* (6), Hobbes (54), Locke (55), Marx and Engels (59), Machiavelli (62), Tocqueville (66). Not all the Papers need be read; Mr. Gabriel's selection is a judicious one. A fairly thorough knowledge of this classic may be gained by a reading of Numbers 1-51, 84, 85.

85. JEAN-JACQUES ROUSSEAU (1712–1778)
Confessions

Of all the great writers we have met, Rousseau is the most irritating. His whole character offends any reasonable mind. Socially awkward; sexually ill-balanced; immoral; nauseatingly sentimental; mean and quarrelsome; a liar; manic-depressive; the victim of a large number of unpleasant ills, from persecution delusions to bladder trouble; a defender of the rights of little children who states calmly that he abandoned his five illegitimate offspring to a foundling institution: that is Rousseau, or part of him. It is simply exasperating that this absurd fellow, who died half-cracked, should also have been one of the most powerful forces of his time, the virtual ancestor of the Romantic movement in literature and art, and one of the major intellectual sources of the French Revolution. Even more annoying is the fact that this vagabond-valet-music teacher, whose formal education ended at about twelve, should be a writer of such persuasion that, though his arguments have been refuted by many, his rhetoric still bewitches. The whole Rousseau case is highly irregular . . .

We have encountered the title *Confessions* once before, with St. Augustine (13). In one respect the two men are alike. Both had and recorded a decisive spiritual experience which changed the course of history. St. Augustine's occurred in a garden, Rousseau's on the road to Vincennes outside of Paris. He was reading a paper as he walked along, on his way to visit the famous philosopher Diderot. He noticed an announcement. The Dijon Academy was offering a prize for the best essay on the subject: Has the progress of the arts and sciences contributed to the purification or the corruption of morals?

"All at once," says Rousseau, "I felt myself dazzled by a thousand sparkling lights; crowds of vivid ideas thronged into my head with a force and confusion that threw me into unspeakable agitation; I felt my head whirling in a giddiness like that of intoxication." Out of this trance or vision or fit came his first work, the *Discourse on the Arts and Sciences.* It won the prize, it gained him European fame, and it led to his establishment as the most revolutionary writer of his time. In it and succeeding works he attacked progress as a corrupter of man's natural goodness. He assailed private property. He inveighed against the evil influence of educational discipline on the child mind. He pointed out the constricting power of organized religion. In his crucial *Social Contract* he cried out against those political institutions which are so contrived that "man is born free and everywhere he is in chains."

It is easy to say that Rousseau was a misfit, that his championship of nature and of man's innate goodness sprang from his inability to adjust to the demands of organized society. That may be true. But what he said—it was not new, merely never before so irresistibly expressed—was what his century wanted to hear. This eccentric prophet, this wild "man without a skin," as Hume called him, came at exactly the right time. And his power still persists. Some of it, particularly in the field of education, has worked constructively. For Rousseau, unlike Voltaire, was a positive man; he meant his ideas to form the future.

The *Confessions* is his masterpiece. One of its opening statements arrests attention at once, and has never ceased to do so: "I am commencing an undertaking, hitherto without precedent, and which will never find an imitator. I desire to set before my fellows the likeness of a man in all the truth of nature, and that man myself. . . . If I am not better, at least I am different."

Rousseau lies, exaggerates, and often misunderstands himself. Yet, except for one thing, he makes good his boast. He was wrong in saying that his book would never find an imitator. It has found thousands. The whole literature of modern autobiography, when it is designedly confessional, stems from this one book. Renowned writers like Chateaubriand and Amiel stem from it; dubious self-revelations like those of Frank Harris stem from it; magazines like *True Confessions* stem from it.

But, in its eye-opening candor on the one hand and its remarkable free-flowing and often lyrical style on the other, it has never been equaled.

Rousseau is easy to read. You need no one's guidance to help you make up your mind about him. However, just to confuse you a little, here are two judgments. The first is Romain Rolland's: "He opened into literature the riches of the subconscious, the secret movements of being, hitherto ignored and repressed." The second judgment is by Samuel Johnson. To Boswell's question whether he considered Rousseau as bad a man as Voltaire, Johnson replied: "Why, Sir, it is difficult to settle the proportion of iniquity between them."

86. JAMES BOSWELL (1740–1795)
Life of Samuel Johnson

Rousseau we have called the father of modern autobiography. Boswell may claim to be the father of modern biography. His *Life* is the best in the language, perhaps the best in any language. It was published seven years after the death of its subject, in 1791. Ever since, Samuel Johnson has been the most intimately known figure in English literature. But he is more than a literary character. Many who have never read a line of his essays or his *Lives of the Poets* or his grave, rather impressive poetry nevertheless claim him as a familiar friend. He will never cease to be quoted, often by people innocent of the source of the quotation.

This is all the consequence of a meeting in Davies' London bookshop on May 16, 1763, between the literary dictator of England, then aged fifty-three, and an eager, hero-worshiping Scot, then aged twenty-two. At once Boswell, sensing his vocation, began to take notes of the great man's talk and habits and opinions. He continued this activity, with intermissions, up to

Johnson's death in 1784. The result is a full-length portrait, complete with warts, of a stunning character; plus an equally lively picture of the swarming, noisy, brilliant literary and social life of the latter part of the eighteenth century, which boasted, in addition to Johnson, such colorful men as Burke, Garrick, Goldsmith, and Sir Joshua Reynolds; plus an unconscious revelation of Boswell himself, who has turned out to be the most interesting of them all.

Boswell was of good Scottish family. Trained in the law, he preferred other modes of experience: good conversation, liquor, wenching, travel, some abortive meddling in politics, and the company of any great man he could contrive to meet, including Voltaire (38) and Rousseau (85). Above all, however, he was a natural writer. He possessed most of the attributes of a supremely great reporter. He wrote easily. He had a phenomenal memory. He knew how to take notes, written or mental. He put things down when he heard them. He had a nose for the striking, concrete detail. He loved gossip and scandal. And he always happened to be around when something new was happening or being said.

But beyond this, he knew how to *create* news. Had Boswell never existed, Johnson would still have been a great personality. But we might never have known it. Boswell *made* Johnson talk—not that he encountered any innate reluctance. But he forced Johnson into full flower, with the aid of naive or cunning questions, by irritating or flattering him, by caressing or exacerbating his prejudices, even by demeaning himself so as to permit Johnson to enjoy a recordable triumph over him. Johnson is a creation. And that is why Boswell is more than a superb reporter. He is an artist, just as surely as Rembrandt or Hals or any other first-rate portrait painter is one.

In the last forty years or so our view of Boswell has changed radically. Back of this shift lies what Christopher Morley called "the most exciting adventure in English letters." In 1927 Lieutenant Colonel Ralph Isham, a rich and persuasive connoisseur, bought from the owners of Malahide Castle in Ireland some

Boswell Papers that had been lying there untouched for generations. This discovery had been preceded by others of a similar nature and was at once followed by more. Finally there was amassed an enormous collection of eighteenth-century material, by or about Boswell and other contemporaries, which has given us radically new insights into the period. Of this material nine volumes (as of this writing) have been published. The first volume, *Boswell's London Journal 1762-1763*, is the most interesting to the general reader (see Suggestions).

What we now see is a Boswell who is no longer merely the faithful recorder of Johnson's thunder. We have a fantastic fellow, an odd genius, with a little of Hamlet in him, a damaged soul, a divided mind, a shrewd fool, a libertine—and a far finer writer than we had ever thought him. The fact is that though Johnson was a great man and Boswell was not, the disciple is beginning to overshadow the master. In his subtleties, his despairs, his divisions of mind, his violent alternations of emotion, he seems to make a special appeal to our time. Consequently his masterpiece gains a dimension.

87. HENRY ADAMS (1838–1918)
The Education of Henry Adams

Henry Adams was born with a complete set of sterling silver in his mouth. A scion of what is probably the First Family of the United States, he was the great-grandson of John Adams, the grandson of John Quincy Adams, and the son of Charles Francis Adams, who represented us at the Court of St. James. The fascination of his life lies in the unexpectedness of what he did with his inheritance.

The family tradition of service virtually demanded that he grow up to wield high political power for his country's good. The presidency itself would not have been inconceivable. Henry

Adams became a scholar, a major historian, an influential teacher, a philosopher, a marvelous letter writer, a world traveler of genius, and the author of the finest of American autobiographies. He never became a leader. His influence has been profound, but it has been indirect. At one point he remarked: "So far as [I] had a function in life, it was as stable-companion to statesmen." Acquainted with everyone of importance here and in England, he rarely departed from his role of ironic observer, the irony directed inward as well as outward.

From one standpoint (and it was also his own) he was a failure. From another, he was a success, though largely a posthumous one. His failure lay in disappointed ambitions, in his inability to live up to the family tradition. He felt—this is a major motif in the *Education*—that his eighteenth-century upbringing, with its emphasis on humane letters and strict moral accountability, had ill-equipped him for the twentieth century, with its emphasis on energy, science, and industry. His success lay in the fact that this very dissatisfaction with himself (a dissatisfaction out of which he made a virtual career) led him to probe deeply the age for which he was temperamentally unsuited. His books, particularly the *Education*, are pearls produced by irritation.

The Education of Henry Adams, written in a severely ironical third person, is an attempt to explain the author to himself and his time to the author. Adams was greatly influenced by late nineteenth-century physics. He felt that civilizations, like matter, were subject to inexorable laws of change and degradation. In the thirteenth century (see his beautiful book of medieval studies, *Mont-Saint-Michel and Chartres*) he believed Western civilization to have achieved a state of coherence and unity, symbolized by the figure of the Virgin. Our time, symbolized by the Dynamo, he saw as one moving further and further away from unity toward multiplicity. The rate of disintegration was rapidly increasing; mankind had little to look forward to beyond a series of graver and graver catastrophes. The *Education* is remarkable for wit, elegance, wonderful on-the-scene reporting; but what gives it its sharp edge of emotion is Adams' constant cold prescience of tragedy. It makes the *Education* a work of poetry as well as truth.

The critic Paul Elmer More has decried its "sentimental nihilism," and it is true that Adams' special brand of pessimism sometimes strikes tediously on the ear. Yet, when one looks about at the world today, it is hard to find many writers who foresaw as clearly as did Adams the shape of the future. We have experienced several of the catastrophes he foretold; and it is clear that we are to experience others. Disintegration rather than coherence seems more and more to mark our era. It required a considerable depth of imagination to say in 1862, as Adams did: "Some day science may have the existence of mankind in its power, and the human race may commit suicide by blowing up the world."

Henry Adams was by nature a rather unhappy man, and his beloved wife's suicide in 1885 further predisposed him to pessimism. He was snobbish, intellectually cocky, and his self-depreciation is often spurious. Yet from these weaknesses, as well as his strengths, he drew the materials that make the *Education* a great book. Being an Adams, he could not write a *Confessions*. His aim is not the revelation of a human heart but the unflinching consideration of a historical character, who happens to be the writer himself. As an intellectual analysis of a labyrinthine mind and of the changing and, as he thought, disintegrating society he knew intimately, the *Education* remains unrivaled.

Some Contemporaries

88. ROBERT FROST (1874–) *Collected Poems (1949 edition)*

Though not *very* near, Frost is probably the nearest thing we have to a national poet. He is constantly anthologized. School children are regularly exposed to his simpler work. The television screen, the lecture platform, and the college classroom have made his remarkable personality familiar to many Americans who do not think of themselves as poetry lovers. A citizen of a prize-respecting country, he has won the Pulitzer Prize four times. Finally, together with other talents, he possesses that of longevity. All these factors combine to make him a kind of unofficial poet laureate. Insofar as this has helped to raise the status of poetry in a poetry-resistant age, it is a fine thing. Insofar as it has created a fuzzy or sentimentalized or incomplete image of a great writer, it is less so.

"Literature begins with geography," says Frost. The literature he has created did indeed begin with the hilly, lonely, past-conserving Yankeeland north of Boston. Yet Frost is no "regional" poet. He may begin with geography but he advances into unmappable country. Nor is Frost, though deeply American, a representative "voice"; Frost is his own man. Nor is he a "poet of the people," as Sandburg may be. He writes often about farmers, hill folk, lonely "small" souls. But the slope of his temperament is as aristocratic as Yeats's, though more sociable, flexible, and humorous. As is often the case with him, he is half serious, half kidding in such a casual remark as: "I have given up my democratic prejudices and have willingly set the lower classes free to be completely taken care of by the upper classes." Finally, though he uses simple words and weaves into his verse the actual tones of common speech (so that it "says" itself), his technique and imagination are both extraordinarily complex. In other words, Frost is no Yankee sage, rhyming cracker-barrel philosophy, but a sophisticated mind who scorns the usual lingo of sophistication. His understatement conceals a rich growth of statement.

Frost is an uncornerable man. He will say, "I never take my own side in a quarrel." He will say, "I'm never serious except when I'm fooling." About his own art he has ideas no one else ever seems to have thought of: "Like a piece of ice on a hot stove the poem must ride on its own melting." He has absorbed Thoreau and Emerson and reflects some of their independence, even their crankiness; but, that said, we have said little. Frost outwits classification, as he has outwitted his own time, refusing to bow to it, refusing to be intimidated by it, using it always for his own secret, sly purposes: "I would have written on me on my stone: I have a lover's quarrel with the world."

The poems most of us know—"Mending Wall," "After Apple Picking," "The Road Not Taken," "Stopping by Woods on a Snowy Evening"—remain beautiful. But to find and wind your way into this ironic, humorous, elusive mind it is necessary to read the less familiar Frost of the later years. He has grown more difficult, more philosophical, far more daring, satirical, funny, scathing. Absorb him slowly, over a long period. Who touches Frost touches Proteus.

89. WILLIAM FAULKNER (1897-   )
The Sound and the Fury, As I Lay Dying

William Faulkner has been hailed (except by a few uninfluential dissenters) as the greatest American novelist of his generation. Some critics rank him among the greatest of all time. In France and England his reputation stands even higher than it does among us. In 1949 the award of the Nobel Prize marked at least an official peak in an extraordinary career which shows no sign of slackening vitality.

The front matter of his most recent novel, *The Mansion,* lists twenty-three other Faulkner titles. Most of these are novels and short stories laid in Yoknapatawpha County, Mississippi. This invented region has now become hallowed literary ground, like Hardy's Wessex. The novels' time span covers almost a century and a half, beginning in 1820. They form a connected series, something like Zola's Rougon-Macquart family chronicle or Balzac's more loosely linked "Human Comedy." Through accounts of the fortunes of a number of related families, Faulkner exposes, in a style of great complication and variety, the tragedy, and some of the comedy, of his violent, haunted, guilt-ridden Deep South. Mainly represented are three worlds: that of the Negro; that of the degenerate aristocracy, typified by the Compsons in *The Sound and the Fury*; and that of the even more degenerate emergent commercial class, whose emblem is the horrifying Lem Snopes.

The two novels above recommended are by most critics considered among Faulkner's finest; they are certainly among his most violent in theme and trail-blazing in technique. His champions also single out for high praise *Light in August* and *Absalom, Absalom!* as well as the Snopes trilogy (*The Hamlet, The Town, The Mansion*).

Mr. Faulkner is a serious, difficult, and daring writer. He is also, to some, a shocking writer. And finally, to a few, he is a writer only intermittently readable. The latter do not have the key to his mind, which may well be their loss. To this class I belong. If you need guidance through Mr. Faulkner's special inferno, the only fair thing for me to do is to refer you to any of the books and essays listed in the Suggestions. To my mind the best of these commentaries is Malcolm Cowley's Introduction to his *Portable Faulkner,* a brilliant exercise in sympathetic clarification.

90. ERNEST HEMINGWAY (1898-)
Short Stories

Mr. Hemingway may and, one hopes, will scale new heights in the novel. But at this date, and with the perspective we now have on his brilliant career, it is his short stories, rather than his more ambitious fiction, that stand out. In them the defects of his attitudes have neither time nor space in which to expose themselves. The bellicosity, the conscious virility, the exaltation of violence and toughness, the bravado, the conception of women as romantic receptacles—these are all muted or depersonalized in his marvelous tales. By the same token the famous style, perfectly suited to the illumination of intense moments or isolated situations, gains a power in the short story it does not always possess in the longer works. Another twenty-five years must pass before any mandarin judgment can be laid down. But at this moment it seems fair to say that, by virtue of his reverence for truth, the originality of his prose, the bone-bare exactness of his dialogue, and the charge of his emotion, Hemingway already ranks among the first half dozen of the world's masters of the short story.

Though he seems to grapple with ultimates, such as death, passion, and the defeat or persistence of men's hopes, Hemingway's total world is actually not a large one. In even the lesser novelists we have already met more and wider gateways to human nature. To match him with the greatest is probably pointless. Beside Stendhal he seems young; beside Henry James, primitive; beside Tolstoy, simply minor. Yet his achievement is solid. Building on a foundation laid down by Mark Twain (46), he has quite literally remodeled the English sentence. He has forced it to reveal, without waste motion, the exact truth of a moment, an insight, an experience. This contribution to literature is not merely technical. It is moral. Hemingway has taught language honesty.

His greater tales (with which we must class the *novella The Old Man and the Sea*) are now as much a part of our American heritage as is *Rip Van Winkle* or *The Fall of the House of Usher*. *The Snows of Kilimanjaro, The Undefeated, My Old Man, The Killers, Fifty Grand,* and dozens of others, compel us, no matter how often reread, to relive the experience the creator once felt so deeply. Whether or not we accept Hemingway's view of life, we cannot reject these tales of the veld, the bull ring, the barroom, the ski slope, the race track, the prize ring, the Michigan woods. For they pass beyond the novel settings and beyond the still novel style. Emotion and the control of emotion are here held in exquisite poise. An artist who is also an honest man succeeds in telling the truth.

91. W. SOMERSET MAUGHAM (1874–   )
Of Human Bondage

Here are some facts about the indestructible Maugham:

1. He has written a great deal, much of it for the market.
2. Virtually all of his output has been wildly profitable, and he has made no secret of the fact that he enjoys royalties.
3. None of it has been experimental or novel in form. Because he has never written an obscure line, critics cannot live off Maugham.
4. He has always played down his own achievement, never issued lofty pronouncements on man's destiny, never set himself up as moralist or prophet, but only as a professional writer offering high-grade entertainment.
5. He can be read with ease; unlike Henry James or Faulkner, he has not had to create the taste by which he may be judged.
6. His hallmark is neither passion nor depth. It is good sense.

7. His most solid book appeared almost half a century ago, in 1915.

If you will reflect on these seven facts, you may see why many critics and historians of literature would not include him in any such reading program as ours.

But think of it this way. The great forward leaps in the thought and imagination of the last three millennia have been made by originators. Most of our writers have issued primal communications, for which the duller name is classics. But for any tradition to keep its balance and to permeate the mass of men, there must also be conservators, consolidators, men of acute but not necessarily powerful intelligence. Genius needs the support of high talent. Among contemporary writers of fiction of this order Maugham takes a high, perhaps the highest place. And that is why, apart from his charm, his superb craftsmanship, and his general readability, he is included in this Plan.

To know Maugham is to know an urbane but not superficial mind, thoughtful, tolerant, observant, deeply impressed by the "unaccountability of human beings." He has traveled more widely than any of his contemporaries, always as a detached but not frigid observer. His life has been of a nature to produce a balanced view of things, with no mystical inflections. He is a sensible man. In our neurotic era there is room for such a man, for the play of good sense, cultivation of manner, general enlightenment. These are Maugham's virtues. They may not be the virtues of genius, but they are rare and valuable.

Most of you have probably read *Of Human Bondage*. It deserves rereading. It belongs on the same shelf with *Sons and Lovers* (34), *A Portrait of the Artist as a Young Man*, and *The Magic Mountain* (36), being, like them, a classic picture of the education of a young man, his search for the meaning of life, his quest of freedom. The title (drawn from Spinoza's *Ethics*) suggests what it is about—slavery and partial emancipation. Philip Carey's slavery is to a woman unworthy of him. But the book is more than a study of sexual infatuation. Philip's bondage is unconsciously self-imposed. It symbolizes his self-destructive drives, themselves the consequence of his miserable childhood and his physical handicap, a clubfoot. *Of Human Bondage* is autobiographical, the issue of certain tensions in Maugham's own life which were never to be repeated. Hence it stands alone in his copious output and has a quality of emotion he never quite regained.

I suggest three other books by Maugham. *Cakes and Ale* is a delicious masterpiece, probably the neatest ironical portrait in English of the weaknesses of the literary temperament. Maugham prefers it to his other novels. Small scale, it is not shallow; and as pure composition it has the perfection of a Vermeer. Read also, if possible, at least two of his books of reflective memoirs, *Don Fernando* and *The Summing Up*. They contain the essence of one of the most civilized, illusionless minds now at large among us.

92. E. M. FORSTER (1879–) *A Passage to India*

Compared with a Faulkner or a Hemingway, E. M. Forster has made little noise in the world. He has written only five novels, none of them radiating a portentous air. Of these, four date from before the *First* World War. The fifth, *A Passage to India*, was published in 1924. As a novelist he has since then been silent, though numerous books of essays and biography have appeared. Of the novels only *A Passage to India* has had anything like a popular reception. Why, then, is he included in this short, highly debatable list of contemporary writers?

One reason is that, by the most perceptive critics, he is generally considered the finest of living English novelists. Finest, not greatest. The latter adjective somehow seems inappropriate to Forster; he would reject it himself. The second reason is that though his output is small and almost historical in date, it is weighty in import and as modern as you wish. A third reason: his reputation continues to increase, while that of many of his near contemporaries (Wells, Galsworthy, Bennett, Walpole) ebbs.

Forster's quiet power of survival springs from his special gift for treating crucial problems in human relations in a style showing not even a chemical trace of journalism, a style marked by grace, delicacy, and a pervasive sense of comedy. Comedy rather than satire. Except for a generally liberal viewpoint (which he is quite capable of mocking) he is an uncommitted writer. His values are those of civilization—not Anglo-Saxon civilization or even European civilization, but a kind of civilization of the heart unlinked to any special group or creed.

In *A Passage to India* there are no heroes or villains. The Hindus, the Moslems, the English—they are all at times "right," at times "wrong." Each character, even those the author dislikes, has a certain dignity; each character, even those the author admires, has a certain absurdity. But one quality they all share: they are incapable of perfect communication. This strange and wonderful book (see whether the worn adjective wonderful does not properly apply to the scene in the Marabar Caves) is not about the claims of Indian nationalism; nor about the stupidities of English imperialism; nor about the appeal of Hindu mysticism. All three themes are involved. But if their involvement were the book, *A Passage to India* would now, since the liberation and partition of that subcontinent, be unreadable. This novel is about separateness, about the reverse of Donne's sentence, for every man is also an island unto himself. It is about the barriers we or Fate or God throw up and that isolate us one from another. It is about that possibly permanent tragic condition in human intercourse arising from poor connections.

If you have read *A Passage to India*, reread it. If you have reread it, try Forster's other major novel, *Howards End*. Many consider it his masterpiece.

93. T. S. ELIOT (1888–)
Collected Poems and Plays

In our short list of leading contemporary writers the inclusion of T. S. Eliot is inescapable. Not because, in 1948, he won the Nobel Prize—on balance the prize has more often gone to mediocrities than men of high talent. Nor because he is the (involuntary) leader of a highly vocal and influential school of poets and critics. Nor because he occupies a position in England held in previous eras by such literary popes as Dryden, Addison, and Samuel Johnson. Nor because he is still, at seventy-one, the most controversial figure in contemporary English letters. Nor because the klieg lights of publicity were switched on him when he declared himself "Anglo-Catholic in religion, royalist in politics, and classicist in literature"—a description fitting hundreds of thousands of virtuous and intelligent Britishers. (The fuss made over it sprang from the liberal temperament's besetting weakness, which is parochialism.)

Except in his lucid essays (some of which I recommend you try) Eliot is a difficult writer, though as the years pass he seems less so, for he has educated us to understand him. Difficult or not, his achievement may be stated in grandly simple terms. More than any other living man, he has altered, deepened, and refined the character of English and American poetry in our time. More than any other living man he has supplied modern criticism with a set of elevated and rigorous standards useful as a counterweight to the prevailing sleazy impressionism. In so doing he has retrieved for us or set in a new light a whole series of writers: the minor Elizabethans, the seventeenth-century divines, Dante, Dryden, Donne. To these two achievements he may (it is too soon to tell) add a third: the revival, along lines suitable to the age of the second rather than the first Elizabeth, of poetic drama.

Read his poetry in chronological order. Eliot—and this is not true of all the Plan's writers—is by nature a developer. His growth has been both technical and spiritual. Technically he has passed from verse filled with allusions and quotations, verse often rather tricky and fantastically clever, to verse of great purity, sonority of rhythm, and symphonic form. Spiritually he has moved from the dandiacal irony of the Prufrock poems of 1917, through the detached, terrible despair of *The Waste Land* (1922) to the brooding metaphysical religiousness of the *Four Quartets* (1943).

During the whole of this evolution he has held fast to his original aim: "to digest and express new objects, new groups of objects, new feelings, new aspects." Many of these objects and feelings are repulsive, corresponding to our modern waste land as the traditionalist eyes of Eliot see it. But his purpose is neither to enjoy the luxury of misery nor to shock us with the disagreeable. "The essential advantage for a poet is not to have a beautiful world with which to deal; it is to be able to see beneath both beauty and ugliness; to see the boredom, and the horror, and the glory." All three—the boredom, the horror, the glory—are woven into his verse.

Though it has forebears, Eliot's poetry is nonetheless truly revolutionary, like the fiction of Proust or Joyce. It is exact and condensed on the one hand and rich in magical suggestion on the other. Every word or allusive echo carries its proper weight, and all is borne upon a rhythmic current whose effect becomes evident when you read the lines aloud or listen to Eliot's own recording of them. At first the language seems private, impossible to penetrate. But as one gains familiarity, it begins to emerge as a marvelously precise and evocative rendering of states of mind peculiar to sensitive Western men at this particular stage of our evolution or devolution. And it shares at least one quality with the greatest verse, Shakespeare's or Dante's: it is rich in lines so finally expressive that they remain in our heads forever and become part of our emotional world.

94. ALDOUS HUXLEY (1894–)
Brave New World, Collected Essays

Eliot and Huxley have much in common. Both are of distinguished lineage—Huxley is the grandson of the biologist Thomas Henry Huxley and the grand-nephew of the poet and critic Matthew Arnold. Both are formidably intelligent, as well as formidably learned. Both sum up in their personalities a large part of the Western tradition that is the subject of this book. Both have moved from a position of destructive critical irony to one of faith—Eliot to Anglo-Catholicism, Huxley toward a mysticism drawn from the East but also from such Western visionaries as Blake, Eckhart, Tauler, and others. Eliot's may be the profounder intellect, as he is certainly the greater artist. But Huxley's intellect is more adventurous, more playful, and more closely involved with insistent concrete problems of our time, particularly those pointing the way to race suicide, such as total war and murderous overpopulation.

The variety, the flexibility, the erudition, the sheer brilliance of Huxley's restless mind may be enjoyed through a reading of his essays. He leaves few of the major concerns of man untouched. His skepticism, never cheap or easy, has a cleansing power still to be properly estimated. I know no other single English or American writer who reflects with such clarity the last forty years of shifts and modulations in the Western intellect, including its latest shift toward the thought of the East.

Huxley was famous before he was thirty, a circumstance perhaps not entirely fortunate for him. But the book that gave him a world-wide audience is *Brave New World,* published in 1932, reissued in 1946 with an important new preface by the author. Probably this terrible fable will lose its point and force as unconsciously we take on in reality the condition he describes in fantasy. For our period, however, it is what might be called a temporary classic. No one who really wishes to learn what is happening, not to our environment but to our souls, should remain unacquainted with this nightmare of a book.

The Utopian literature of the twentieth century, unlike that of the Renaissance, is negative. In it we hear not shouts of encouragement but cries of warning. As Berdiaeff, quoted by Huxley, puts it, our concern is not how to attain but how to avoid Utopia. For that Utopia we are so busy preparing is, according to Huxley, Orwell (in his 1984), and dozens of other thoughtful writers, a heaven or hell of dehumanization.

Huxley's *Brave New World,* projected six hundred years into the future, is populated by managed animals (still known as human beings) and their managers. The managed animal has been taught to love his servitude; he is happy, or, as we proudly say, adjusted. The Constitution of the state has but three articles: Community, Identity, Stability. Religion as we know it, art, theoretical science, the family, emotions, individual strivings and differences—all have vanished.

Not a good novel, *Brave New World* should be read as a prophetic fable, differing from other prophecies in that it is the product not of intuition but of cold intelligence. Its ideas (and all its characters are ideas), first advanced almost thirty years ago, have proved prescient. All the gambits of current cocktail party conversation are prefigured in *Brave New World:* the conformist, the Beat nonconformist, the relapse to primitivism, the new chartered sexuality, the organization man, the man in the gray flannel suit, the lonely crowd, the dweller in the Crystal Palace—they are here extended into a future that seems less remote today than it did in 1932.

I do not suggest that *Brave New World* be taken literally. It is not a textbook of the future but a purposely exaggerated satirical vision, in the tradition of *Gulliver.* Doubtless Huxley will rank below Swift. But not too far below. And what he has to say is perhaps more immediate, if less crushing, than Swift's total misanthropy.

95. ANDRÉ MALRAUX (1901–) *Man's Fate*

With Malraux we reach the last of our major writers and one of the most interesting men now alive. Either of two other figures—the late Albert Camus or Jean-Paul Sartre—might well been have chosen to represent contemporary French writing. Both are distinguished, both influential, and Camus is a Nobel Prize winner. Both deserve close reading; but I cannot help feeling that the biography and work of André Malraux are in a class by themselves.

To convince yourself of this, read the brilliant study "The Human Condition" in Janet Flanner's *Men and Monuments* (see Suggestions). It tells us as much about Malraux's fantastic career as is learnable at the moment. Otherwise a highly modern type, he considers his private life his own property.

As a man of action Malraux has been involved, often responsibly, in several insurrections, revolutions, and wars: China in 1925-1927, the Spanish Civil War (sixty-five flights over enemy territory, two wounds); the Resistance (wounded, captured, escaped, rising to a colonelcy, decorated). As a political figure he has held Kuomintang office, a cabinet ministry in De Gaulle's provisional government, and is currently engaged in reorganizing the French theater as the Minister of State for Information. As an adventurer-explorer-archaeologist he has tracked down virtually unknown works of art in the jungles of Indo-China and has flown over what may have been (considerable doubt here) the fabled capital city of the Queen of Sheba. As esthetician and philosopher of art he has in his monumental *The Voices of Silence* revolutionized our way of looking at the art monuments of the world. He is an orator and conversationalist of major proportions. His erudition is apparently endless. His political evolution, from Popular Frontism to Gaullism, though bizarre, has no trace in it of either the hysterical or the opportunistic. He is generally conceded, in a country where the production of intelligence is virtually a major industry, to be one of the most intelligent Frenchmen alive.

To add to all this, he is a stunning novelist.

Man's Fate, translated into sixteen languages, is probably his masterpiece. Its setting is Shanghai and its ostensible subject the aborted Shanghai insurrection of 1927. What Malraux said of an earlier novel *The Conquerors* is true of *Man's Fate*: "The principal emphasis is on the relation between individuals and a collective action, not in collective action alone . . . The book is first of all a representation of the human condition."

La condition humaine . . . the phrase, now famous, found in Pascal and others, is the French title of *Man's Fate.* It deals with revolution, which Malraux sees as the key tragic experience of our century. But it is not a revolutionary novel in the Marxist sense. It is a terrifying study, which should have been illustrated by El Greco, of the paroxysms of violence, tension, eroticism, sadism, and courage which convulse men engaged in revolutionary action. It is about as far from the proletarian novel as are the fictions of Dostoevski, Malraux's master, if so original a writer may be said to have one.

In another of his novels, *Man's Hope,* a character asks and answers a question: "What can a man best do in his life? Translate into consciousness the largest possible experience." In Malraux's universe of emotion the deepest experience a man can have is the foretaste of death, against which inevitability he marshals all the resources of his tragic but indomitable nature. At their richest these resources produce Art, which Malraux sees as "a revolt against man's fate," as "an attempt to give men a consciousness of their own hidden powers." Thus his novels, though their content is often horrifying, are not negative or depressing. True, they do not reveal us to ourselves in our more normal, our quieter aspects. But for Malraux our century has already dedicated itself to a mode of experience in which quietude and normality are overborne by the increasing domination of catastrophic change, by terror, by recurrent situations in which the human will is tested on the rack of history, sometimes to be broken, sometimes to be exalted.

Malraux is Hemingway grown up.

Miscellaneous

96. E. H. GOMBRICH (1900–   )
The Story of Art

(The Lifetime Reading Plan is concerned mainly with original communications in the domain of words. But the stream of Western culture is made up of more than words, indeed far more than words. The serious reader, with a lifetime in which to do it, should reinforce and supplement his growing knowledge and enjoyment of works of literature and reflection with some study of the closely related achievements of the Western creative imagination and intellect in the arts and sciences. I have therefore noted below and in the Suggestions a few secondary works in only three essential areas: art, mathematics, and the physical sciences. As for the arts, the truly satisfactory way to gain insight is by contemplation of the originals or first-rate reproductions. Nevertheless a well-illustrated, authoritative book can be helpful. I would like to believe that is equally true of music. The facts can be learned from any one of many excellent histories of Western music. But by their nature they cannot affect the only genuine organ of appreciation, which is the ear. Hence I list none. Our Plan concludes with two miscellaneous volumes, one a manual of reading, the other an anthology. Their possible uses are indicated under 99 and 100.)

There is no recognized classic in this fascinating, crowded, and controversial field. The Suggestions list several works, including one confined to modern art since David (1748-1825).

I have chosen Mr. Gombrich's book for several reasons. It is neither so short as to be superficial nor so long as to be overwhelming. The author begins his story with prehistoric and primitive peoples, carrying it through the centuries down to the experimental art of our own day. The emphasis is dominantly on European art, but there are sections on Egypt, Mesopotamia, Islam, and China. The book contains 370 intelligently chosen illustrations, a fair number in full color. No illustration is shown that is not discussed in the text, an excellent feature. The discussion itself deals only with real works of art (including architecture and sculpture) and not with eccentricities, however interesting, or minor examples. Mr. Gombrich stresses well-known masterpieces, a policy that pays dividends to the beginner in this field. His interest is not in rhapsodizing over "beauties" but in tracking down the artist's intention, estimating his success, and placing his work, without undue forcing, in its historical frame.

My preference for this book over many other fine histories, however, is based largely on its style. In planning and writing it, the author tells us, he had in mind first and foremost "readers in their teens who had just discovered the world of art for themselves." But the result is not in the least elementary. Here is a book suitable for any adult except the one whose knowledge is already considerable. The style is marked by simplicity, clarity, and candor. The approach is sensible and humane. There is no jargon, but no patronizing note either. I have learned much from it and, more to the point, enjoyed learning. As I have no expertness in the field, I feel my own experience with Mr. Gombrich may well prefigure that of many of my readers.

For those who wish to pursue the subject the author includes "A Note on Art Books," an excellent bibliography of more specialized works. See also my own Suggestions.

97. ALFRED NORTH WHITEHEAD (1861–1947)
An Introduction to Mathematics

That our modern scientific-technological-industrial-war-making culture rests ultimately on a mathematical base needs no demonstration. The platform of mathematics supports the physical sciences and, increasingly, the biological and even the social sciences, particularly economics. Nowadays a casual acquaintance with a few equations is needed even to satisfy our human curiosity as to just how the next war, or series of wars, hopes to kill, maim, poison, or pulverize us, as well as to deform and/or drive mad our descendants.

Mathematics is not only a magnificent science and a powerful language, but a moving art. It may be contemplated in a humanistic as well as a technical spirit. An interest in mathematics is often found in writers who have won eminence in other fields. Among the artists and thinkers we have met, Plato, Lewis Carroll, Hobbes, Whitehead, Descartes, and Pascal were professional mathematicians. Artists like Leonardo, Uccello, and Dürer were informed with mathematical imagination. The thought of others, such as Dante, Voltaire, Poe, Marx, Donne, and Adams, was to a marked degree influenced by mathematical conceptions. The scientist and the humanist are not opposed types; and, should they feel themselves in opposition, they are, by that very token, inferior scientists or humanists.

If we could all read the original communications of men like Kepler or Fourier or Huygens or Newton or Archimedes, The Lifetime Reading Plan would have included them. But it is unrealistic to think that we can. The best most of us can aim at is some superficial sense of the major ideas underlying scientific and mathematical thought. Thus we may correct and balance the lopsidedness that comes of an exclusive attention to works of the imagination, as conventionally defined.

Whitehead we have met before (58) in other connections. In

his own right he was a mathematician of high, if not the first, order. The little book suggested above was written almost fifty years ago. It takes no account therefore of the tremendous advances made in our own time. That is for our purposes unimportant. Whitehead, writing here for the general nonmathematical public, is not concerned with the evolution of the subject, nor with its higher reaches. He proposes to give a clear explanation of its fundamental ideas and to bound its major compartments. His book runs to only 250 small pages, yet it cannot be read both properly and quickly. On the other hand, though it contains a moderate amount of mathematical symbolism, it is possible for us to grasp the basic notions without working out, or even completely understanding, every formula and equation.

If you have both time and interest, it is advisable to supplement Whitehead with one or more of the titles listed in the Suggestions. I hope you will find this worth while. You may, as I once did myself, think you are neither interested in the subject nor able to understand it. Yet (and this is true equally of that presumed bugaboo, poetry) the more intimate your acquaintance with the mathematical imagination, the more rewarding the experience becomes.

A life passed with no knowledge of mathematics and the physical sciences is to a degree that unexamined life Socrates thought not worth living.

98. LINCOLN BARNETT (1909–)
The Universe and Dr. Einstein

One of the aims of the Plan is to give the Lifetime reader a sense, growing constantly deeper and clearer, of his own location in the world of Western thought and imagination. But it is no less useful and interesting to have some sense of where we stand in the physical universe also, for the two senses reinforce each other. Over the centuries our location has changed, and our minds have changed accordingly. The savage, looking at the stars in wonder or fear, lives at one cosmic address; Periclean man at another; Ptolemaic man at another; Copernican and Newtonian men at still another.

Einstein, quantum physics, and relativity theory have changed our address once more. We today live in a world of space and time—and therefore of thought—somewhat different from that of our grandfathers. One of the consequences of this shift is that we read the literature of the past in a different perspective. The terror of Pascal (65) as he viewed the infinity of space has more meaning for us than it did for his contemporaries, or at least an altered meaning. This shift in perspective is less marked, of course, when we read poets and novelists than when we read philosophers.

My reason for recommending Mr. Barnett's brief exposition (you can read it in two hours) is not only that it outlines the major conclusions of modern quantum and cosmological theory. My reason is also that it suggests to us a feeling of our place in the universe, as far as we can determine it today. Thus we are helped to set the whole Western tradition in the largest possible frame of physical fact and speculation.

There are many excellent books on the same theme. I know of none, however, at once so clear, so condensed, and so suitable for readers like me, who are without scientific training. In a brief foreword Einstein himself endorses Mr. Barnett's work as "a valuable contribution to popular scientific writing," and goes on to praise its presentation of both the theory of relativity and the present state of our knowledge of physics. The interested reader who wishes to pursue this mind-enlarging subject (as well as to delve deeper into related sciences) will find a few other books listed in the Suggestions.

99. MORTIMER J. ADLER (1902–)
How To Read a Book

For half a century I have been an amateur reader and for a third of a century both an amateur and a professional one. But I am still learning how to read. I do not mean how to decipher words. That is merely a useful trick, just slightly above the capacity of a chimpanzee. It is taught, more or less, in the schools, and suffices for the reading of most books and magazines, virtually all newspapers, and absolutely all lavatory signs. I mean the reading of books of some weight and density, into which went hard mental work and out of which comes real mental change. Such are the ones we have been considering in the Plan. Such reading involves a complex, often intense activity, not the passive reception of the author's message. And the result of such reading is not "finishing the book" but starting something endless in the reader's mind.

Mr. Adler's well-known work is an honest one, but it is not quite honestly titled. It should be called something like *How To Read a Great Book* or *How To Read an Original Communication*. He says, "I have tried to write a light book about heavy reading." Always clear, he is not light. But the "heavy reading" part is true enough. His rules, in fact, are more useful for philosophy and the sciences than they are for the reading of pure works of the imagination. Yet they are of some profit in all cases.

I speak of rules; and there are rules here, and concrete tips, and a whole course of instruction. Still, this is no manual. Rather is it, as the author says, "a book about reading in relation to life, liberty, and the pursuit of happiness." It is less about reading as a specific action than about a liberal education in general, about the links that connect great literature with free minds and so with free men. The ideas animating *How To Read a Book* are those animating the book you now hold in your hand; and it was from Mr. Adler, among other great teachers, that I learned them.

As I suggested in the introductory talk with the reader, perhaps you should digest Mr. Adler first, before starting on the Plan. But this is not essential, any more than it is essential that you follow his prescriptions literally. It is the spirit, not the letter, of his exhortation that counts.

The appendix lists a whole library of great books, duplicating our own in part, but laying much greater stress on works of theology, philosophy, and the physical and social sciences.

100. *The American Treasury*, 1455-1955, SELECTED, ARRANGED, AND EDITED BY Clifton Fadiman (1904–), ASSISTED BY Charles Van Doren (1926–)

I wanted to end our Plan with some book that would give us back our own country between two covers. No such book exists, nor can there ever be one. Because I wanted to make a stab at it, however, I once, assisted by Charles Van Doren, spent three years on an anthology which, whatever its faults (and they are many), at least has the virtue of having no exact fellow. I believe it is a good book, but its editors have very little to do with its goodness, for it was written by the people of the United States of America. As I cannot speak of it myself, I here append a brief review by Russell Lynes. This originally appeared in *American Panorama*, edited by Eric Larrabee. I am indebted to the New York University Press for permission to quote.

> Somewhere between a book of quotations and an anthology, *The American Treasury, 1455-1955* is an attempt to provide a portrait of America, its spirit, its landscape, its dominant philosophies, and the nature (both

serious and comic) of its men and women. It is more than a grab bag of excerpts from the writings, speeches, conversations, slogans, and witticisms that have accumulated to form a spoken and written American literature; it is an orderly assemblage from a vast mass of material of those statements that are most characteristic of the workings of the American mind at its best and sometimes at its worst. It is a portrait with all the wrinkles left in. It includes the petulant words of demagogues along with the professions of faith in liberty and justice of America's greatest statesmen. It juxtaposes the solemn with the frivolous, the serious with the witty, the philosophic with the mindless, the inspirational with the cynical. It omits only the pedantic or tiresome.

The American Treasury can be read from start to finish, as its editors planned it, or it can be used for sampling or for reference; it is excellently indexed by subjects, authors, titles, and familiar words and phrases. It includes passages from every American author of enduring stature and from many whom time had all but buried and who are here resurrected, from farmers and historians, from Presidents and burlesque comedians, advertising copywriters, poets, scientists, song writers, and anonymous sages and wits.

In the introductory essays in his "general preface," Mr. Fadiman has not only explained the intentions of this volume but has put the selections into perspective for the reader. In his "Envoi" he draws from the 6,000 items a brief portrait of the American as he is revealed in both the statements he has made about himself and those others have made about him. "Wisdom is not our forte," he writes, "nor perfection of utterance. But the Adamic quality of beginningness is."

Bibliography

Suggestions for Further Reading

Bibliography

1. HOMER. *The Iliad*

Anger of Achilles: Homer's Iliad, trans. by Robert Graves, illus. by Ronald Searle. Doubleday, $4.95.

The Iliad, trans. by Richmond Lattimore. University of Chicago Press, $4.50.

The Iliad, trans. by E. V. Rieu. Penguin Books, $0.95.

The Iliad, trans. by W. H. D. Rouse. New American Library, $0.50.

2. HOMER. *The Odyssey*

The Odyssey, trans. by T. E. Shaw (Lawrence of Arabia). Oxford University Press, Galaxy Books, $1.50.

The Odyssey, trans. by E. V. Rieu. Penguin Books, $0.85.

The Odyssey, trans. by W. H. D. Rouse. New American Library, $0.50.

3. HERODOTUS. *The Histories*

The Persian Wars, trans. by George Rawlinson in *The Greek Historians,* edited by Francis R. B. Godolphin. Random House, 2 vols. boxed, $10.00.

Works, trans. by J. E. Powell. Oxford University Press, 2 vols., $4.80.

History, trans. by George Rawlinson, edited by Manuel Komroff. Tudor Publishing Co., $2.98.

The Persian Wars, trans. by George Rawlinson, introd. by Francis R. B. Godolphin. Modern Library, $1.65.

The Histories, trans. by Aubrey de Selincourt. Penguin Books, $1.25.

4. THUCYDIDES. *The History of the Peloponnesian War*

The Peloponnesian War, trans. by Benjamin Jowett in *The Greek Historians*, edited by Francis R. B. Godolphin. Random House, 2 vols. boxed, $10.00.

The Peloponnesian War, trans. by Thomas Hobbes, edited by David Grene. University of Michigan Press, 2 vols. boxed, $6.95.
(A classic seventeenth-century version.)

The History of the Peloponnesian War, trans. by Richard Crawley, introd. by John Warrington. E. P. Dutton, Everyman's Library, $2.45.

Complete Writings: The Peloponnesian War, trans. by Richard Crawley, introd. by John H. Finley, Jr. Modern Library, $1.65.

History of the Peloponnesian War, edited in trans. by R. W. Livingstone, illus. Oxford University Press, World's Classics, $1.65.

The Peloponnesian War, trans. by Rex Warner. Penguin Books, $1.25.

Complete Writings: The Peloponnesian War, trans. by Richard Crawley, introd. by John H. Finley, Jr. Modern Library College Editions, $0.85.

5. PLATO. *Selected Works*

Dialogues, trans. by Benjamin Jowett, introd. by Raphael Demos. Random House, 2 vols. boxed, $7.50.
(A classic, but markedly Victorian version.)

Works, trans. by Benjamin Jowett, selected by Irwin Edman. Tudor Publishing Co., $4.98.

The Portable Plato (*Protagoras, Phaedo, Symposium, The Republic*), trans. by Benjamin Jowett, edited by Scott Buchanan. Viking Press, $2.95.

The Republic, trans. by F. M. Cornford. Oxford University Press, $2.75.

Works, trans. by Benjamin Jowett, selected and edited by Irwin Edman. Modern Library, $1.65.

Selected Passages, edited by R. W. Livingstone. Oxford University Press, World's Classics, $1.65.

The Republic, trans. by Benjamin Jowett. Modern Library, $1.65.

The Republic, trans. by Benjamin Jowett, introd. by Scott Buchanan, illus. by Laszlo Matulay. World Publishing Co., Living Library, $1.65.

Plato: Portrait of Socrates (*The Apology, Crito, Phaedo*), edited by R. W. Livingstone. Oxford University Press, $1.60.

The Portable Plato (*Protagoras, Phaedo, Symposium, The Republic*), trans. by Benjamin Jowett, edited by Scott Buchanan. Viking Press Paperbound Editions, $1.45.

The Republic, trans. by Benjamin Jowett. Modern Library Paperbacks, $1.25.

The Republic, trans. by F. M. Cornford. Oxford University Press, $1.00.

The Republic, trans. by H. D. P. Lee. Penguin Books, $0.85.

The Symposium, trans. by Walter Hamilton. Penguin Books, $0.65.

Protagoras and Meno, trans. by W. K. C. Guthrie. Penguin Books, $0.65.

Great Dialogues of Plato, trans. by W. H. D. Rouse. New American Library, $0.50.

Dialogues, trans. by Benjamin Jowett, edited by J. D. Kaplan. Pocket Books, $0.35.

6. ARISTOTLE. *Ethics, Politics*

Basic Works, the Oxford trans. by W. R. Roberts and I. Bywater, edited by Richard P. McKeon. Random House, $6.00.

Introduction to Aristotle, edited by Richard P. McKeon. Modern Library, $1.65.

Nicomachean Ethics, trans. by David Ross. Oxford University Press, World's Classics, $1.65.

Ethics, trans. by J. A. K. Thomson. Penguin Books, $0.95.

Politics, trans. by Benjamin Jowett, introd. by H. W. C. Davis. Oxford University Press, $2.40.

Politics, trans. by Benjamin Jowett, introd. by Max Lerner. Modern Library, $1.65.

7. AESCHYLUS. *The Oresteia*

The Complete Greek Tragedies (includes excellent modern versions of the works of Aeschylus, Sophocles, and Euripides), edited by David Grene and Richmond Lattimore. University of Chicago Press, 4 vols. boxed, $20.00.

The Oresteian Trilogy, trans. by George Thomson in *The Portable Greek Reader,* edited by W. H. Auden. Viking Press, $2.95.

The Oresteian Trilogy, trans. by George Thomson in *The Portable Greek Reader,* edited by W. H. Auden. Viking Press Paperbound Editions, $1.45.

The Oresteian Trilogy, trans. by Philip Vellacott. Penguin Books, $0.85.

8. SOPHOCLES. *Oedipus Cycle*

The Complete Greek Tragedies (see above under Aeschylus.)
Oedipus the King, trans. by David Grene; *Oedipus at Colonus,* trans. by Robert Fitzgerald; *Antigone,* trans. by Elizabeth Wyckoff. University of Chicago Press, $3.00.
Oedipus the King, trans. by David Grene; *Oedipus at Colonus,* trans. by Robert Fitzgerald; *Antigone,* trans. by Elizabeth Wyckoff. University of Chicago Press, $1.25.
Three Theban Plays: Antigone, Oedipus the King, Oedipus at Colonus, trans. by T. H. Banks. Oxford University Press, $1.25.
Oedipus Cycle: Oedipus Rex, trans. by Dudley Fitts and Robert Fitzgerald; *Oedipus at Colonus,* trans. by Robert Fitzgerald; *Antigone,* trans. by Dudley Fitts and Robert Fitzgerald. Harcourt, Brace, Harvest Books, $1.15.
Oedipus Plays of Sophocles, trans. by Paul Roche. New American Library, $0.75.
Theban Plays, trans. by E. F. Watling. Penguin Books, $0.65.
Oedipus the King, trans. by Bernard M. W. Knox. Washington Square Press, $0.35.

9. EURIPIDES. *Plays*

The Complete Greek Tragedies (see above under Aeschylus.)
Alcestis, trans. by Richmond Lattimore; *Medea,* trans. by Rex Warner; *Heracleidae,* trans. by Ralph Gladstone; *Hippolytus,* trans. by David Grene. University of Chicago Press, $3.75.
Alcestis, trans. by Richmond Lattimore; *Medea,* trans. by Rex Warner; *Heracleidae,* trans. by Ralph Gladstone; *Hippolytus,* trans. by David Grene. University of Chicago Press, $1.25.
Three Great Plays of Euripides: Medea, Hippolytus, Helen, trans. by Rex Warner. New American Library, $0.75.

Alcestis and Other Plays (*Hippolytus, Iphigenia in Tauris*), trans. by Philip Vellacott. Penguin Books, $0.65.

Hippolytus, trans. by Rex Warner. Michigan State University Press, $1.50.

10. LUCRETIUS. *Of the Nature of Things*

On the Nature of Things, trans. by W. H. D. Rouse. Harvard University Press, Loeb Library, $3.50.

On the Nature of Things, trans. by H. A. J. Munro in *The Stoic and Epicurean Philosophers*, edited by Whitney J. Oates. Modern Library Giants, $2.95.

Of the Nature of Things, trans. by W. E. Leonard. E. P. Dutton, Everyman's Library, $2.45.

Of the Nature of Things, trans. by W. E. Leonard. E. P. Dutton, Everyman's Paperbacks, $0.95.

Nature of the Universe, trans. by R. E. Latham. Penguin Books, $0.85.

11. VIRGIL. *The Aeneid*

The Aeneid, trans. by Rolfe Humphries. Charles Scribner's Sons, $3.50.

The Aeneid, trans. by Michael Oakley, introd. by E. M. Forster. E. P. Dutton, Everyman's Library, $1.85.

The Aeneid, trans. by Rolfe Humphries. Charles Scribner's Sons, $1.45.

The Aeneid, trans. by C. Day Lewis. Doubleday, Anchor Books, $0.95.

The Aeneid, trans. by W. F. Jackson Knight. Penguin Books, $0.95.

The Aeneid, edited and trans. by Kevin Guinagh. Rinehart, $0.75.

12. MARCUS AURELIUS. *Meditations*

Meditations, trans. by George Long in *The Stoic and Epicurean Philosophers*, edited by Whitney J. Oates. Modern Library Giants, $2.95.

Thoughts, trans. by John Jackson. Oxford University Press, World's Classics, $1.65.

Meditations, trans. by George Long. Peter Pauper Press, Pocket Editions, $1.00.

Thoughts of Marcus Aurelius, edited and trans. by George Long. David McKay Co., $1.00.

13. ST. AUGUSTINE. *Confessions*

Basic Writings of St. Augustine (includes the *Confessions*, large sections of *The City of God*, plus other works), edited by Whitney J. Oates. Random House, 2 vols. boxed, $7.50 each; set $12.50.

Confessions, edited by F. J. Sheed. Sheed and Ward, $3.50.

Confessions of Saint Augustine, trans. by E. B. Pusey, introd. by Fulton J. Sheen. Modern Library, $1.65.

Confessions of St. Augustine, trans. by E. B. Pusey. Thomas Nelson, Nelson Classics, $1.25.

Confessions of St. Augustine, introd. by H. C. Gardiner. Pocket Books, $0.35.

14. DANTE. *The Divine Comedy*

The Divine Comedy, trans. by Laurence Binyon. St. Martin's Press, 3 vols., $7.50.

The Divine Comedy, Carlyle-Wicksteed trans., Italian text and English trans. on facing pages. E. P. Dutton, 3 vols., $4.50.

The Divine Comedy, trans. by Laurence Binyon in *The Portable Dante*, edited by Paolo Milano. Viking Press, $2.95.

The Divine Comedy, Carlyle-Wicksteed trans., introd. by C. H. Grandgent. Modern Library, $1.65.

The Divine Comedy, trans. by M. B. Anderson. Oxford University Press, World's Classics, $1.65.

The Divine Comedy, trans. by Laurence Binyon in *The Portable Dante*, edited by Paolo Milano. Viking Press Paperbound Editions, $1.45.

The Divine Comedy, Carlyle-Wicksteed trans., introd. by C. H. Grandgent, Modern Library Paperbacks, $1.25.

The Divine Comedy, trans. by Thomas G. Bergin. Appleton-Century-Crofts, Crofts Classics, $0.95.

The Divine Comedy, trans. by H. R. Huse. Rinehart, $0.95.

The Divine Comedy, Carlyle-Wicksteed trans., introd. by C. H. Grandgent. Modern Library College Editions, $0.85.

The Inferno, trans. by John Ciardi. New American Library, $0.50.

15. CHAUCER. *The Canterbury Tales*

Works (Facsimile of *Kelmscott Chaucer*), introd. by J. T. Winterich, illus. by Edward Burne-Jones. World Publishing Co., $17.50.

Complete Works, edited by W. W. Skeat. Oxford University Press, $3.50.

Complete Works, edited by A. W. Pollard. St. Martin's Press, $3.00.

The Canterbury Tales, trans. by J. U. Nicolson, introd. by G. H. Gerould, illus. by Rockwell Kent. Doubleday, Garden City, $2.95.

The Canterbury Tales, edited by W. W. Skeat, introd. by Louis Untermeyer. Modern Library, $1.65.

The Canterbury Tales, edited by W. W. Skeat. Oxford University Press, World's Classics, $1.65.

The Canterbury Tales, trans. by Nevill Coghill. Penguin Books, $1.45.

The Canterbury Tales, edited and trans. by R. M. Lumiansky. Rinehart, $0.95.

The Canterbury Tales, edited by Robert D. French. Appleton-Century-Crofts, Crofts Classics, $0.45.

16. SHAKESPEARE. *Complete Works*

(Single-volume editions are listed first and then collections.)

Complete Works, edited by G. B. Harrison. Harcourt, Brace, $11.75.

Complete Works, edited by G. L. Kittredge. Ginn, $8.50.

Complete Plays and Poems, edited by W. A. Neilson and C. J. Hill. Houghton Mifflin Co., $7.50.

Works (Shakespeare Head Edition), edited by A. H. Bullen. Oxford University Press, $6.50.

Complete Works (Temple Edition notes), preface by Christopher Morley, illus. by Rockwell Kent. Doubleday, Garden City, $5.95.

Complete Works, edited by W. J. Craig. Oxford University Press, $4.00.

Complete Works (Globe Library), edited by W. G. Clark and W. A. Wright. Grosset and Dunlap, $3.95.

Complete Works (Globe Library), edited by W. G. Clark and W. A. Wright. St. Martin's Press, $3.75.

Complete Works (Temple Edition notes), illus. by T. M. Matterson. World Publishing Co., $3.50.

Complete Works (*Comedies, Histories and Poems, Tragedies*), edited by Edward Dowden, introd. by A. C. Swinburne. Oxford University Press, 3 vols., $12.00.

Comedies, 2 vols; *Histories; Histories and Poems; Tragedies,* 2 vols. Modern Library, 6 vols., $1.65 each; set $9.90.

Comedies; Historical Plays; Tragedies, vol. 1; *Tragedies and*

Poems, vol. 2; edited by Peter Alexander. W. W. Norton, New Collins Classics, 4 vols., $1.45 each; set $5.80.

Comedies, Histories and Poems, Tragedies, edited by W. G. Clark and W. A. Wright. E. P. Dutton, Everyman's Library, 3 vols., $5.55.

(In addition, there are many individual plays in paperbound editions: the new Laurel Shakespeare which now has twelve volumes (Dell Books, $0.35 each); Pocket Library Shakespeare, twelve volumes, including the new Folger Library editions (Pocket Books, $0.35 each); also the more scholarly treatments of the Yale Shakespeare, with twelve volumes in paper (Yale University Press, $0.75 each). Pelican Shakespeare has seventeen titles published, five in preparation (Penguin Books, $0.50-$0.65 each). Sixteen titles of Kittredge's edition are in paperbacks (Ginn, $0.75 each).)

17. MOLIÈRE. *Selected Plays*

Six Prose Comedies of Molière, trans. by George Graveley. Oxford University Press, $3.75.

Eight Plays, trans. with an introd. by Morris Bishop. Modern Library, $1.65.

Misanthrope and Other Plays, trans. by John Wood. Penguin Books, $0.95.

Eight Plays, trans. with an introd. by Morris Bishop. Modern Library College Editions, $0.85.

18. GOETHE. *Faust*

Faust, trans. by George Priest. Alfred A. Knopf, $5.75.

Faust, trans. by Bayard Taylor, introd. by Victor Lang. Modern Library, $1.65.

Faust: A Tragedy in Two Parts, trans. by Bayard Taylor, introd.

by Marshall Montgomery. Oxford University Press, World's Classics, $1.65.

Faust, trans. by Philip Wayne. Penguin Books; Part 1, $0.65; Part 2, $0.95.

Faust, edited and trans. by Louis MacNeice. Oxford University Press, $1.50.

Faust, trans. by Bayard Taylor, introd. by Victor Lang. Modern Library College Editions, $0.75.

19. IBSEN. *Selected Plays*

Eleven Plays, introd. by Eric Bentley. Modern Library Giants, $2.95.

Six Plays: A Doll's House, Ghosts, An Enemy of the People, Rosmersholm, Hedda Gabler, The Master Builder, trans. and edited by Eva Le Gallienne. Modern Library, $1.65.

Six Plays: A Doll's House, Ghosts, An Enemy of the People, Rosmersholm, Hedda Gabler, The Master Builder, trans. and edited by Eva Le Gallienne. Modern Library College Editions, $0.75.

Three Plays: Ghosts, An Enemy of the People, The Wild Duck, edited by Benfield Pressey. Rinehart, $0.75.

Three Plays: The Wild Duck, Hedda Gabler, A Doll's House, introd. by Seymour L. Flaxman. Dell Books, $0.50.

Four Great Plays: A Doll's House, Ghosts, An Enemy of the People, The Wild Duck. Bantam Books, $0.50.

20. SHAW. *Selected Plays and Prefaces*

Seven Plays (With Prefaces and Notes). Dodd, Mead, $6.00.

Four Plays: Candida, Caesar and Cleopatra, Pygmalion, Heartbreak House, introd. by Louis Kronenberger. Modern Library, $1.65.

Selected Plays and Other Writings: Arms and the Man,

Candida, Man and Superman, introd. by William Irvine, foreword by R. Martin Browne. Rinehart, $0.95.

Four Plays: Candida, Devil's Disciple, Caesar and Cleopatra, Captain Brassbound's Conversion. Dell Books, $0.50.

(In addition, many plays may be bought separately in Penguin editions for $0.35-$0.65.)

21. BUNYAN. *The Pilgrim's Progress*

The Pilgrim's Progress, introd. by G. B. Harrison. E. P. Dutton, Everyman's Library, $1.85.

The Pilgrim's Progress. Oxford University Press, World's Classics, $1.65.

The Pilgrim's Progress, introd. by H. R. Williamson. W. W. Norton, New Collins Classics, $0.95.

The Pilgrim's Progress, edited by Louis L. Martz. Rinehart, $0.95.

The Pilgrim's Progress, introd. by Alexander M. Witherspoon. Pocket Books, $0.35.

22. DEFOE. *Robinson Crusoe*

Robinson Crusoe, introd. by May Lamberton Becker, illus. by Roger Duvoisin. World Publishing Co., Rainbow Classics, $2.50.

Robinson Crusoe, introd. by Guy N. Pocock. E. P. Dutton, Everyman's Library, $1.85.

Life and Adventures of Robinson Crusoe. Oxford University Press, World's Classics, $1.65.

Robinson Crusoe and Journal of the Plague Year, introd. by Louis Kronenberger. Modern Library, $1.65.

Robinson Crusoe (the Shakespeare Head text), introd. by Frederick Brereton. W. W. Norton, New Collins Classics, $1.25.

Robinson Crusoe, introd. by Douglas Knight. Pocket Books, $0.50.

23. SWIFT. *Gulliver's Travels and Other Works*

The Portable Swift, edited by Carl Van Doren. Viking Press, $2.95.

Gulliver's Travels and Other Writings, introd. by Ricardo Quintana. Modern Library, $1.65.

The Portable Swift, edited by Carl Van Doren. Viking Press Paperbound Editions, $1.45.

Gulliver's Travels and Other Writings, introd. by Ricardo Quintana. Modern Library Paperbacks, $0.95.

Gulliver's Travels and Other Writings, introd. by Ricardo Quintana. Modern Library College Editions, $0.75.

Gulliver's Travels and Other Writings, edited by Louis A. Landa. Houghton Mifflin Co., Riverside Editions, in prep.

Gulliver's Travels, introd. by May Lamberton Becker, illus. by R. M. Powers. World Publishing Co., Rainbow Classics, $2.50.

Gulliver's Travels, introd. by George Sherburn. Harper, Harper's Modern Classics, $1.25.

Gulliver's Travels (the Nonesuch Edition text), edited by John Hayward, introd. by Peter Quennell. W. W. Norton, New Collins Classics, $0.95.

Gulliver's Travels, edited by John F. Ross. Rinehart, $0.65.

Gulliver's Travels, introd. by Maxwell Geismar. Pocket Books, $0.35.

24. STERNE. *Tristram Shandy*

Tristram Shandy, introd. by Bergen Evans. Modern Library, $1.65.

Life and Opinions of Tristram Shandy, Gentleman. Oxford University Press, World's Classics, $1.65.

Tristram Shandy, introd. by T. C. Livingstone. W. W. Norton, New Collins Classics, $1.45.

Tristram Shandy, edited by Samuel Holt Monk. Rinehart, $0.95.

Tristram Shandy, introd. by Bergen Evans. Modern Library College Editions, $0.85.

Life and Opinions of Tristram Shandy, Gentleman, introd. by Maxwell Geismar. Pocket Books, $0.50.

25. FIELDING. *Tom Jones*

Tom Jones, introd. by George Sherburn. Modern Library, $1.65.

Tom Jones, introd. by Alan Pryce-Jones. W. W. Norton, New Collins Classics, $1.65.

Tom Jones, introd. by George Sherburn. Modern Library Paperbacks, $1.25.

Tom Jones, introd. by George Sherburn. Modern Library College Editions, $0.85.

26. AUSTEN. *Pride and Prejudice, Emma*

Pride and Prejudice, introd. by May Lamberton Becker, illus. by Edgard Cirlin. World Publishing Co., Rainbow Classics, $2.50.

Pride and Prejudice, introd. by R. W. Chapman. Oxford University Press, $1.65.

Pride and Prejudice, introd. by Austin Dobson, illus. by Charles E. Brock. St. Martin's Press, $1.50.

Pride and Prejudice, introd. by Louis Kronenberger. Harper, Harper's Modern Classics, $1.25.

Pride and Prejudice, introd. by V. S. Pritchett. W. W. Norton, New Collins Classics, $0.95.

Pride and Prejudice, introd. by Mark Schorer. Houghton Mifflin Co., Riverside Editions, $0.75.

Pride and Prejudice, edited by Robert Daniel. Rinehart, $0.75.

Pride and Prejudice. Dell Books, $0.50.

Emma, edited by E. V. Lucas. Oxford University Press, World's Classics, $1.65.

Emma, introd. by Austin Dobson, illus. by Hugh Thomson. St. Martin's Press, $1.50.

Emma, introd. by G. B. Stern. W. W. Norton, New Collins Classics, $1.25.

Emma, introd. by Lionel Trilling. Houghton Mifflin Co., Riverside Editions. $0.95.

Emma, Bantam Books, $0.50.

Complete Novels. Modern Library Giants, $2.95.

27. EMILY BRONTË. *Wuthering Heights*

Wuthering Heights, introd. by May Lamberton Becker, illus. by Nell Booker. World Publishing Co., Rainbow Classics, $2.50.

Wuthering Heights and Selected Poems, introd. by Margaret Lane. E. P. Dutton, Everyman's Library, $1.85.

Wuthering Heights, introd. by H. W. Garrod. Oxford University Press, World's Classics, $1.65.

Wuthering Heights, introd. by Bruce McCullough. Harper, Harper's Modern Classics, $1.25.

Wuthering Heights, introd. by Bonamy Dobrée. W. W. Norton, New Collins Classics, $0.95.

Wuthering Heights, introd. by V. S. Pritchett. Houghton Mifflin Co., Riverside Editions, $0.75.

Wuthering Heights, introd. by Mark Schorer. Rineheart, $0.75.

Wuthering Heights, introd. by Geoffrey Moore. New American Library, $0.50.

Wuthering Heights, introd. by Albert J. Guérard. Pocket Books, $0.35.

28. DICKENS. *Novels*

Pickwick Papers, introd. by Charles Dickens the Younger, illus. by "Phiz." St. Martin's Press, $2.75.

Pickwick Papers, introd. by G. K. Chesterton. E. P. Dutton, Everyman's Library, $1.85.

Pickwick Papers. Modern Library, $1.65.

David Copperfield, introd. by G. K. Chesterton. E. P. Dutton, Everyman's Library, $1.85.

David Copperfield, introd. by E. K. Brown, illus. by "Phiz." Modern Library, $1.65.

David Copperfield, edited with introd. by George H. Ford. Houghton Mifflin Co., Riverside Editions, $1.35.

David Copperfield, introd. by E. K. Brown, illus. by "Phiz." Modern Library College Editions, $0.85.

David Copperfield, introd. by Joseph Mersand. Pocket Books, $0.75.

Bleak House, introd. by Charles Dickens the Younger, illus. by "Phiz." St. Martin's Press, $2.75.

Bleak House, introd. by G. K. Chesterton. E. P. Dutton, Everyman's Library, $1.85.

Bleak House, introd. by R. Brimley Johnson. W. W. Norton, New Collins Classics, $1.65.

Bleak House, edited with introd. by Morton D. Zabel. Houghton Mifflin Co., Riverside Editions, $1.25.

Great Expectations and Hard Times, introd. by Charles Dickens the Younger, illus. St. Martin's Press, $2.75.

Great Expectations, introd. by G. K. Chesterton. E. P. Dutton, Everyman's Library, $2.45.

Great Expectations, Oxford University Press, World's Classics, $1.65.

Great Expectations, edited by Earle Davis. Rinehart, $0.95.

Great Expectations, introd. by Edward Wagenknecht. Pocket Books, $0.35.

Hard Times, introd. by G. K. Chesterton. E. P. Dutton, Everyman's Library, $1.85.
Hard Times, introd. by Frederick Brereton. W. W. Norton, New Collins Classics, $0.95.
Hard Times, edited by W. W. Watt. Rinehart, $0.65.
Our Mutual Friend, introd. by Charles Dickens the Younger, illus. by Marcus Stone. St. Martin's Press, $2.75.
Our Mutual Friend, introd. by G. K. Chesterton. E. P. Dutton, Everyman's Library, $1.85.
Little Dorrit, introd. by Charles Dickens the Younger, illus. by "Phiz." St. Martin's Press, $2.75.
Little Dorrit, introd. by G. K. Chesterton. E. P. Dutton, Everyman's Library, $1.85.
New Oxford Illustrated Dickens. Oxford University Press, 21 vols., $3.75 each.

29. THACKERAY. *Vanity Fair*

Vanity Fair, introd. by Whitelaw Reid. E. P. Dutton, Everyman's Library, $1.85.
Vanity Fair, introd. by George H. Ford. Harper, Harper's Modern Classics, $1.65.
Vanity Fair, introd. by Joseph Warren Beach. Modern Library, $1.65.
Vanity Fair, introd. by Joseph Warren Beach. Modern Library Paperbacks, $1.25.
Vanity Fair, edited by John W. Dodds. Rinehart, $1.25.
Vanity Fair, introd. by Joseph Warren Beach. Modern Library College Editions, $0.85.
Vanity Fair, introd. by Lionel Stevenson. Pocket Books, $0.75.

30. GEORGE ELIOT. *The Mill on the Floss*

The Mill on the Floss, introd. by W. Robertson Nicoll. E. P. Dutton, Everyman's Library, $1.85.
The Mill on the Floss. Oxford University Press, World's Classics, $1.65.
The Mill on the Floss, introd. by Gerald Bullett. W. W. Norton, New Collins Classics, $1.25.
The Mill on the Floss, introd. by Maxwell Goldberg. Pocket Books, $0.50.
Best-Known Novels: Adam Bede, The Mill on the Floss, Silas Marner, Romola. Modern Library Giants, $2.95.

31. LEWIS CARROLL. *Alice in Wonderland and Through the Looking-Glass*

Alice in Wonderland and Through the Looking Glass, illus. by John Tenniel. Heritage Press, $3.00
Alice's Adventures in Wonderland and Through the Looking-Glass, introd. by May Lamberton Becker, illus. by John Tenniel. World Publishing Co., Rainbow Classics, $2.50.
Alice in Wonderland, Through the Looking Glass, Hunting of the Snark, introd. by Alexander Woollcott, illus. by John Tenniel and Henry Holiday. Modern Library, $1.65.
Alice's Adventures in Wonderland and Through the Looking Glass, illus. by John Tenniel. St. Martin's Press, $0.95.
Complete Works, introd. by Alexander Woollcott, illus. by John Tenniel. Modern Library Giants, $2.95.

32. HARDY. *The Mayor of Casterbridge*

The Mayor of Casterbridge, introd. by S. C. Chew. Modern Library, $1.65.

The Mayor of Casterbridge, introd. by J. F. A. Pyre. Harper, Harper's Modern Classics, $1.25.
The Mayor of Casterbridge, edited by V. de Sola Pinto. St. Martin's Press, $0.95.
The Mayor of Casterbridge, edited by Harvey C. Webster. Rinehart, $0.75.
The Mayor of Casterbridge, introd. by S. C. Chew. Modern Library College Editions, $0.65.
The Mayor of Casterbridge, introd. by Albert J. Guérard. Pocket Books, $0.35.

33. CONRAD. *Nostromo*

Nostromo, introd. by Robert Penn Warren. Modern Library, $1.65.

34. LAWRENCE. *Sons and Lovers*

Sons and Lovers, introd. by John Macy. Modern Library, $1.65.
Sons and Lovers. Viking Press, Compass Books, $1.65.
Sons and Lovers, introd. by Mark Schorer. Harper, Harper's Modern Classics, $1.25.
Sons and Lovers. New American Library, $0.50.

35. JOYCE. *Ulysses*

Ulysses, foreword by Morris Ernst. Random House, $4.75.
Ulysses, foreword by Morris Ernst. Modern Library Giants, $2.95

36. MANN. *The Magic Mountain*

The Magic Mountain, trans. by H. T. Lowe-Porter. Alfred A. Knopf, $5.00.

37. RABELAIS. *Gargantua and Pantagruel*

Works, trans. by Jacques Le Clercq. Tudor Publishing Co., $2.98.

Complete Works, trans. by Jacques Le Clercq. Modern Library Giants, $2.95.

The Portable Rabelais, edited and trans. by Samuel Putnam. Viking Press, $2.95.

Gargantua and Pantagruel, trans. by J. M. Cohen. Penguin Books, $1.50.

The Portable Rabelais, edited and trans. by Samuel Putnam. Viking Press Paperbound Editions, $1.45.

38. VOLTAIRE. *Candide and Other Works*

Candide, trans. by Richard Aldington, illus. by Rockwell Kent. Doubleday, $3.50.

The Portable Voltaire, edited by Ben Ray Redman. Viking Press, $2.95.

Candide and Other Writings, edited with introd. by Haskell M. Block. Modern Library, $1.65.

Candide, introd. by Carl Van Doren, illus. by S. A. Adler. World Publishing Co., Living Library, $1.65.

The Portable Voltaire, edited by Ben Ray Redman. Viking Press Paperbound Editions, $1.45.

Candide, trans. by John Butt. Penguin Books, $0.50.

Candide, trans. by Lowell Bair, illus. Bantam Books, $0.35.

39. STENDHAL. *The Red and the Black*

The Red and the Black, trans. by C. K. Scott-Moncrieff. Modern Library, $1.65.

Scarlet and Black, trans. by M. R. B. Shaw. Penguin Books, $1.25.

The Red and the Black, trans. by Lowell Bair, introd. by Clifton Fadiman. Bantam Books, $0.75.

40. BALZAC. *Père Goriot, Eugénie Grandet*

Père Goriot and Eugénie Grandet, trans. by E. K. Brown and others, introd. by E. K. Brown. Modern Library, $1.65.

Père Goriot and Eugénie Grandet, trans. by E. K. Brown and others, introd. by E. K. Brown. Modern Library College Editions, $0.65.

Père Goriot, trans. by J. M. Sedgwick, edited by Wallace Fowlie. Rinehart, $0.75.

Old Goriot, trans. by Marion Crawford. Penguin Books, $0.65.

Eugénie Grandet, trans. by Marion Crawford. Penguin Books, $0.50.

Eugénie Grandet, trans. by Lowell Bair. Bantam Books, $0.35.

41. FLAUBERT. *Madame Bovary*

Madame Bovary, trans. by Francis Steegmuller. Modern Library, $1.65.

Madame Bovary, trans. by Alan Russell. Penguin Books, $0.95.

Madame Bovary, trans. by Francis Steegmuller. Modern Library College Editions, $0.75.

Madame Bovary, trans. by Lowell Bair. Bantam Books, $0.35.

42. PROUST. *Remembrance of Things Past*

Remembrance of Things Past, trans. by C. K. Scott-Moncrieff and Frederick A. Blossom, introd. by Joseph Wood Krutch. Random House, 2 vols. boxed, $15.00.

Remembrance of Things Past, trans. by C. K. Scott-Moncrieff and Frederick A. Blossom. Modern Library, 7 vols., $1.65 each. (*Swann's Way, Within a Budding Grove, The Guermantes Way, The Cities of the Plain, The Captive, The Sweet Cheat Gone, The Past Recaptured*)

43. POE. *Short Stories and Other Works*

Complete Tales and Poems. Modern Library Giants, $2.95.
The Portable Poe, edited by Philip Van Doren Stern. Viking Press, $2.95.
Tales of Mystery and Imagination, introd. by Padraic Colum. E. P. Dutton, Everyman's Library, $1.85.
Selected Poetry and Prose, introd. by T. O. Mabbott. Modern Library, $1.65.
Tales of Mystery and Imagination. Oxford University Press, World's Classics, $1.65.
The Portable Poe, edited by Philip Van Doren Stern. Viking Press Paperbound Editions, $1.45.
Selected Writings, edited by E. H. Davidson. Houghton Mifflin Co., Riverside Editions, $0.95.
Selected Prose and Poetry, edited by W. H. Auden. Rinehart, $0.95.
Selected Poetry and Prose, introd. by T. O. Mabbott. Modern Library College Editions, $0.85.
Selected Tales. Penguin Books, $0.85.
Great Tales and Poems. Pocket Books, $0.35.

44. HAWTHORNE. *The Scarlet Letter, Selected Tales*

Complete Novels and Selected Tales. Modern Library Giants, $2.95.
The Portable Hawthorne, edited by Malcolm Cowley. Viking Press, $2.95.

The Scarlet Letter, introd. by John C. Gerber. Modern Library, $1.65.

The Scarlet Letter, introd. by Carl Van Doren, illus. by Nell Booker. World Publishing Co., Living Library, $1.65.

The Portable Hawthorne, edited by Malcolm Cowley. Viking Press Paperbound Editions, $1.45.

Short Stories, edited by Newton Arvin. Alfred A. Knopf, Vintage Books, $1.25.

The Scarlet Letter, introd. by Newton Arvin. Harper, Harper's Modern Classics, $1.25.

The Scarlet Letter, introd. by John C. Gerber. Modern Library College Editions, $0.65.

The Scarlet Letter, edited by Austin Warren. Rinehart, $0.65.

The Scarlet Letter. New American Library, $0.50.

The Scarlet Letter, afterword by Maxwell Geismar. Pocket Books, $0.35.

45. MELVILLE. *Moby Dick*

Moby Dick or The White Whale, edited by L. S. Mansfield and H. P. Vincent. Farrar, Straus and Cudahy, $3.50.

Moby Dick, illus. by Rockwell Kent. Modern Library Giants, $2.95.

Moby Dick, introd. by Sherman Paul. E. P. Dutton, Everyman's Library, $2.45.

Moby Dick, introd. by Leon Howard. Modern Library, $1.65.

Moby Dick or The Whale, edited by Willard Thorpe. Oxford University Press, World's Classics, $1.65.

Moby Dick, introd. by Clifton Fadiman. Harper, Harper's Modern Classics, $1.25.

Moby Dick, edited by Newton Arvin. Rinehart, $0.95.

Moby Dick, edited with introd. by Alfred Kazin. Houghton Mifflin, Riverside Editions, $0.85.

Moby Dick, introd. by Leon Howard. Modern Library College Editions, $0.75.

Moby Dick, introd. by William M. Gibson. Dell Books, $0.75.
Moby Dick. New American Library, $0.50.

46. MARK TWAIN. *Huckleberry Finn*

Adventures of Huckleberry Finn, introd. by May Lamberton Becker, illus. by Baldwin Hawes. World Publishing Co., Rainbow Classics, $2.50.
Adventures of Huckleberry Finn, introd. by Brander Matthews and Dixon Wecter. Harper, Harper's Modern Classics, $1.25.
Adventures of Huckleberry Finn, edited by H. N. Smith. Houghton Mifflin Co., Riverside Editions, $0.80.
Adventures of Huckleberry Finn. Penguin Books, $0.65.
Adventures of Huckleberry Finn, edited by Lionel Trilling. Rinehart, $0.65.
Adventures of Huckleberry Finn. New American Library, $0.50.
Adventures of Huckleberry Finn, illus. by Harold Minton. Pocket Books, $0.35.

47. HENRY JAMES. *The Ambassadors*

The Ambassadors, edited with introd. by R. W. Stallman. Doubleday, Anchor Books, $1.25.
The Ambassadors, introd. by Martin W. Sampson and John C. Gerber. Harper, Harper's Modern Classics, $1.25.
The Ambassadors, edited with introd. by Leon Edel. Houghton Mifflin Co., Riverside Editions, in prep.

48. CERVANTES. *Don Quixote*

Ingenious Gentleman Don Quixote de la Mancha, trans. by Samuel Putnam. Viking Press, $6.00.

The Portable Cervantes, trans. by Samuel Putnam. Viking Press, $2.95.

Adventures of Don Quixote (abridged), trans. by J. M. Cohen. Penguin Books, $1.85.

The Portable Cervantes, trans. by Samuel Putnam. Viking Press, Paperbound Editions, $1.45.

Don Quixote (abridged), trans. by Walter Starkie. New American Library, $0.50.

49. GOGOL. *Dead Souls*

Dead Souls, trans. by George Reavey, introd. by Maurice Bowra. Oxford University Press, World's Classics, $2.50.

Dead Souls, trans. by C. J. Hogarth, introd. by John Cournos. E. P. Dutton, Everyman's Library, $1.85.

Dead Souls, trans. by B. G. Guerney, introd. by René Wellek. Rinehart, $0.95.
(This is the best.)

50. TURGENEV. *Fathers and Sons*

Fathers and Sons, trans. by C. J. Hogarth, introd. by V. S. Pritchett. E. P. Dutton, Everyman's Library, $1.85.

Fathers and Sons, trans. by George Reavey, introd. by Alan Hodge. Noonday Press, $1.45.

Fathers and Children, trans. by Richard Hare, introd. by Ernest J. Simmons. Rinehart, $0.75.

Fathers and Sons, trans. by Barbara Makanowitzky, introd. by Alexandra Tolstoy. Bantam Books, $0.50.

51. DOSTOEVSKI. *Crime and Punishment, The Brothers Karamazov*

Crime and Punishment, trans. by Jessie Coulson. Oxford University Press, $3.75.

Crime and Punishment, trans. by Constance Garnett, introd. by Laurence Irving. E. P. Dutton, Everyman's Library, $1.85.

Crime and Punishment, trans. by Constance Garnett, introd. by Ernest J. Simmons. Modern Library, $1.65.

Crime and Punishment, trans. by Constance Garnett, introd. by Alfred Kazin, illus. by Ruth Gikow. World Publishing Co., Living Library, $1.65.

Crime and Punishment, trans. by Constance Garnett, introd. by Avrahm Yarmolinsky. Harper, Harper's Modern Classics, $1.25.

Crime and Punishment, trans. by Constance Garnett, introd. by Ernest J. Simmons. Modern Library Paperbacks, $1.25.

Crime and Punishment, trans. by David Magarshack. Penguin Books, $0.95.

Crime and Punishment, trans. by Constance Garnett, introd. by Ernest J. Simmons. Dell Books, $0.75.

Crime and Punishment, trans. by Constance Garnett, introd. by Ernest J. Simmons, Modern Library College Editions, $0.75.

Crime and Punishment, trans. by Constance Garnett. Bantam Books, $0.50.

The Brothers Karamazov, trans. by Constance Garnett, introd. by Edward Garnett. E. P. Dutton, Everyman's Library, 2 vols., $3.70.

The Brothers Karamazov, trans. by Constance Garnett. Modern Library Giants, $2.95.

The Brothers Karamazov, trans. by David Magarshack. Penguin Books, $1.90.

The Brothers Karamazov, trans. by Constance Garnett, introd. by Marc Slonim. Modern Library, $1.65.

The Brothers Karamazov, trans. by Constance Garnett, introd. by Marc Slonim. Modern Library Paperbacks, $1.25.

The Brothers Karamazov, trans. by Constance Garnett, introd. by Marc Slonim. Modern Library College Editions, $0.85.

The Brothers Karamazov, trans. by Constance Garnett, edited by Manuel Komroff. New American Library, $0.75.

52. TOLSTOY. *War and Peace*

War and Peace, trans. by Louise and Aylmer Maude. Oxford University Press, World's Classics, 3 vols., $5.00.

War and Peace, trans. by Rosemary Edmonds. Penguin Books, 2 vols. boxed, $3.50.

War and Peace, trans. by Constance Garnett. Modern Library Giants, $2.95.

War and Peace (abridged), edited by Manuel Komroff. Bantam Books, $0.75.

War and Peace (abridged), edited by Edmund Fuller. Dell Books, $0.50.

53. UNDSET. *Kristin Lavransdatter*

Kristin Lavransdatter, trans. by A. G. Chater. Alfred A. Knopf, $6.50.

54. HOBBES. *Leviathan*

Leviathan, edited by Michael Oakeshott. Macmillan Co., Blackwell's Political Texts, $2.85.

Leviathan, introd. by A. D. Lindsay. E. P. Dutton, Everyman's Library, $2.45.

Leviathan. Oxford University Press, $2.40.

55. LOCKE. *Second Treatise on Government*

Second Treatise on Civil Government and a Letter Concerning Toleration, edited by Charles L. Sherman. Appleton-Century-Crofts, Crofts Classics, $1.25.

Second Treatise of Government, introd. by Thomas P. Peardon. Liberal Arts Press, $0.80.

Of Civil Government, 2nd Essay. Henry Regnery Co., Gateway Editions, $0.75.

56. HUME. *An Enquiry Concerning Human Understanding*

Enquiries Concerning the Human Understanding, edited by L. A. Selby-Bigge. Oxford University Press, $2.40.

An Enquiry Concerning Human Understanding, introd. by Russell Kirk. Henry Regnery Co., Gateway Editions, $0.95.

An Enquiry Concerning Human Understanding. Open Court, $0.85.

An Inquiry Concerning Human Understanding. Liberal Arts Press, $0.80.

57. MILL. *On Liberty*

On Liberty, Representative Government, The Subjection of Women, introd. by M. G. Fawcett. Oxford University Press, World's Classics, $1.65.

On Liberty. Henry Regnery Co., Gateway Editions, $0.85.

On Liberty, edited by Currin V. Shields. Liberal Arts Press, $0.65.

58. WHITEHEAD. *Science and the Modern World*

Science and the Modern World. Macmillan Co., $5.00.
Science and the Modern World. New American Library, $0.50.

59. MARX AND ENGELS. *The Communist Manifesto*

The Communist Manifesto, introd. by Stefan T. Possony. Henry Regnery Co., Gateway Editions, $0.65.
The Communist Manifesto, edited by Samuel H. Beer. Appleton-Century-Crofts, Crofts Classics, $0.45.

60. NIETZSCHE. *Thus Spoke Zarathustra, Selected Other Works*

Philosophy (*Thus Spoke Zarathustra, Beyond Good and Evil, Genealogy of Morals, Ecce Homo, Birth of Tragedy*). Modern Library Giants, $2.95.
The Portable Nietzsche, edited by Walter Kaufmann. Viking Press Paperbound Editions, $1.45.

61. FREUD. *Selected Works*

The Origin and Development of Psychoanalysis. Henry Regnery Co., Gateway Editions, $0.65.
The Interpretation of Dreams, trans. by A. A. Brill. Modern Library, $1.65.
A General Introduction to Psychoanalysis, trans. by Joan

Rivière, preface by Ernest Jones and G. Stanley Hall. Pocket Books, $0.50.

New Introductory Lectures on Psychoanalysis, trans. by W. J. H. Sprott. W. W. Norton, $3.95.

Beyond the Pleasure Principle, trans. by James Strachey. Bantam Books, $0.50.

The Ego and the Id, trans. by Joan Rivière. Hillary House, $1.75.

Civilization and Its Discontents, trans. by Joan Rivière. Doubleday, Anchor Books, $0.95.

Basic Writings, trans. and edited by A. A. Brill. Modern Library Giants, $2.95.

A *General Selection from the Works of Sigmund Freud,* edited by John Rickman. Doubleday, Anchor Books, $1.25.

62. MACHIAVELLI. *The Prince*

The Prince, trans. by W. K. Marriott, introd. by H. Butterfield. E. P. Dutton, Everyman's Library, $1.85.

The Prince and Discourses, trans. by Luigi Ricci, introd. by Max Lerner. Modern Library, $1.65.

The Prince, trans. by Luigi Ricci, rev. by E. R. P. Vincent. Oxford University Press, World's Classics, $1.65.

The Ruler, trans. by Samuel Rodd. Henry Regnery Co., Gateway Editions, $0.85.

The Prince, trans. by Luigi Ricci, rev. by E. R. P. Vincent, introd. by Christian Gauss. New American Library, $0.50.

63. MONTAIGNE. *Selected Essays*

Complete Essays, edited and trans. by Donald M. Frame. Stanford University Press, $5.75.

Essays, trans. by E. J. Trechmann, introd. by J. M. Robertson. Oxford University Press, $3.50.

Selected Essays, edited and trans. by Donald M. Frame. D. Van Nostrand Co., $1.35.
Essays, trans. by J. M. Cohen. Penguin Books, $0.95.

64. DESCARTES. *Discourse on Method*

Discourse on Method, trans. by John Veitch. Open Court. $1.10.
Discourse on Method, trans. by John Veitch. Open Court Paperback, $0.60.
Discourse on Method, trans. by Laurence J. Lafleur. Liberal Arts, $0.50.

65. PASCAL. *Thoughts (Pensées)*

Pensées, trans. by W. F. Trotter, introd. by T. S. Eliot. E. P. Dutton, Everyman's Library, $1.85.
Thoughts: An Apology for Christianity, edited by Thomas S. Kepler. World Publishing Co., $1.75.
Pensées, trans. by W. F. Trotter, and *Provincial Letters,* trans. by Thomas McCrie. Modern Library, $1.65.
Pensées, trans. by W. F. Trotter, introd. by T. S. Eliot. E. P. Dutton, Everyman's Paperbacks, $1.15.

66. TOCQUEVILLE. *Democracy in America*

Democracy in America (the Henry Reeve text rev. by Francis Bowen), edited with introd. by Phillips Bradley. Alfred A. Knopf, Vintage Books, 2 vols., $2.90.
Democracy in America, trans. by Henry Reeve, edited by Henry Steele Commager. Oxford University Press, World's Classics, $2.50.

67. THOREAU. *Walden, Civil Disobedience*

The Portable Thoreau, edited by Carl Bode. Viking Press, $2.95.

Walden and Other Writings, edited by Brooks Atkinson, foreword by T. Scudder. Modern Library, $1.65.

The Portable Thoreau, edited by Carl Bode. Viking Press Paperbound Editions, $1.45.

Walden and Other Writings, edited by Brooks Atkinson, foreword by T. Scudder. Modern Library College Editions, $0.75.

Walden and the Famous Essay on Civil Disobedience. New American Library, $0.50.

Walden and Civil Disobedience, edited by Norman H. Pearson. Rinehart, $0.50.

Works, edited by H. S. Canby, illus. Houghton Mifflin Co., Cambridge Editions, $6.50.

68. EMERSON. *Selected Works*

The Portable Emerson, edited by Mark Van Doren. Viking Press, $2.95.

Essays and Other Writings, introd. by Brooks Atkinson. Modern Library, $1.65.

Essays, Representative Men, Poems, introd. by De Lancey Ferguson. W. W. Norton, New Collins Classics, $1.45.

The Portable Emerson, edited by Mark Van Doren. Viking Press Paperbound Editions, $1.45.

Essays, Representative Men, Poems. D. Van Nostrand Co., $1.35.

Selections, edited by Stephen E. Whicher. Houghton Mifflin Co., Riverside Editions, $1.15.

Selected Prose and Poetry, edited by Reginald L. Cook. Rinehart, $0.95.

A Modern Anthology, edited by Alfred Kazin and Daniel Aaron. Dell Books, 0.50.

Basic Selections, edited by Eduard C. Lindeman. New American Library, $0.50.

69. WILLIAM JAMES. *Selected Works*

Principles of Psychology. Dover Publications, 2 vols., $5.00.
Pragmatism and Four Related Essays from the Meaning of Truth, edited by Ralph Barton Perry. Longmans, Green, $3.25.
Pragmatism and Other Essays from the Meaning of Truth. Meridian Books, $1.35.
Varieties of Religious Experience. Modern Library, $1.65.
Varieties of Religious Experience, foreword by Jacques Barzun. New American Library, $0.50.

70. DEWEY. *Human Nature and Conduct*

Human Nature and Conduct, introd. by the author. Modern Library, $1.65.

71. SANTAYANA. *Skepticism and Animal Faith, Selected Other Works*

Skepticism and Animal Faith. Dover Publications, $3.50.
Skepticism and Animal Faith. Dover Publications, $1.50.
The Last Puritan: A Memoir. Charles Scribner's Sons, $5.00.
Dialogues in Limbo. University of Michigan Press, $1.45.
Interpretations of Poetry and Religion. Harper, Torchbooks, $1.45.
Persons and Places: Background of My Life, The Middle Span, My Host the World. Charles Scribner's Sons, 3 vols. boxed, $9.00.

72. *Poets of the English Language,* EDITED BY Auden AND Pearson

Poets of the English Language (Viking Portables). Viking Press, 5 vols., $2.95 each; set $14.75.

Poets of the English Language (Viking Paperbound Portables). Viking Press, 5 vols., $1.45 each; set $7.25.

73. *An Anthology of World Poetry,* EDITED BY Mark Van Doren

An Anthology of World Poetry. Harcourt, Brace, $8.50.

74. DONNE. *Selected Works*

Poems, edited by H. J. C. Grierson. Oxford University Press, $3.50.

Poems, edited by Hugh I'Anson Fausset. E. P. Dutton, Everyman's Library, $1.85.

Complete Poetry and Selected Prose, edited by Charles M. Coffin. Modern Library, $1.65.

Poetry and Prose, edited by A. M. D. Hughes. Oxford Univer-Press, $1.40.

Sermons, edited by Theodore A. Gill. Meridian Books, $1.35.

Poetry and Prose, edited by A. Desmond Hawkins. Thomas Nelson, $1.25.

Selected Poems, edited by J. Hayward. Penguin Books, $0.65.

The Complete Poetry of John Donne and William Blake, introd. by Robert Silliman Hillyer. Modern Library Giants, $2.95.

75. MILTON. *Selected Works*

Complete Poetical Works, edited by Harris Francis Fletcher. Houghton Mifflin Co., Cambridge Editions, $6.50.

Poetical Works, rev. edition, edited by Helen Darbishire. Oxford University Press, $3.75.

The Portable Milton, edited by Douglas Bush. Viking Press, $2.95.

Complete Poetry and Selected Prose, introd. by Cleanth Brooks. Modern Library, $1.65.

The Portable Milton, edited by Douglas Bush. Viking Press Paperbound Editions, $1.45.

Poetry and Prose, edited by A. M. D. Hughes. Oxford University Press, $1.40.

Paradise Lost and Selected Poetry and Prose, edited by Northrop Frye. Rinehart, $0.95.

Complete Poetry and Selected Prose, introd. by Cleanth Brooks. Modern Library College Editions, $0.85.

76. BLAKE. *Selected Works*

Poetical Works, edited by John Sampson. Oxford University Press, $3.50.

The Portable Blake, edited by Alfred Kazin, illus. Viking Press, $2.95.

Poems and Prophecies, edited by Max Plowman. E. P. Dutton, Everyman's Library, $1.85.

Selected Poetry and Prose, edited by Northrop Frye. Modern Library, $1.65.

Selected Poems. Oxford University Press, World's Classics, $1.65.

The Portable Blake, edited by Alfred Kazin, illus. Viking Press Paperbound Editions, $1.45.

Poems and Prose, edited by J. Bronowski. Penguin Books, $0.85.

The Complete Poetry of John Donne and William Blake, introd. by Robert Silliman Hillyer. Modern Library Giants, $2.95.

77. WORDSWORTH. *Selected Works*

Complete Poetical Works, introd. by John Morley. St. Martin's Press, $2.50.

Selected Poetry, edited by Mark Van Doren. Modern Library, $1.65.

Selected Poems. Oxford University Press, World's Classics, $1.65.

Poems, edited by H. M. Margoliouth. W. W. Norton, New Collins Classics, $1.45.

Prelude With Selected Sonnets and Minor Poems, edited by Carlos Baker. Rinehart, $0.95.

Selected Poetry, edited by Mark Van Doren. Modern Library College Editions, $0.85.

Selected Poems, edited by Richard Wilbur, introd. by David Ferry. Dell Books, $0.35.

78. COLERIDGE. *Selected Works*

Poems, edited by E. H. Coleridge. Oxford University Press, $3.50.

The Portable Coleridge, edited by I. A. Richards. Viking Press, $2.95.

Selected Poetry and Prose, edited by Donald A. Stauffer. Modern Library, $1.65.

Poems, edited by A. T. Quiller-Couch. Oxford University Press, World's Classics, $1.65.

The Portable Coleridge, edited by I. A. Richards. Viking Press Paperbound Editions, $1.45.

Selected Poetry and Prose, edited by Elisabeth Schneider. Rinehart, $0.95.
Selected Poetry and Prose, edited by Donald A. Stauffer. Modern Library College Editions, $0.85.
Selected Poetry and Prose, edited by K. Raine. Penguin Books, $0.85.
Selected Poems, edited by Richard Wilbur, introd. by G. Robert Stang. Dell Books, $0.35.

79. YEATS. *Collected Poems, Plays, Autobiography*

Collected Poems, definitive edition. Macmillan Co., $6.00.
Collected Plays. Macmillan Co., $5.50.
Autobiography. Macmillan Co., $5.00.
Autobiography. Doubleday, Anchor Books, $1.25.

80. WHITMAN. *Selected Works*

The Portable Whitman, edited by Mark Van Doren. Viking Press, $2.95.
Leaves of Grass, edited by Emory Holloway. E. P. Dutton, Everyman's Library, $1.85.
Leaves of Grass and Selected Prose, introd. by John Kouwenhoven. Modern Library, $1.65.
The Portable Whitman, edited by Mark Van Doren. Viking Press Paperbound Editions, $1.45.
Complete Poetry and Selected Prose, edited by James E. Miller, Jr. Houghton Mifflin Co., Riverside Editions, $1.15.
Leaves of Grass and Selected Prose, introd. by John Kouwenhoven. Modern Library College Editions, $0.85.
Leaves of Grass, introd. by Gay Wilson Allen. New American Library, $0.50.
The Whitman Reader, edited by Maxwell Geismar. Pocket Books, $0.50.

Selected Poems, edited by Richard Wilbur, introd. by Leslie A. Fiedler. Dell Books, $0.35.

81. DURANT. *The Story of Civilization*

The Story of Civilization, illus. Simon and Schuster, 6 vols., $10.00 each.
Our Oriental Heritage, The Life of Greece, Caesar and Christ, The Age of Faith, The Renaissance, The Reformation

82. TREVELYAN. *History of England*

History of England. Doubleday, Anchor Books, 3 vols., $2.85.

83. NEVINS AND COMMAGER. *A Short History of the United States*

A Short History of the United States. Modern Library, $1.65.

84. *Basic Documents*, EDITED BY Morris *On the Constitution*, EDITED BY Gabriel

Basic Documents in American History. D. Van Nostrand Co., Anvil Books, $1.25.
On the Constitution: Selections from the Federalist Papers. Liberal Arts Press, $0.95.

85. ROUSSEAU. *Confessions*

Confessions. E. P. Dutton, Everyman's Library, 2 vols., $3.70.
Confessions. Modern Library, $1.65.

Confessions of J. J. Rousseau, trans. by J. M. Cohen. Penguin Books, $0.95.

Confessions, edited by Lester G. Crocker. Pocket Books, $0.50.

86. BOSWELL. *Life of Samuel Johnson*

Life of Samuel Johnson, preface by R. W. Chapman. Oxford University Press, $6.00.

Life of Dr. Johnson. E. P. Dutton, Everyman's Library, 2 vols., $3.70.

Life of Samuel Johnson. Doubleday, Garden City, $2.95.

Life of Samuel Johnson, introd. by Herbert Askwith. Modern Library Giants, $2.95.

87. ADAMS. *The Education of Henry Adams*

The Education of Henry Adams. Houghton Mifflin Co., $5.50.

The Education of Henry Adams. Modern Library, $1.65.

88. FROST. *Collected Poems*

Complete Poems of Robert Frost. Henry Holt, $6.00.

Poems. Modern Library, $1.65.

89. FAULKNER. *The Sound and the Fury, As I Lay Dying*

The Sound and the Fury and As I Lay Dying. Modern Library, $1.65.

The Sound and the Fury and As I Lay Dying. Modern Library Paperbacks, $0.95.

The Sound and the Fury. Modern Library, $1.25.
The Sound and the Fury. New American Library, $0.50.

90. HEMINGWAY. *Short Stories*

Short Stories. Charles Scribner's Sons, $4.95.

91. MAUGHAM. *Of Human Bondage*

Of Human Bondage. Doubleday, $4.50.
Of Human Bondage, introd. by R. A. Cordell. Modern Library, $1.65.
Of Human Bondage, introd. by R. A. Cordell. Modern Library Paperbacks, $1.25.

92. FORSTER. *A Passage to India*

A Passage to India. Harcourt, Brace, $2.25.

93. T. S. ELIOT. *Collected Poems and Plays*

The Complete Poems and Plays, 1909-1950. Harcourt, Brace, $6.00.

94. HUXLEY. *Brave New World, Collected Essays*

Brave New World, foreword by the author. Modern Library, $1.65.
Brave New World, foreword by the author, introd. by Charles J. Rolo. Harper, Harper's Modern Classics, $1.25.

Brave New World, foreword by the author. Bantam Books, $0.35.

Collected Essays. Harper, $5.00.

95. MALRAUX. *Man's Fate*

Man's Fate, trans. by Haakon M. Chevalier. Modern Library, $1.65.

96. GOMBRICH. *The Story of Art*

The Story of Art. Doubleday, Phaidon, $7.50.

97. WHITEHEAD. *An Introduction to Mathematics*

An Introduction to Mathematics. Oxford University Press, $1.50.

98. BARNETT. *The Universe and Dr. Einstein*

The Universe and Dr. Einstein, foreword by Albert Einstein. New American Library, $0.50.

99. ADLER. *How To Read a Book*

How To Read a Book. Simon and Schuster, $1.75.

100. *The American Treasury*, EDITED BY Fadiman, WITH Van Doren

The American Treasury, 1455-1955. Harper, $7.95.

Suggestions for Further Reading

For a selection of editions of the one hundred titles, giving price and publisher, see the listings in the Bibliography. The following lists a small number of reference and secondary works that will be helpful to the reader who wants to acquire more background than my brief notes can well supply. When only author and title are given, without publisher and price, the book is out of print. It may be found in libraries and secondhand bookstores. Where the price is given, the book is of this writing available in bookstores. Every effort has been made to check this information, but prices (and even publishers) are subject to change. Wherever possible I have listed cheap, paperbound editions, though these are of course less durable than the hardcover editions. The reader who wishes to build up a library, whether of original or secondary material, at a price most of us can afford is earnestly advised to buy *Paperbound Books in Print,* listing six thousand inexpensive reprints. It is revised semiannually; $3.00 a year, $2.00 a single copy; R. R. Bowker Co., 62 West 45th Street, New York 36.

THE BEGINNING (1-12)

A comprehensive reference volume covering the entire field of Greek and Roman civilization is the *Oxford Companion to Classical Literature* (Oxford University Press, $3.75), compiled and edited by Paul Harvey. Excellent also is Oskar Seyffert, A

Dictionary of Classical Antiquities (Meridian Books, $1.95).

A good standard history of Greece is J. B. Bury, *A History of Greece* (Modern Library, $2.95). Less elaborate: C. E. Robinson, *Hellas: A Short History of Ancient Greece* (Beacon Press, $1.45).

For this section some knowledge of the classical gods and heroes is useful. Two excellent small volumes: H. J. Rose, *Gods and Heroes of the Greeks* (Meridian Books, $1.25); Edith Hamilton, *Mythology* (New American Library, $0.50).

Three serviceable general surveys of Greek literature, covering all the Greek authors on our list plus a great many others, are: C. M. Bowra, *Ancient Greek Literature* (Oxford University Press, $1.20); H. C. Baldry, *Greek Literature for the Modern Reader* (Cambridge University Press, $1.95); Gilbert Murray, *The Literature of Ancient Greece* (University of Chicago Press, Phoenix Books, $1.75).

A few suggestions on Greek drama: H. D. F. Kitto, *Greek Tragedy* (Doubleday, Anchor Books, $1.25); Gilbert Norwood, *Greek Tragedy* (Hillary House, $5.00); Gilbert Murray, *Aeschylus: The Creator of Tragedy* (Oxford University Press, $4.00); Gilbert Murray, *Euripides and His Age* (Oxford University Press, $1.20).

For the philosophers: A. E. Taylor, *Socrates* (Doubleday, Anchor Books, $0.75); R. W. Livingstone, editor, *Plato: Portrait of Socrates*, introduction particularly valuable (Oxford University Press, $1.60); W. D. Ross, *Aristotle* (Meridian Books, $1.45); Rex Warner, *The Greek Philosophers* (New American Library, $0.50). Matthew Arnold's famous essay on Marcus Aurelius is available in *The Portable Matthew Arnold* (Viking Press, $1.25), edited by Lionel Trilling.

J. B. Bury's *The Ancient Greek Historians* (Dover Publications, $1.50) covers other Greek historians, as well as Herodotus and Thucydides, and is a classic in its field.

Your study of the Latin classics might be aided by a reading of: R. H. Barrow, *The Romans* (Penguin Books, $0.85); Michael Grant, *Roman Literature* (Penguin Books, $0.85); the essay on Lucretius by George Santayana in his *Three Philosophical Poets* (Doubleday, Anchor Books, $0.75)—this also contains penetrating essays on Dante (14) and Goethe (18) who are part of The Lifetime Reading Plan.

THE MIDDLE AGES (13-15)

Henry Osborn Taylor's two-volume *The Mediaeval Mind* (Harvard University Press, $10.00), though written many years ago, is still a valuable and comprehensive study of "thought and emotion in the Middle Ages." Will Durant's *The Age of Faith* (Simon and Schuster, $10.00) is one of the six volumes comprising his *Story of Civilization* (81), which is part of The Lifetime Reading Plan. These two books will give you a good general picture of a fascinating period. For specific writers see the following:

13. St. Augustine. Martin C. D'Arcy, editor, *St. Augustine: His Age, Life and Thought* (Meridian Books, $1.45).

14. Dante. Jefferson Butler Fletcher, *Dante*; essay on Dante in George Santayana's *Three Philosophical Poets* (Doubleday, Anchor Books, $0.75); essay on Dante in T. S. Eliot, *Selected Essays* (Harcourt, Brace, $5.75).

15. Chaucer. John Livingston Lowes, *Geoffrey Chaucer* (Indiana University Press, $1.50); Marchette Chute, *Geoffrey Chaucer of England* (E. P. Dutton, Everyman's Library, $1.55).

PLAYS (16-20)

16. Shakespeare. To aid in your reading of Shakespeare, I have listed seven cheaply priced books, each approaching the subject from a different angle, each useful in a different way.

A. C. Bradley, *Shakespearean Tragedy* (Meridian Books, $1.35); E. K. Chambers, *Shakespeare: A Survey* (Hill and Wang, Dramabooks, $1.45); Mark Van Doren, *Shakespeare*

(Doubleday, Anchor Books, $0.95); G. B. Harrison, *Introducing Shakespeare* (Penguin Books, $0.95); Henri Fluchère, *Shakespeare and the Elizabethans* (Hill and Wang, Dramabooks, $1.25); Marchette Chute, *Shakespeare of London* (E. P. Dutton, Everyman's Library, $1.65); Margaret Webster, *Shakespeare Without Tears* (Fawcett Publications, Premier Books, $0.50).

17. MOLIÈRE. Ramon Fernandez, *Molière: The Man Seen Through the Plays* (Hill and Wang, $3.75); D. B. Wyndham Lewis, *Molière: The Comic Mask* (Coward McCann, $4.00).

18. GOETHE. It is worth while, so versatile is Goethe's mind, to get some idea of what he did and thought exclusive of *Faust*. For this purpose you might find useful *Great Writings of Goethe* (New American Library, $0.75), edited and with an introduction by Stephen Spender. This also contains MacNeice's excellent English translation of *Faust*, Part 1. Other suggestions: G. H. Lewes, *The Life and Works of Goethe* (E. P. Dutton, Everyman's Library, $1.85); the essay on Goethe in Santayana's *Three Philosophical Poets* (Doubleday, Anchor Books, $0.75); and various essays on Goethe in Thomas Mann's *Essays of Three Decades* (Alfred A. Knopf, Vintage Books, $1.25).

19. IBSEN. A slanted but brilliant essay is Shaw's *The Quintessence of Ibsenism* (Hill and Wang, Dramabooks, $0.95).

20. SHAW. On Shaw himself the commentaries are legion. Completely uninspired and indeed not very perceptive but a vast storehouse of facts is Archibald Henderson's monumental and expensive *George Bernard Shaw: Man of the Century* (Appleton-Century-Crofts, $12.00). For an interesting collection of essays by various hands try Louis Kronenberger, editor, *G. B. Shaw: A Critical Survey* (World Publishing Co., $6.00). Three quite different studies, of which Chesterton's is truly brilliant (but also highly personal), are: Eric Bentley's *Bernard Shaw* (New Directions, $1.25); G. K. Chesterton's *George Bernard Shaw* (Hill and Wang, Dramabooks, $0.95); and Hesketh Pearson's lively biography *G. B. S. A Full Length Portrait* (Harper, $6.00).

NARRATIVES (21-53)

For a good general survey of English fiction see Walter Allen, *The English Novel* (E. P. Dutton, Everyman's Library, $1.75). F. R. Leavis' influential *The Great Tradition* (Doubleday, Anchor Books, $0.95) has long chapters on George Eliot, Henry James, Joseph Conrad, as well as a general discussion of English fiction. For Dickens, Thackeray, Emily Brontë, and George Eliot see David Cecil's *Victorian Novelists* (University of Chicago Press, Phoenix Books, $1.75). On the individual novelists I list herewith a few standard works, not all of them easily available in bookstores or small libraries.

21. BUNYAN. G. B. Harrison, *Bunyan: A Study in Personality.*

22. DEFOE. James Sutherland, *Defoe* (British Book Centre, $0.50); essay by Virginia Woolf in *The Common Reader* (Harcourt, Brace, Harvest Books, $1.15).

23. SWIFT. Carl Van Doren, *Swift*; John Middleton Murray, *Jonathan Swift: A Critical Biography.*

24. STERNE. There are later studies but I still like Wilbur L. Cross's old-fashioned *Life and Times of Sterne.* For a Victorian view see Thackeray's *The English Humourists of the Eighteenth Century,* which also discusses Swift and Fielding. For a more modern appraisal see Virginia Woolf's essay "The Sentimental Journey" in her *Second Common Reader* (Harcourt, Brace, Harvest Books, $1.15). This also discusses, among other topics, *Robinson Crusoe* (22), Swift's *Journal to Stella,* and the novels of Thomas Hardy (32).

25. FIELDING. The latest biography is the two-volume *Henry Fielding: His Life, Works, and Times,* by F. Homes Dudden. For most readers this is pretty formidable, as is the even more basic and earlier three-volume work by Wilbur L. Cross, *The History of Henry Fielding.* Thackeray's estimate of Fielding is good but deeply Victorian: see his *The English Humourists of the Eighteenth Century.*

26. AUSTEN. The standard life is *Jane Austen: Her Life and Letters,* by W. and R. A. Austen-Leigh. See also Elizabeth Jenkins, *Jane Austen* (Farrar, Straus and Cudahy, $5.00) and essay by Virginia Woolf in *The Common Reader* (Harcourt, Brace, Harvest Books, $1.15).

27. EMILY BRONTË. The standard older biography, partly outmoded by others, but still a most interesting picture of the family, is Elizabeth Gaskell's *Life of Charlotte Brontë* (Oxford University Press, World's Classics, $1.65 or E. P. Dutton, Everyman's Library, $1.85). The focus is of course not on Emily. Irene Cooper Willis' *The Brontës* (Macmillan Co., $1.50) is an adequate condensed account.

28. DICKENS. The Dickens literature is formidable. For a really comprehensive biography you must go to Edgar Johnson's two-volume *Charles Dickens: His Tragedy and Triumph.* Two penetrating estimates are G. K. Chesterton's *Charles Dickens: A Critical Study* and Edmund Wilson's crucial essay "Dickens: The Two Scrooges" in his *Eight Essays* (Doubleday, Anchor Books, $0.85). Also see pp. 58-73 of *Soliloquies in England,* by George Santayana.

29. THACKERAY. The standard life is now Gordon N. Ray's two-volume work *Thackeray: The Uses of Adversity (1811-1846)* (McGraw-Hill Book Co., $7.00) and *Thackeray: The Age of Wisdom* (1847-1863) (McGraw-Hill Book Co., $8.00).

30. GEORGE ELIOT. See Lawrence and Elizabeth Hanson, *Marian Evans and George Eliot,* (Oxford University Press, $4.40). Interesting views of George Eliot may be found in Virginia Woolf's *The Common Reader* (Harcourt, Brace, Harvest Books, $1.15), F. R. Leavis' *The Great Tradition* (Doubleday, Anchor Books, $0.95), David Cecil's *Victorian Novelists* (University of Chicago Press, Phoenix Books, $1.75), and Henry James's *Partial Portraits.*

31. LEWIS CARROLL. Official, dull, and reticent is S. Dodgson Collingwood's *Life and Letters of Lewis Carroll.* It's rather hard to find. Derek Hudson's *Lewis Carroll* takes advantage of the diaries and many hitherto unpublished letters. Florence Becker

Lennon's *Victoria Through the Looking-Glass* offers an interesting analysis of Carroll's peculiar temperament, as refracted through his work. Shorter studies are legion, one of the best being Edmund Wilson's "C. L. Dodgson: The Poet-Logician" in his *The Shores of Light* (Farrar, Straus and Cudahy, $6.50).

32. HARDY. The official life is by Florence E. Hardy, in two volumes: *The Early Life of Hardy, 1840-1891* and *The Later Years, 1892-1928*. Professor Guérard's introduction to the Pocket Library edition of *The Mayor of Casterbridge* (Pocket Books, $0.35) is excellent.

33. CONRAD. The chief source is G. Jean-Aubry's *Sea Dreamer: A Definitive Biography of Joseph Conrad* (Doubleday, $4.50). See also F. R. Leavis, *The Great Tradition* (Doubleday, Anchor Books, $0.95); E. M. Forster, "Joseph Conrad: A Note" in *Abinger Harvest* (Meridian Books, $1.25). *The Portable Conrad* (Viking Press, $2.95), edited by Morton D. Zabel, contains excellent examples of Conrad's work in several fields.

34. LAWRENCE. Books about Lawrence are bewilderingly numerous; he was the kind of controversial figure who, like Byron, invites attack and defense, much of it biased. I suggest H. T. Moore's *The Intelligent Heart* (Farrar, Straus and Cudahy, $6.50); F. R. Leavis' *D. H. Lawrence, Novelist* (Alfred A. Knopf, $5.00); *D. H. Lawrence: A Composite Biography*, 3 vols. (University of Wisconsin Press, $7.50 each), edited by Edward Nehls. Also see the essay on Lawrence by Aldous Huxley in his *Collected Essays* (Harper, $5.00).

35. JOYCE. The literature, already vast, will grow vaster. The fullest, as well as most recent, biography is Richard Ellmann's *James Joyce* (Oxford University Press, $12.50). Also excellent are Harry Levin's brief *James Joyce: A Critical Introduction*; Magalaner and Kain's *Joyce: The Man, the Work, the Reputation* (New York University Press, $5.00); W. Y. Tindall, *A Reader's Guide to James Joyce* (Noonday Press, $1.65). Edmund Wilson's brilliant short estimate is in his *Axel's Castle* (Charles Scribner's Sons, $1.45). The standard commentary on *Ulysses* itself remains Gilbert Stuart's *James Joyce's "Ulysses."*

36. MANN. There is no really good full-length study of Mann in English; for some reason our finest critics tend to neglect him. The reader may find useful commentary in *The Stature of Thomas Mann*, edited by Charles Neider; J. G. Brennan's *Thomas Mann's World;* and my own anthology *Reading I've Liked* (Simon and Schuster, $2.25).

37. RABELAIS. The best one-volume life I know is the translation by Louis P. Roche of Jean Plattard's *The Life of François Rabelais*, but this is hard to come by. Samuel Putnam's *Rabelais, Man of the Renaissance* is good too. D. B. Wyndham Lewis' *Doctor Rabelais* (Sheed and Ward, $4.00), by a Catholic and a humorist, offers a sympathetic interpretation of both these aspects of Rabelais. Most translations contain useful introductions.

38. VOLTAIRE. S. G. Tallentyre's *Life of Voltaire* is a sound standard biography. See also Richard Aldington's *Voltaire.*

39. STENDHAL. For a sound biography in English see Matthew Josephson's *Stendhal.* Martin Turnell's brilliant *The Novel in France* (Alfred A. Knopf, Vintage Books, $1.25) offers penetrating analyses of three other Lifetime authors, in addition to Stendhal: Balzac, Flaubert, Proust. The excellent Lowell Bair translation of *The Red and the Black* (Bantam Books, $0.75) contains a longish introduction by Clifton Fadiman.

40. BALZAC. A good biography is Stefan Zweig's *Balzac.* Shorter studies are to be found in Harry Levin's *Toward Balzac* (New Directions, $1.50) and particularly Henry James's "The Lesson of Balzac" in *The Future of the Novel* (Alfred A. Knopf, Vintage Books, $1.25), edited by Leon Edel. The latter also contains estimates of Flaubert, Turgenev, Tolstoy, and Conrad.

41. FLAUBERT. Francis Steegmuller's *Flaubert and Madame Bovary* (Alfred A. Knopf, Vintage Books, $1.25) is a masterly study.

42. PROUST. An excellent brief biography is André Maurois' *Proust* (Meridian Books, $1.45). Another is Richard H. Barker's *Marcel Proust* (Criterion Books, $6.50). George D. Painter's *Proust: The Early Years* (Little, Brown, Atlantic Monthly Press,

$6.50) is the first part of a detailed, comprehensive, well-researched, projected two-volume biography. For a brief appreciation see Edmund Wilson's *Axel's Castle* (Charles Scribner's Sons, $1.45).

43. POE. The standard authority is Arthur H. Quinn's *Edgar Allan Poe: A Critical Biography* (Appleton-Century-Crofts, $8.00). See also Joseph Wood Krutch's excellent *Edgar Allan Poe: A Study in Genius*. One of the finest critical works (but it requires close attention) on the major American writers of the mid-nineteenth century is F. O. Matthiessen's *American Renaissance* (Oxford University Press, $10.00). While this discusses Poe, the major emphasis is on Melville, Thoreau, Hawthorne, and Whitman. It may be consulted in connection with these four writers particularly.

44. HAWTHORNE. Two excellent short treatments: Mark Van Doren's *Nathaniel Hawthorne: A Critical Biography* (Viking Press, Compass Books, $1.25); Randall Stewart's *Nathaniel Hawthorne: A Biography* (Yale University Press, $4.50).

45. MELVILLE. The literature is vast and various. Some interesting treatments: Leon Howard's *Herman Melville: A Biography* (University of California Press, $1.95); Newton Arvin's *Herman Melville* (Viking Press, Compass Books, $1.25); Richard Chase's *Herman Melville: A Critical Study* (Macmillan Co., $4.50). The Harper Modern Classics edition of *Moby Dick* (Harper, $1.25) contains an introduction by Clifton Fadiman.

46. MARK TWAIN. Carl Van Doren's *The American Novel 1789-1939*, revised and enlarged edition (Macmillan Co., $5.50), contains a sensible judgment of Mark Twain, as well as good estimates of three other Lifetime novelists: Hawthorne, Melville, Henry James. Highly recommended is Bernard De Voto's *Mark Twain's America* (Houghton Mifflin Co., $4.00). A special but interesting interpretation is Van Wyck Brooks's *The Ordeal of Mark Twain* (Meridian Books, $1.35). See also Charles Neider's remarkable edition of *The Autobiography of Mark Twain* (Harper, $6.00).

47. HENRY JAMES. James is his own best commentator: see

his *The Art of the Novel* (Charles Scribner's Sons, $1.95), edited by R. P. Blackmur. An excellent short study is F. W. Dupee's *Henry James: His Life and Writings* (Doubleday, Anchor Books, $0.95). The probably definitive biography will be Leon Edel's projected three-volume work. At this writing only the first installment has appeared: *Henry James: The Untried Years* (J. B. Lippincott Co., $6.00).

48. CERVANTES. The bibliography is of course enormous. Gerald Brenan's *Literature of the Spanish People* (Meridian Books, $1.95) contains a fine Cervantes chapter and is well worth reading complete. Ditto for Joseph Wood Krutch's *Five Masters* (Indiana University Press, $1.75). Also recommended: Mark Van Doren's *Don Quixote's Profession* (Columbia University Press, $2.50); Aubrey F. G. Bell's *Cervantes* (University of Oklahoma Press, $4.00); Salvador de Madariaga's *Don Quixote: An Introductory Essay in Psychology* (Oxford University Press, $1.40).

49. GOGOL. As you read Gogol, Turgenev, Tolstoy, and Dostoevski, you will find useful Marc Slonim's *Outline of Russian Literature* (New American Library, $0.50). Two excellent fuller treatments of Gogol: Vladimir Nabokov's somewhat eccentric *Nikolai Gogol* (New Directions, $1.25) and David Magarshack's more conventional *Gogol: A Life* (Grove Press, $6.50).

50. TURGENEV. Two reliable biographies: Avrahm Yarmolinsky's *Turgenev, the Man, His Art and His Age* (Orion Press, $6.00) and David Magarshack's *Turgenev* (Grove Press, $6.00). Edmund Wilson contributes an interesting, lengthy introduction to a Turgenev collection *Literary Reminiscences and Autobiographical Fragments* (Grove Press, Evergreen Books, $1.95).

51. DOSTOEVSKI. Avrahm Yarmolinsky's *Dostoevsky, His Life and Art* (Criterion Books, $7.50); Janko Lavrin's *Dostoevsky.*

52. TOLSTOY. The standard full-dress biography in English is Aylmer Maude's *The Life of Tolstoy: First Fifty Years* (Oxford University Press, World's Classics, $2.50). Janko Lavrin's *Tolstoy: An Approach* and Ernest Simmons' *Leo Tolstoy* are

excellent shorter works. Isaiah Berlin's *The Hedgehog and the Fox* (New American Library, $0.35) is a brilliant essay on Tolstoy's view of history. Essays on *War and Peace* can be found in Clifton Fadiman's *Party of One* (World Publishing Co., $5.00) and *Any Number Can Play* (World Publishing Co., $5.00).

53. Undset. A. H. Winsnes' *Sigrid Undset: A Study in Christian Realism* offers a sympathetic interpretation.

PHILOSOPHY, PSYCHOLOGY, POLITICS, ESSAYS (54-71)

Bertrand Russell's *History of Western Philosophy* (Simon and Schuster, $2.25) covers the entire period, from the Greeks to our own day, not always to the satisfaction of academic minds. Will Durant's *Story of Philosophy* (Pocket Books, $0.50) remains a highly readable account, particularly strong on the biographical side. New American Library publishes five useful little books at $0.50 each. These are:

Giorgio De Santillana, *The Age of Adventure* (Renaissance Philosophers); Stuart Hampshire, *The Age of Reason* (Seventeenth Century); Isaiah Berlin, *The Age of Enlightenment* (Eighteenth Century); Henry D. Aiken, *The Age of Ideology* (Nineteenth Century); Morton White, *The Age of Analysis* (Twentieth Century).

54. Hobbes. Richard Peters, *Hobbes* (Penguin Books, $0.85). Basil Willey's *The Seventeenth Century Background* (Doubleday, Anchor Books, $0.95) discusses, in addition to Hobbes, these figures on our list: Milton, Descartes, Locke.

55. Locke. R. I. Aaron, *John Locke* (Oxford University Press, $4.50); Maurice Cranston, *John Locke* (Macmillan Co., $8.00).

56. Hume. J. Y. T. Greig, *David Hume*.

57. Mill. Maurice Cranston, *J. S. Mill* (British Book Centre, $0.50); Michael St. John Packe, *The Life of John Stuart Mill* (Macmillan Co., $6.50).

58. WHITEHEAD. As far as I know, no formal biography has as yet appeared. An intimate delightful picture is given in *Dialogues of Alfred North Whitehead* (New American Library, $0.50), as recorded by Lucien Price.

59. MARX (AND ENGELS). Isaiah Berlin's *Karl Marx: His Life and Environment* (Oxford University Press, $1.20) is a brilliant short account. See also, especially if you are interested in economics, Robert L. Heilbroner, *The Worldly Philosophers* (Simon and Schuster, $1.50); George Soule, *Ideas of the Great Economists* (New American Library, $0.50). Jacques Barzun, *Darwin, Marx, Wagner* (Doubleday, Anchor Books, $1.25) interprets Marx as part of his whole century.

60. NIETZSCHE. Walter Kaufmann's *Nietzsche: Philosopher, Psychologist, Antichrist* (Meridian Books, $1.55) is a useful, highly learned work that does its best to defend Nietzsche against the kind of charges rather persuasively made by such critics as Bertrand Russell in his *History of Western Philosophy* (Simon and Schuster, $2.25). See also George Allen Morgan, Jr., *What Nietzsche Means.*

61. FREUD. The standard biography, one of the classics of our time, is Ernest Jones's three-volume *Life and Work of Sigmund Freud* (Basic Books, vols. 1 and 2, $6.75 each; vol. 3, $7.50; set $21.00). An interesting critical monograph is Erich Fromm's *Sigmund Freud's Mission* (Harper, $3.00). See also Lionel Trilling's *Freud and the Crisis of Our Culture* (Beacon Press, $1.00). Beyond this further suggestions are not feasible, for the literature is at once too vast and too tendentious.

62. MACHIAVELLI. Ralph Roeder, *The Man of the Renaissance* (Meridian Books, $1.95).

63. MONTAIGNE. Marvin Lowenthal's *The Autobiography of Michel de Montaigne* (Alfred A. Knopf, Vintage Books, $1.25) arranges and excerpts the *Essays* so as to follow the course of Montaigne's life. Donald M. Frame's *Montaigne's Discovery of Man* (Columbia University Press, $3.50) is a serious, scholarly work. Two first-class essays are by Virginia Woolf in *The Common Reader* (Harcourt, Brace, Harvest Books, $1.15) and Ralph

Waldo Emerson in *The Portable Emerson* (Viking Press, $1.45) or the *Complete Essays* (Modern Library College Editions, $0.85).

64. DESCARTES. E. S. Haldane's *Descartes, His Life and Times* was published in 1905 but is still useful. The relevant chapters in the histories of philosophy by Will Durant in his *Story of Philosophy* (Pocket Books, $0.50) and Bertrand Russell in *History of Western Philosophy* (Simon and Schuster, $2.25) may also be consulted.

65. PASCAL. Morris Bishop, *Pascal: The Life of Genius* is a sound biography. See also T. S. Eliot's essay on Pascal in his *Selected Essays* (Harcourt, Brace, $5.75).

66. TOCQUEVILLE. Recommended: a careful reading of Phillips Bradley's long and thoughtful introduction to his monumental two-volume edition of *Democracy in America* (Alfred A. Knopf, Vintage Books, $2.90). See also: G. W. Pierson, *Tocqueville in America,* abridged by Dudley C. Lunt (Doubleday, Anchor Books, $1.45); J. P. Mayer, *Alexis de Tocqueville: Journey to America* (Yale University Press, $6.50).

67. THOREAU. The fullest satisfactory account is H. S. Canby's *Thoreau* (Beacon Press, $2.75). Two first-rate shorter books are J. W. Krutch's *Henry David Thoreau* (William Sloane, $4.75) and Mark Van Doren's *Henry David Thoreau: A Critical Study.*

68. EMERSON. The definitive biography is Ralph L. Rusk's *The Life of Ralph Waldo Emerson* (Columbia University Press, $10.00). Van Wyck Brooks' *The Flowering of New England* (E. P. Dutton, Everyman's Library, $1.85) gives a splendid picture of the whole Concord group. F. O. Matthiessen's *American Renaissance* (Oxford University Press, $10.00) offers the deepest interpretation of our American mid-nineteenth-century major figures. See also Bliss Perry, editor, *The Heart of Emerson's Journals* (Dover Publications, $1.85) and George Santayana's essay on Emerson in *Interpretations of Poetry and Religion* (Harper, $1.45).

69. WILLIAM JAMES. The basic account is Ralph Barton Perry's *The Thought and Character of William James,* 2 vols.

(Harvard University Press, $6.00), of which there is a good one-volume briefer version (Braziller, $3.00). See also Perry's *In the Spirit of William James* (Indiana University Press, $1.50) and the chapter on James in Santayana's *Character and Opinion in the United States* (Doubleday, Anchor Books, $0.75).

70. DEWEY. *Intelligence in the Modern World: John Dewey's Philosophy* (Modern Library, $2.95) contains excellent selections from most of Dewey's major works, plus a long, professional philosopher's introduction by the editor, Joseph Ratner. See also Sidney Hook's *John Dewey: An Intellectual Portrait.*

71. SANTAYANA. Willard Arnett, *Santayana and the Sense of Beauty* (Indiana University Press, $1.25); George W. Howgate, *George Santayana.* The latter is useful but not definitive. *The Philosophy of George Santayana* (Tudor Publishing Co., $6.95) offers a well-chosen selection, with an introduction by the editor, Paul Arthur Schilpp.

POETRY (72-80)

72. Anthologies of English and American verse are legion. Space does not permit the naming of even a representative selection, and there are many others just as good as those here listed. The Auden and Pearson anthology I have recommended seems to me a first-rate large-scale job. But so is *The Viking Book of Poetry of the English-Speaking World,* 2 vols. (Viking Press, $12.50), edited by Richard Aldington. A standard one-volume work, a bit conventional but excellent, is *The Oxford Book of English Verse* (Oxford University Press, $6.50), edited by Arthur Quiller-Couch. A small-scale general anthology is *Six Centuries of Great Poetry* (Dell Publishing Co., $0.75), edited by Robert Penn Warren and Albert Erskine.

A first-rate collection of modern verse is *Modern Verse in English, 1900-1950* (Macmillan Co., $5.00), edited by David Cecil and Allen Tate. This contains splendid introductions by the distinguished editors. A few inexpensive small anthologies of modern verse: *New Poems by American Poets #2* (Ballantine Books, $0.35); *New Poets of England and America* (Meridian Books, $1.45), edited by Hall, Pack, and Simpson; *The Pocket Book of Modern Verse* (Pocket Books, $0.50), edited by Oscar Williams; *100 Modern Poems* (New American Library, $0.50), edited by Selden Rodman.

Books about poetry are not generally very helpful. There are exceptions. One is Mark Van Doren's *Introduction to Poetry* (Henry Holt, $3.75). This precedes a good general anthology with 135 pages of sharp, intelligible, no-nonsense commentaries on thirty varied examples of first-rate verse. Another excellent work is Elizabeth Drew's *Poetry: A Modern Guide to Understanding and Enjoyment* (W. W. Norton, $3.95).

Louis Untermeyer's *Lives of the Poets* (Simon and Schuster, $7.95) is a good readable compendium of biography plus critical summary. It deals with English and American poets, from *Beowulf* to Dylan Thomas.

73. Van Doren's is as good a general anthology as any. However, Hubert Creekmore's *A Little Treasury of World Poetry* (Charles Scribner's Sons, $4.50), though built on a smaller scale, is excellent. A unique and delightful collection is Henry Wells's *1001 Poems of Mankind* (Tupper and Love, $5.00). This is limited to *very* short poems from the world's chief literatures. For translations from the Greek: F. L. Lucas, *Greek Poetry for Everyman* (Beacon Press, $1.75); Dudley Fitts, *Anthologia Graeca: Poems From the Greek Anthology* (New Directions, $1.00); Higham and Bowra, *The Oxford Book of Greek Verse in Translation* (Oxford University Press, $5.00); Moses Hadas, *The Greek Poets* (Modern Library, $1.65). From the Latin: L. R. Lind, *Latin Poetry in Verse Translation* (Houghton Mifflin, Riverside Editions, $1.45); F. R. B. Godolphin, *The Latin Poets* (Modern Library, $1.65). A delightful book on the Latin poets, containing some superb translations, is Gilbert Highet's *Poets in a Landscape* (Alfred A. Knopf, $6.50). From the Middle Ages (fourteen languages): Hubert Creekmore's *Lyrics of the Middle Ages* (Grove Press, $4.75). From the

French: C. F. MacIntyre, *French Symbolist Poetry* (University of California Press, \$1.50); Wallace Fowlie, *Mid-Century French Poets* (Grove Press, Evergreen Books, \$1.95); Angel Flores, *An Anthology of French Poetry From Nerval to Valéry in English Translation* (Doubleday, Anchor Books, \$1.45). From the Spanish: J. M. Cohen, *The Penguin Book of Spanish Verse* (Penguin Books, \$0.95). From the Italian: George Kay, *The Penguin Book of Italian Verse* (Penguin Books, \$0.95). The two last-named accompany the originals with plain prose translations. From the German: Angel Flores, *An Anthology of German Poetry From Hölderlin to Rilke* (Doubleday, Anchor Books, \$1.45). From the Irish: *Kings, Lords, and Commons* (Alfred A. Knopf, \$3.75), an anthology, selected and translated by Frank O'Connor.

74. DONNE. Though later studies have partly superseded it, the standard biography still remains Edmund Gosse's two-volume *Life and Letters of John Donne* (Peter Smith, \$12.00). See also: Hugh I. Fausset, *John Donne, A Study in Discord*; George Williamson, *The Donne Tradition* (Noonday Press, \$1.45); Theodore Spencer, editor, *A Garland for John Donne* (Peter Smith, \$3.75); and T. S. Eliot's influential essay on "The Metaphysical Poets" in his *Selected Essays* (Harcourt, Brace, \$5.75).

75. MILTON. Rose Macaulay's *Milton* (Macmillan Co., \$1.50) is a sound brief biography. The leading Milton authority is E. M. W. Tillyard. His *Milton* is a standard work. See also Basil Willey, *The Seventeenth Century Background* (Doubleday, Anchor Books, \$0.95), Chapter 10, and the two interesting Milton essays in T. S. Eliot's *On Poetry and Poets* (Farrar, Straus and Cudahy, \$4.00).

76. BLAKE. Mona Wilson, *The Life of William Blake* (Oxford University Press, \$3.40); S. Foster Damon, *William Blake: His Philosophy and Symbols* (Peter Smith, \$12.50); Mark Schorer, *William Blake* (Alfred A. Knopf, Vintage Books, \$1.45); H. C. Goddard, *Blake's Fourfold Vision* (Pendle Hill

Pamphlets, $0.35); essay on Blake in T. S. Eliot's *Selected Essays* (Harcourt, Brace, $5.75).

77. WORDSWORTH. The standard biography is George McLean Harper's two-volume *William Wordsworth, His Life, Works, and Influence.* See also Mary Moorman's large-scale *William Wordsworth, A Biography: The Early Years* (1770-1803) (Oxford University Press, $8.00). For diverse critical appraisals see H. I. Fausset, *The Lost Leader, A Study of Wordsworth;* H. W. Garrod, *Wordsworth: Lectures and Essays* (Oxford University Press, $1.70); Coleridge's *Biographia Literaria* (E. P. Dutton, Everyman's Library, $1.85).

78. COLERIDGE. E. K. Chambers, *Samuel Taylor Coleridge* (Oxford University Press, $4.80) is a sound biographical study. For the early years see Lawrence Hanson, *The Life of Samuel Taylor Coleridge.* The finest book on Coleridge's genius and a masterpiece in its own right is John Livingston Lowes, *The Road to Xanadu* (Alfred A. Knopf, Vintage Books, $1.95).

79. YEATS. The standard biography is J. M. Hone, *William Butler Yeats.* Two interesting critical appraisals: T. R. Henn, *The Lonely Tower;* Richard Ellmann, *Yeats: The Man and the Masks* (E. P. Dutton, Everyman's Library, $1.55). See also John Unterecker, *A Reader's Guide to William Butler Yeats* (Noonday Press, $1.65); and essays on Yeats in Arland Ussher, *Three Great Irishmen* (New American Library, $0.50); Edmund Wilson, *Axel's Castle* (Charles Scribner's Sons, $1.45); T. S. Eliot, *On Poetry and Poets* (Farrar, Straus and Cudahy, $4.00).

80. WHITMAN. The most satisfactory biography is Gay Wilson Allen, *The Solitary Singer* (Grove Press, Evergreen Books, $2.95). Two other good book-length treatments: H. S. Canby, *Walt Whitman, An American;* Emory Holloway, *Whitman: An Interpretation in Narrative.* See also F. O. Matthiessen, *American Renaissance* (Oxford University Press, $10.00) and the essay "The Poetry of Barbarism," which may be found in a useful collection, edited by Irving Singer, *Essays in Literary Criticism of George Santayana* (Charles Scribner's Sons, $7.50).

HISTORY, BIOGRAPHY, AUTOBIOGRAPHY (81-87)

81. It is probably foolish, in view of the vastness of the subject of world history, or even of our Western subdivision, to list any books at all. However, for different purposes, and purses, the following titles may prove helpful:

Three once-over-lightly histories of the world: René Sédillot, *History of the World in 240 Pages* (New American Library, $0.50); *Pelican History of the World*, 6 vols. (Penguin Books, $0.85-$0.95); Hendrik Van Loon, *The Story of Mankind* (Pocket Books, $0.50). The most famous one-volume treatment: H. G. Wells, *The Outline of History* (Doubleday, Garden City, $3.95). In preparation: Goldwin Smith's vast *The Heritage of Man: A History of the World* (Charles Scribner's Sons). Handsome, with pictures: *Life's Picture History of Western Man* (Simon and Schuster, $13.50). For reference: William R. Shepherd, *Historical Atlas* (Barnes and Noble, $15.00); William Langer, editor, *An Encyclopedia of World History* (Houghton Mifflin Co., $8.50).

82. I have already suggested that you buy *Paperbound Books in Print*. In it, listed under History, you will find a large number of good, modestly priced titles dealing with special periods or phases of history and with countries other than England and the United States. Let your special interests be your guide.

For England: the Trevelyan totals only one thousand pages, a handleable length. If you prefer a shorter view: J. A. Rickard, *History of England* (Barnes and Noble, $1.50); *Pelican History of England*, 8 vols. (Penguin Books, $0.85-$0.95); A. M. Low, *England's Past Presented* (E. P. Dutton, $3.75). J. R. Green, *A Short History of the English People*, 2 vols. (E. P. Dutton, Everyman's Library, $3.70) is a Victorian classic, now somewhat outmoded.

83. No special claim is made for Nevins and Commager

against other one-volume treatments. Here are a few alternatives: Charles and Mary Beard, *Basic History of the United States* (Doubleday, Garden City, $3.95); J. T. Adams, *The Epic of America* (Little, Brown, Atlantic Monthly Press, $6.50); William Miller, *The History of the United States* (Dell Publishing Co., $0.75); Hendrik Van Loon, *The Story of America* (Dell Publishing Co., $0.35)—this is rather elementary. A highly praised recent two-volume work is Kraus and Dulles, *The United States: A Modern History* (University of Michigan Press, $15.00). For reference: Richard B. Morris, editor, *Encyclopedia of American History* (Harper, $6.95). D. W. Brogan, *The American Character* (Alfred A. Knopf, Vintage Books, $0.95) is a brilliant short book that you may wish to compare with Tocqueville (66).

84. For a wider sampling of American historical documentary records, see Richard Hofstadter, editor, *Great Issues in American History*, 2 vols. (Alfred A. Knopf, Vintage Books, $2.50). For a brilliant study of the Declaration, see Carl Becker, *The Declaration of Independence* (Alfred A. Knopf, Vintage Books, $1.25). For an interesting account of the making of the Constitution, see Carl Van Doren, *The Great Rehearsal* (Viking Press, $3.75).

85. ROUSSEAU. The best biographer of Rousseau is of course Rousseau, but he has no great passion for accuracy. If you care to check up on him, the full-dress biography in English is John Morley, *Rousseau and His Era*, but it's pretty dull. See also Matthew Josephson, *Jean-Jacques Rousseau*. For a fine slashing attack on everything Rousseau stands for, see Irving Babbitt, *Rousseau and Romanticism* (Meridian Books, $1.45).

86. BOSWELL. No solid biography based on the new Boswell finds has yet appeared and the old 1891 *Life* by Percy Fitzgerald is now so outmoded as to be misleading. Hesketh Pearson's *Johnson and Boswell* (Harper, $5.50) is a lively, readable, and recent account. See also: *Boswell's London Journal* (New American Library, $0.50), edited by F. A. Pottle; C. B. Tinker, *Young*

Boswell; Macaulay's "Boswell's Life of Johnson" in *Critical and Historical Essays,* Vol. I (E. P. Dutton, Everyman's Library, $1.85).

87. ADAMS. Ernest Samuels, *The Young Henry Adams* (Harvard University Press, $5.50) and *The Middle Years* (Harvard University Press, $7.50) will presumably be followed by a third volume. The whole should prove the standard life. Other admirable studies: J. C. Levenson, *The Mind and Art of Henry Adams* (Houghton Mifflin Co., $6.00); Elizabeth Stevenson, *Henry Adams: A Biography* (Macmillan Co., $6.00); R. A. Hume, *Runaway Star: An Appreciation of Henry Adams* (Cornell University Press, $3.75). See also the handy collection, A *Henry Adams Reader* (Doubleday, Anchor Books, $1.25), edited by Elizabeth Stevenson.

SOME CONTEMPORARIES (88-95)

88. FROST. Lawrance Thompson, *Fire and Ice: The Art and Thought of Robert Frost.* Sidney Cox, A *Swinger of Birches: A Portrait of Robert Frost* (New York University Press, $3.75); R. L. Cook, *The Dimensions of Robert Frost* (Rinehart, $3.95). See also two essays on Frost in Randall Jarrell's witty *Poetry and the Age* (Alfred A. Knopf, Vintage Books, $0.95).

89. FAULKNER. Ward L. Miner, *The World of William Faulkner* (Grove Press, Evergreen Books, $1.45); Robert Coughlan, *The Private World of William Faulkner* (Harper, $2.75); Irving Howe, *William Faulkner: A Critical Study;* William Van O'Connor, *The Tangled Fire of William Faulkner* (University of Minnesota Press, $4.00). In preparation: Edmond L. Volpe, A *Reader's Guide to William Faulkner* (Noonday Press). See also: Alfred Kazin, *On Native Grounds* (Doubleday, Anchor Books, $1.25); F. J. Hoffman, *The Modern Novel in America* (Henry Regnery Co., Gateway Editions, $1.25); Malcolm Cowley's introduction to *The Portable Faulkner* (Viking Press, $2.95).

90. HEMINGWAY. Carlos Baker, *Hemingway: The Writer as Artist* (Princeton University Press, $5.00); Philip Young, *Ernest Hemingway* (University of Minnesota Press, $1.00). See also: Alfred Kazin, *On Native Grounds* (Doubleday, Anchor Books, $1.25); F. J. Hoffman, *The Modern Novel in America* (Henry Regnery Co., Gateway Editions, $1.25); Edmund Wilson's essay on Hemingway in *Eight Essays* (Doubleday, Anchor Books, $0.85).

91. MAUGHAM. R. A. Cordell, *W. Somerset Maugham*; Richard Aldington, *W. Somerset Maugham: An Appreciation*; John Brophy, *Somerset Maugham* (British Book Centre, $0.50); Klaus W. Jonas, editor, *The World of Somerset Maugham* (British Book Centre, $3.50).

92. FORSTER. Lionel Trilling, *E. M. Forster* (New Directions, $2.00); Rose Macaulay, *The Writings of E. M. Forster*. See also Virginia Woolf, *The Death of the Moth and Other Essays*.

93. T. S. ELIOT. The best book is still the third edition of F. O. Matthiessen's *The Achievement of T. S. Eliot* (Oxford University Press, $4.50). Also useful: George Williamson, *A Reader's Guide to T. S. Eliot* (Noonday Press, $1.45); Hugh Kenner, *The Invisible Poet: T. S. Eliot* (McDowell, Obolensky, $5.00); Helen Gardner, *The Art of T. S. Eliot* (E. P. Dutton, Everyman's Library, $1.15); essay on Eliot in Edmund Wilson, *Axel's Castle* (Charles Scribner's Sons, $1.45).

94. HUXLEY. John Atkins, *Aldous Huxley* (Roy Publishers, $5.00); Jocelyn Brooke, *Aldous Huxley* (British Book Centre, $0.50). See also: *The World of Aldous Huxley* (Grosset and Dunlap, $1.45), an omnibus volume with an excellent introduction by the editor, Charles J. Rolo; David Daiches, *The Novel and the Modern World*.

95. MALRAUX. W. M. Frohock, *André Malraux and the Tragic Imagination* (Stanford University Press, $4.00). See also Janet Flanner, *Men and Monuments* (Harper, $5.00); Wallace Fowlie, *A Guide to Contemporary French Literature* (Meridian Books, $1.45); Henri Peyre, *The Contemporary French Novel*

(Oxford University Press, $5.00); Brée and Guiton, *An Age of Fiction* (Rutgers University Press, $5.00).

MISCELLANEOUS (96-100)

96. There are a great many fine histories of art, and you may prefer one of them to the Gombrich book. Erwin O. Christenson's *History of Western Art* (New American Library, $0.75) costs you very little. It is clear, concise, illustrated, and has a bibliography. Helen Gardner's *Art Through the Ages* (Harcourt, Brace, $8.95) is a standard text, well illustrated, rather pedagogical. The same is true of Upjohn, Wingert, and Mahler, *History of World Art* (Oxford University Press, $12.00). Germain Bazin's *History of Art From Prehistoric Times to the Present* (Houghton Mifflin Co., $9.00) has a good bibliography, authoritative text. Another recent book is Dr. Frederick Hartt, *A History of Art in the Western World* (Charles Scribner's Sons, in prep.). For those who wish to learn more about modern art a notable recent work is John Canaday's *Mainstreams of Modern Art: David to Picasso* (Simon and Schuster, $12.50). See also Sara Newmeyer, *Enjoying Modern Art* (New American Library, $0.50). Most good art books are pretty expensive, but you get something for your money in the way of format and illustrations.

97. The most interesting, most varied reading *about* mathematics I know of is to be found in James R. Newman's magnificent four-volume anthology *The World of Mathematics* (Simon and Schuster, $25.00). At least half of it is perfectly comprehensible to anyone who has had two years of high school math. For fascinating biographies of the great figures in the field see E. T. Bell, *Men of Mathematics* (Simon and Schuster, $6.50). See also: Tobias Dantzig, *Number, The Language of Science* (Doubleday, Anchor Books, $0.95); Kasner and Newman, *Mathematics and the Imagination* (Simon and Schuster, $4.50); G. H. Hardy, *A Mathematician's Apology*; Clifton Fadiman,

editor, *Fantasia Mathematica* (Simon and Schuster, $4.95). None of these books demands any extensive technical knowledge.

98. It would probably be more sensible to list no books at all; the field is too vast, and any bibliography under ten pages is almost meaningless. I note here a few titles that I happen to have found useful or interesting. There are hundreds of others as good, perhaps better. Two modestly priced treatments of modern physics and cosmology: E. N. da C. Andrade, *An Approach to Modern Physics* (Doubleday, Anchor Books, $0.95); Fred Hoyle, *Nature of the Universe* (New American Library, $0.50). From the horse's mouth: Albert Einstein, *Relativity, the Special and General Theory* (Peter Smith, $2.50). Schwartz and Bishop, editors, *Moments of Discovery* (Basic Books, $15.00) is a remarkable two-volume anthology of long extracts from the original writings of about one hundred scientists, most of them great. Shapley, Rapport, and Wright, editors, *A Treasury of Science* (Harper, $6.95) is a somewhat similar job in one volume, stressing modern writers, many of them good journalists rather than original researchers.

99. For our purposes Mr. Adler's book is the best I know. Alfred Stefferud, editor, *The Wonderful World of Books* (New American Library, $0.50) contains dozens of short essays on the joys of reading, with occasionally some good concrete advice, plus useful bibliographies.

100. A note on anthologies: that recommended in the text is but one of many excellent anthologies of related character. Paul M. Angle, editor, *The American Reader: From Columbus to Today* (Rand McNally, $7.50) is a compilation of eyewitness historical narratives. Brockway and Winer, editors, *Homespun America* (Simon and Schuster, $10.00) presents folk and folkish material. Ralph L. Woods, *The Family Reader of American Masterpieces* (Thomas Y. Crowell, $5.95) is a pleasant ragbag of familiar stories, essays, speeches, humorous pieces, and poems. The greatest anthology I know, itself a superb work of art, is a general rather than an American one, but I would like to recom-

mend it anyway. It is edited by Huntington Cairns and is called *The Limits of Art* (Pantheon Books, $7.50). It consists of selections of poetry and prose from Homer to Joyce that have been held by competent critics to be supreme of their kind. In each case the opinion of the critic is cited along with the selection. Where the selections are in languages other than English, the original is given, along with a translation. In a way this wonderful anthology is a kind of Lifetime Reading Plan in miniature.

ABOUT THE AUTHOR

Clifton Fadiman was born in New York City in 1904, and got his A.B. from Columbia University in 1925. He has been a translator, a teacher, an advisor to Samuel Goldwyn, editor at Simon and Schuster, lecturer, platform reader, and book review editor of *The New Yorker*. During these years writing —and editing such books as *Reading I've Liked, The Short Stories of Henry James, The American Treasury, Fantasia Mathematica,* and other books and anthologies—played a concurrent part. His radio and TV chores have included: host of *Information Please,* M.C. of *This Is Show Business,* and conductor of the NBC radio series *Conversation.* He serves regularly as The Roving Reporter on the Saturday afternoon Metropolitan Opera broadcasts. Mr. Fadiman is a member of the Board of Judges of the Book-of-the-Month Club, essayist for *Holiday* magazine, consultant to the Ford Fund for the Advancement of Education, and one of the Board of Editors of the Encyclopaedia Britannica. His "Read It Now" department in *This Week Magazine* is followed by many millions. He is the author of two books of essays, *Party of One* and *Any Number Can Play.*

This book was set in

Electra and Bulmer types.
It was designed by

Abe Lerner and Larry Kamp